ASP.NET 2.0
Revealed

PATRICK A. LORENZ

ASP.NET 2.0 Revealed
Copyright © 2004 by Patrick A. Lorenz

ISBN (pbk): 1-59059-337-5

Printed and bound in the United States of America 12345678910

Trademarked names may appear in this book. Rather than use a trademark symbol with every occurrence of a trademarked name, we use the names only in an editorial fashion and to the benefit of the trademark owner, with no intention of infringement of the trademark.

Openwave and the Openwave logo are registered trademarks and/or trademarks of Openwave Systems Inc. in various jurisdictions. All rights reserved.

Technical Reviewer: Marc Höppner

Editorial Board: Dan Appleman, Craig Berry, Gary Cornell, Tony Davis, Steven Rycroft, Julian Skinner, Martin Streicher, Jim Sumser, Karen Watterson, Gavin Wray, John Zukowski

Assistant Publisher: Grace Wong

Project Manager: Kylie Johnston

Copy Editors: Ami Knox, Nicole LeClerc

Production Manager: Kari Brooks

Production Editor: Laura Cheu

Proofreaders: Lori Bring, Linda Seifert

Compositor: Diana Van Winkle, Van Winkle Design Group

Indexer: Nancy A. Guenther

Cover Designer: Kurt Krames

Manufacturing Manager: Tom Debolski

Distributed to the book trade in the United States by Springer-Verlag New York, Inc., 175 Fifth Avenue, New York, NY 10010 and outside the United States by Springer-Verlag GmbH & Co. KG, Tiergartenstr. 17, 69112 Heidelberg, Germany.

In the United States: phone 1-800-SPRINGER, email orders@springer-ny.com, or visit http://www.springer-ny.com. Outside the United States: fax +49 6221 345229, email orders@springer.de, or visit http://www.springer.de.

For information on translations, please contact Apress directly at 2560 Ninth Street, Suite 219, Berkeley, CA 94710. Phone 510-549-5930, fax 510-549-5939, email info@apress.com, or visit http://www.apress.com.

The source code for this book is available to readers at http://www.apress.com in the Downloads section. You will need to answer questions pertaining to this book in order to successfully download the code.

This book is dedicated to my father, who never
had a chance to see me grow up and write books like he did.
And it's also dedicated to my mother for always bearing with her annoying son.

Contents at a Glance

Contents

About the Author

Patrick A. Lorenz lives in Germany. He works as CTO for a software development and consulting company based in southern Germany. PGK Software & Communication GmbH (www.pgk.de) focuses on .NET technologies, especially ASP.NET. In 2003 the company introduced QualiSite, one of the first enterprise content-management systems developed 100% with .NET technologies.

Patrick is well known in the German developer community as an author and also as a trainer and speaker. He has published over half a dozen books covering C# and ASP.NET, including two famous German code books *ASP.NET mit C# Kochbuch* and *ASP.NET mit VB .NET Kochbuch*. Patrick is recognized by Microsoft as an MVP for .NET technologies, and he's also a founder member of the German Microsoft Code Wise program. You can reach Patrick via his web site, www.aspnet2.de.

About the Technical Reviewer

Marc Höppner is a software developer and architect with 15+ years of experience in object-oriented design and programming. He's a founding member and managing director for NeoGeo New Media (`www.neogeo.com`) in Germany, a software development and consulting company specializing in custom .NET-based applications and thin-client client/server systems for both national and international clients. As an early adopter of many Microsoft technologies such as ASP.NET, the .NET Framework, Office 2003, and SQL Server Yukon, NeoGeo has several years of pure .NET development for real-life projects under its belt.

Marc also is a member of Microsoft's Quality Board for MSDN. Sometimes he writes technical articles and helps out Microsoft as a speaker and expert at technical conferences. Sometimes he even has time left over to enjoy family life with his wife and son, and he enjoys music and karate.

Acknowledgments

WOW, THERE ARE so many people that helped me realize this book project. First of all, I would like to thank my team at PGK, the company I'm working for. Michael Brunnhuber did a really good job in translating the book just in time while I wrote it in German. I only had a few weeks to learn the technology, write a book, translate it—yeah, I really need to thank him! Thanks also to Marc Höppner from NeoGeo, who reviewed the book and who gave me a lot of inspiration.

I want to thank the team at Apress as well. Gary and Julian hadn't seen any content or even a table of contents before we completed the whole book. They just believed we could do it in the given timeframe. Thanks to all the other people at Apress who supported this book and its really tough timeline. Thanks to Kylie Johnston for leading the project. Thanks to Nicole LeClerc and Ami Knox for giving so many excellent hints while copy editing. Thanks to Laura Cheu and her "senior citizen" cat for getting the book through production smoothly. Thanks to Doris Wong and all the other people at Apress I didn't mention. I'm looking forward to working with you again!

The biggest "thank you" goes to the folks at Microsoft. Scott Guthrie (fearless leader of the ASP.NET team) introduced me and a few other guys from around Europe to version 2.0 during TechEd in Barcelona. He also answered a lot of questions I had while writing this book. I want to say thanks to Rob Howard for leading the best Alpha program I ever participated in. I'm actually proud to be part of it. Stacey Giard did a great job in bringing it all together and getting the folks at Apress under NDA. A lot of other people from the ASP.NET team have worked on the Alpha forums. My special thanks go to andlin, AndresS, appana, bash_MS, bleroy, bobbyv, BradMi, CarlosAg, ClayCo, danmor, Eilon, glenko, jdixon, johndund, kashif, keithsmith, mharder, mikepope, omar_k, phuff, russellc, samsp, sangitap, Scott Louvau, scottim, ShankuN, SimonCal, SusanC, SWarren, tinghaoy, Wayne King, YugangW, and all the other people I've unfortunately not mentioned here.

Introduction

WELCOME TO THE SHOW!

The new version of Microsoft .NET is being developed in Redmond under the code name "Whidbey." Whidbey consists of a package including the .NET Framework; various user interface types, such as Windows Forms, ASP.NET, and the Compact Framework; the official languages C#, Visual Basic .NET (VB .NET), and J#; the development environment Visual Studio .NET (VS .NET); and more. This book focuses on a specific part of Whidbey: the innovations of the second version of ASP.NET.

Compared to the eight books I've written previously, this book was really an adventure and a big challenge! There were just 6 weeks between the start of the Whidbey Alpha program and the deadline for the manuscript draft. Six weeks on one side to learn all the essentials and details about a new technology well enough to qualitatively describe them in a book. Six weeks on the other side to write down everything. After all, there were more than 300 pages to be handled within this time frame.

The book was first created in the German language. My colleague Michael Brunnhuber (CEO and CFO of my company, PGK) subsequently translated each chapter while I wrote the next chapter. The finished translated chapters were then reviewed by me and later on by Marc Höppner of NeoGeo, the book's technical reviewer.

What This Book Covers

As you may have guessed, this book is one of the first available worldwide on the new ASP.NET version 2.0. It's based on the Alpha build version 1.2.30703, which Microsoft made available to me. As far as I know, this Alpha version is nearly identical to the Technical Preview, which will be distributed for the first time to the attendees of Microsoft's Professional Developers Conference (PDC) in October 2003.

Apart from ASP.NET, the first chapter of this book tells you briefly about improvements in C# and VB .NET. The examples in this book are all based on C#. Peripheral topics, such as Yukon and its corresponding framework support (System.Data.Sql) and Object Spaces aren't covered explicitly. The various enlargements to the base class library itself aren't discussed here either. These topics are beyond the scope of this book and will certainly be discussed on a different occasion in the near future.

Who This Book Is For

The book describes the innovations of ASP.NET version 2.0 under consideration of the current version. Therefore, a good (or even better, a very good) understanding of the current versions of ASP.NET (1.0 or 1.1) is absolutely essential. Thus, this book isn't intended for beginners; rather, it's aimed at advanced and professional-level users.

Accessing the Technology

If you attended PDC in 2003 (or you're attending PDC now and you're holding this book in your hands), you probably received the Technical Preview with the conference's documentation. (Just check the various CDs you received.) If you didn't attend the PDC event in 2003, it will probably be quite difficult for you at present to get your hands on the bits. In my opinion, this won't be possible until 2004, when the Beta will become available for public download. Your best bet is to check the usual web sites, such as www.asp.net, to find out if something changed since this book was printed.

I've tried to include significant screenshots for those of you who won't have the chance to "play around" with the technology while you read this book. This way, you can realize at least offline how the new features work and the changes the innovations bring about.

Questions About Whidbey

For questions about Whidbey, I recommend that you visit www.asp.net. This web site is directly supported by the ASP.NET developer team and offers the latest news about ASP.NET. You'll be able to download the Beta version from this site when it becomes available.

The web site also provides a long listing of forums relating to different ASP.NET features and technologies. Even Whidbey, the new ASP.NET version, will presumably get its own forum soon. Many questions posted to the forums on www.asp.net are directly answered by developers on the Microsoft team, by MVPs, or by ASP.NET insiders.

Author Contact Information

This is my seventh book about ASP.NET, but my first about version 2.0 and, more important, my first in the English language. Despite working under some tough deadlines, my team and I have worked hard to avoid any mistakes in terms of content and language. I'm sure I didn't succeed completely, but I hope that only very few mistakes are left.

If you should find a mistake, I'd be very grateful for your message. Any comments or suggestions, constructive criticism, and compliments are welcome. The e-mail address for this book is as follows: aspnet2preview@asp-buch.de.

Furthermore, you're welcome to visit one of my web sites. These sites are mostly in the German language, but I'll try to offer more content in English in the future:

- www.aspnet2.de: Information about ASP.NET version 2.0

- www.asp-buch.de: Information on all of my books

- www.pgk.de: My company's web site

- www.qualisite.de: Information about my company's .NET content-management system, QualiSite

MSN Messenger played a big part in this book's communications, apart from some private forums. Please feel free to add me to your buddy list. My Passport address is pl@p-l.de.

Please be aware that I can't offer any support on ASP.NET by e-mail or by Messenger. Please use the corresponding forums, especially those on www.asp.net, if you have any questions.

CHAPTER 1

ASP.NET 2.0 at a Glance

WHAT'S NEW IN ASP.NET? What's changed in C# and VB .NET? In this chapter, I'll take you on a whirlwind tour of the new features to whet your appetite. The rest of the book will look at these features and how they're implemented in more detail.

What's New in ASP.NET 2.0?

The ASP.NET team lead by Scott Guthrie resolved to do a lot of things in the second version of ASP.NET to leave the competitors behind in the hard-fought e-business market. The team in Redmond defined some main goals:

- Increase development productivity by reducing the lines of code by about 70%; ideally this means you'll only need about 300 lines of code from now on for something that took 1,000 lines of code in the past. In this context, the so-called zero-code scenarios are important, as they avoid unnecessary coding and keep the source code short. For the developer, ASP.NET version 2.0 offers frequently used features out of the box. This could be an enhanced Data Control or application-wide services like user administration. Furthermore, improved support by the development environment, including a significantly extended IntelliSense integration, will increase your efficiency.

- Easier use of ASP.NET with existing devices like web browsers, PDAs, cell phones, and so on, and openness to connect new devices in the future.

- Simplification of the administration and management of web applications for developers and administrators.

- Increase in performance and scalability to develop the fastest web applications platform possible—for example, by extending the caching functionality.

- Enhanced hosting opportunities for Internet service providers (ISPs).

- In addition to these goals, one of the main issues was to ensure 100% backwards compatibility. It must be possible to transfer existing code without any modifications to avoid breaking changes.

The team has split the development into three logical units and set up an architecture stack, as depicted in Figure 1-1. At the base of this stack are the application services, which offer basic framework features. On top of this, the page functions implement page-specific functionalities. Last but not least, the developer gets a set of rich web controls built on these page functions. These controls are more specific to particular requirements than they have been up to now.

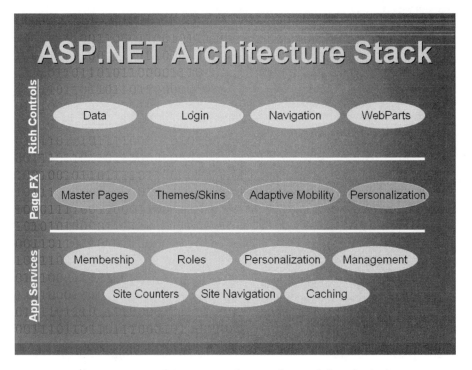

Figure 1-1. The ASP.NET architecture stack is made up of three logical units.

New Controls

The final release of ASP.NET 2.0 will include more than 40 (!) additional controls. All existing controls will, of course, remain to ensure backwards compatibility.

The Data Controls especially turn up with a lot of enhancements. For example, the "new DataGrid control," called GridView, now offers features like sorting, paging, selection, and editing of its content right out of the box. Compared to the DataGrid control, GridView requires no extra code thanks to a brand new Data Source Provider. Communication between database (or other sources) and the control is handled by this new data source model in a transparent way and includes both reading data from and writing data to the data source.

Another new Data Control is DetailsView. It displays only one record instead of a list. The output is usually a vertical listing of the data fields, but can be configured by a custom template.

Both of these controls can be used together (see Figure 1-2). In this example, the GridView control is used to display a list of the items of the Northwind Customer table. The currently selected item is shown in a DetailsView control below the list, which allows you either to edit or to delete the entry. Of course, you can add a new item this way, too. Did I mention that the whole example was developed without a single line of code?

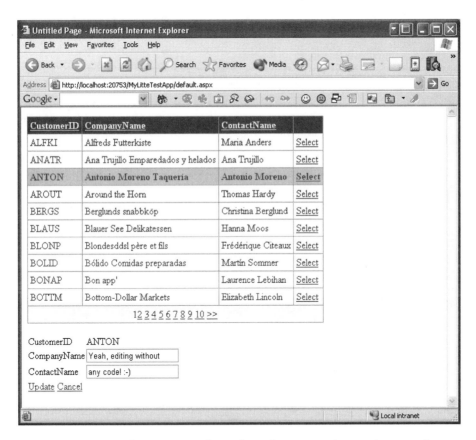

Figure 1-2. Here are the new Data Controls as they appear in a real zero-code scenario.

You'll have real fun using the TreeView control, because it can display hierarchical data. In case you know the existing Internet Explorer Web Controls, it's important for me to mention that this control has nothing to do with the IE TreeView control in version 1.x, and it doesn't use the IE behavior, either. Because it supports the Data Source Provider concept explained earlier, you can bind several different source types to the TreeView control. This includes XML data, for example.

BulletedList is another control designed for data binding. It displays data in a highly configurable HTML list and includes support for hyperlinks and link buttons.

A number of other controls will help you with the output of dynamic pictures, the use of image maps, the upload of files (as web controls!), the rapid implementation of wizards, and much more.

Master Pages

In ASP.NET 1.0 and 1.1, there was no support for so-called Master Pages. Master Pages enable you to place parts of a page (such as header and footer sections) that are commonly used on many pages of a web site into a single file instead of repeating them in the code of every page. If you didn't want to set up a layout for each and every page, you had two choices: Place a User Control on each page, or use one of several published workarounds.

With ASP.NET 2.0, this process is going to be much easier. Master Pages are now one of the standard features (see Figure 1-3 for an example). This includes the support of several content placeholders. The use of Master Pages is quite simple, so you can now rely on the visual design support of the development environment.

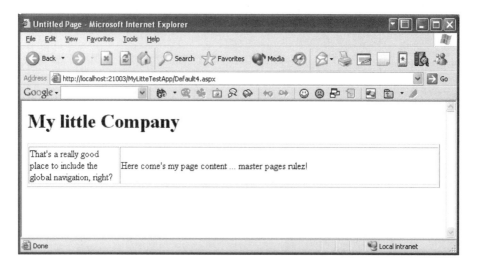

Figure 1-3. Master Pages help to ensure a consistent design.

Site Navigation

Like Master Pages, the implementation of navigation is a necessity for any web application, and it doesn't matter if it's designed for the Internet, or an intranet or extranet. From now on, you can benefit from an integrated navigation structure, based on XML data, for example. Additional controls like positioning indicators (known as *breadcrumbs*) and a DHTML menu make it easy to offer a clearly arranged structure to the user.

Again, a provider does the job of feeding the navigation with data. This gives you the chance to use your own database instead of the integrated site map support. A provider in general acts as a bridge between a common framework functionality and a custom implementation, such as a custom data store. This new approach allows you to provide your own implementation wherever the default doesn't meet your needs, while still taking advantage of the overall model, and is also used in several other parts of version 2.0.

The web site in Figure 1-4 is based on the previous Master Page example and demonstrates the usage of a data-bound TreeView control and the SiteMapPath control to display the current position within the whole web site structure. And still the example contains no code!

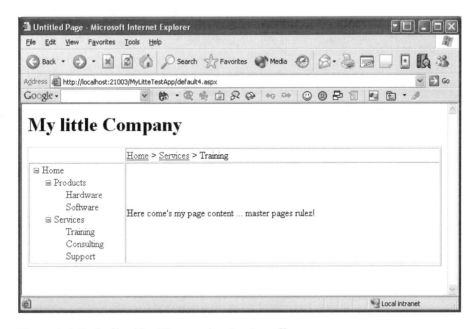

Figure 1-4. Including TreeView navigation is really easy now.

User Management

How often did you develop a user management system? Did you ever try to combine Forms Authentication with individual roles? This is a lot to do, and it's really tricky, too. Again, the new version of ASP.NET provides numerous ways to relieve this problem.

ASP.NET version 2.0 contains a complete user management system out of the box. It comes with an extensive API; special controls for registration, login, and so on; and data providers that handle the data storage without any code from your side. This way you can set up a secured web site—again without have to write a single line of code!

For your convenience, the configuration of the user management system and the creation of the database are assisted by the wizard shown in Figure 1-5 as part of the new ASP.NET web administration feature. Here you can decide how the passwords are stored and whether users are allowed to reset their passwords after answering a question, which they define during registration. Furthermore, the tool enables you to manage the users and their roles (see Figure 1-6).

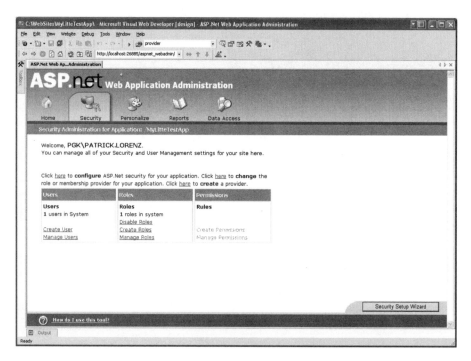

Figure 1-5. The Security Setup Wizard helps set up a secured web site.

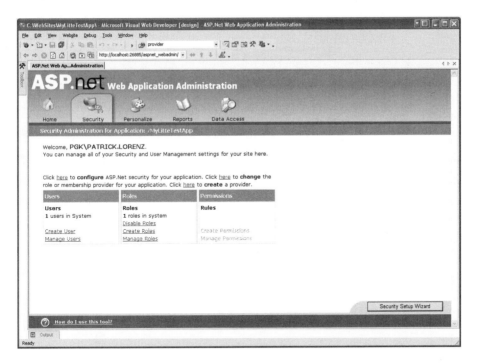

Figure 1-6. You can now manage users and roles out of the box.

Personalization

Personalization is another exciting topic, and ASP.NET version 2.0 comes up with a variety of solutions. It can be used with the integrated user management system as well as with anonymous users. The latter will be recognized by a cookie on a subsequent visit.

Personalization storage makes it possible to assign any information to a user account, save it to persistent storage, and automatically load it back in for the next session. This could be the user's time zone, the user's name, and other preferences—simply put, the type of information you want to be able to save in the web.config file and easily access, even with IntelliSense support. Yet complex data structures like a shopping cart with some product data can be persisted using XML serialization in the same way.

Another feature of personalization is based on pages and the so-called Web Parts, and it allows you to define one or more zones. In each of these zones, a user can arrange the information elements (known as *Web Parts*) using drag and drop. This means moving, deleting, or even changing the content. A zip code can be assigned to the Weather Web Part shown in Figure 1-7, and the local weather will be displayed as a result.

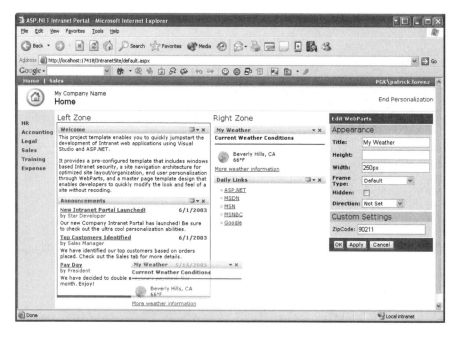

Figure 1-7. It's not that hot in L.A. today.

And the best part is, you don't even have to take care of data storage while using personalization, as the Data Provider does this job for you. All information will be stored in a SQL Server or Microsoft Access database, for example. Plug and play at its best!

Themes/Skins

Do you know the forums on www.asp.net? This voluminous and comfortable system of forums was completely developed in ASP.NET. And members of the ASP.NET team offer you to download the entire source code for free. One of the features the code supports is the capability to adjust the design by various Themes similar to some trendy desktop applications like WinAmp. In the case of the forums application, Theme support is implemented manually by individually loading different designs.

With the new ASP.NET version, you can use functionalities like this with no additional effort other than defining the Theme itself. The standard installation already includes some sample Themes. Just activate them by a little entry in the configuration of your application. Figures 1-8 and 1-9 show exactly the same page but with different Themes. Of course, you can design your own Themes for your application or modify the existing ones to fit to your needs.

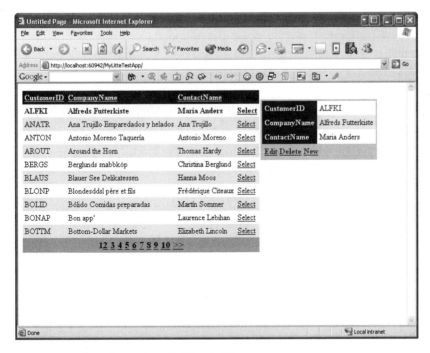

Figure 1-8. This Theme is called Basic Blue ...

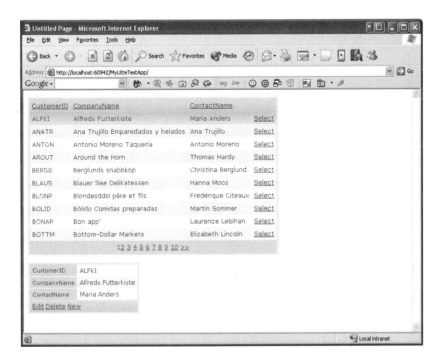

Figure 1-9. ... and this one is called Smoke And Glass.

Other than design properties, the implementation of the Themes functionality includes CSS support and allows the integration of individual graphics. You can define which Theme or sub-Theme (called a *Skin*) will be used per application, per page, or per control in a very sophisticated way.

Mobile Devices

In the first versions of ASP.NET, the development of web applications for mobile devices was only possible with an add-on called Mobile Internet Toolkit, which contained a set of special controls. Since version 1.1, these controls, now named *Mobile Controls,* are shipped with the framework.

Again, in version 2.0 there are some changes. The old controls are still included, but only for compatibility reasons. They aren't recommended for use.

The new magic phrase is "adaptive rendering." In other words, no special controls are needed for mobile devices anymore! Regular web controls will change their presentation depending on the target device. A set of adapter classes can be assigned to each control. A number of these adapters are included for common browsers and mobile devices, but you can define your own, too. These classes will do the alternative rendering. The advantage is that updates or enhancements for existing or new controls can be integrated at a later date—for example, when a new type of mobile device comes to market.

Irrespective of this new generic concept, a set of new controls still target mobile devices (see Figure 1-10). For example, a troika of controls, MultiView, View, and Pager, will help you to implement the presentation of content like the cards in Wireless Markup Language (WML).

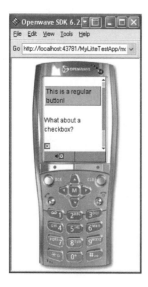

Figure 1-10. Use common controls to create mobile web apps. (Image courtesy Openwave Systems Inc.)

Site Counters

This is a nice feature for counting not only page requests but also clicks of controls like AdRotator, Button, LinkButton, or even HyperLink. The ASP.NET Framework will provide you with an extensive API to analyze, visualize, and process the data.

Configuration

In former versions of ASP.NET, the configuration of both desktop and web applications was hardly perfect. Granted, XML configuration files had a big advantage over the IIS Metabase (a registry-like configuration store used mainly in "classic" ASP). But the increasingly large amount of information placed inside these web configuration files made them very quickly become complex to administer. Until now, changes were possible only by modifying the file manually or by editing the XML data individually, for example, by using use a third-party tool. Not to mention that every change in the web.config file required a complete restart of the application.

Now with ASP.NET version 2.0, a voluminous API to read and write configuration files like web.config in a type-safe manner is delivered with the new .NET Framework. In typical OOP manner, you get one corresponding object per configuration segment and a whole collection where necessary. You can edit these objects and finally save them back to the file. From now on, you can control every setting of your web application within the application, at your local system and remotely.

Two examples for the use of the API are already shipped with the framework. You've seen a new tool called *Web Site Administration* in the earlier description of the user management system (refer back to Figures 1-5 and 1-6). This extensive back end is automatically available for administrators of a web site. Users and roles, for example, can be managed with this tool. Starting with the Beta version, a number of additional functions such as features for analyzing the site counters will be available.

Although the Web Site Administration tool, as the name implies, addresses the administration of web applications by web masters and editors, a second tool, known as the *Configuration Settings Editor,* is optimized for the needs of the server administrator. Naturally, server administrators are recognized as having better knowledge of the details, and therefore will get much more out of the Configuration Settings Editor to fine-tune the application. Basically, this feature is an extension of the IIS MMC Snap-In, which enables you to edit virtually every setting in the web.config file and more. Several parts can be locked down, so an ISP or hosting company can restrict the configuration possibilities for specific web accounts. This is both an advantage in terms of security and in offering new, interesting business models, such as the activation and deactivation of features for a higher monthly fee. All functions of this tool are also available if you use remote access. Figure 1-11 shows the tool in action.

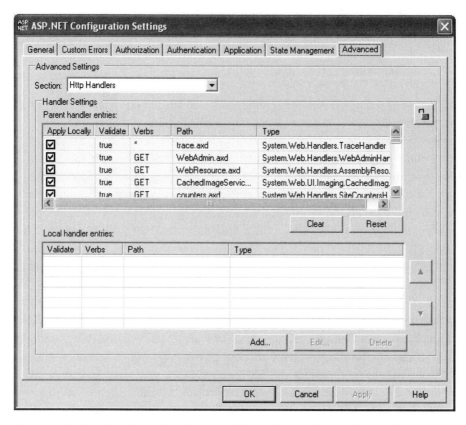

Figure 1-11. The Configuration Settings Editor allows editing of virtually any setting by enhancing the IIS MMC Snap-In.

Deployment

Installation and distribution of applications is an important issue, but no convenient end-to-end solution existed in the previous versions of ASP.NET. The new version offers several new possibilities. First, you can now create or open projects by using either the file system, the local IIS, FrontPage Extensions, or even FTP. An assistant called *Web Copy*, which will be implemented in the upcoming Beta version, supports you by synchronizing your local development version with the live server.

Next, there is an interesting new functionality for compiling complete web applications. The primary results of this compilation are some dynamic link libraries (DLLs), which can easily be copied to the web server. These DLLs not only include the compiled source code, but also contain the content of the ASPX and ASCX files. This means that no design-time files will need to be placed on the server, and therefore the application itself can't be modified.

Summary

So what's up? A little bit curious? The new features promise a lot, don't you think? The enhanced features cover many scenarios that you've previously had to implement manually in the past. The ASP.NET team has come very close to the goal of reducing by 70% the source code you as the developer have to write.

What's New in C# 2.0?

After the previous short preview of the new ASP.NET version, I'd like to present to you the main features of the new C# version 2.0, which is the basis for the rest of the book. You may already know the new features from when Anders Hejlsberg introduced them at OOPSLA in Seattle in autumn 2002. Microsoft Research and the C# team have published some information, too. In comparison to the released news, some syntax changes have been made in the present version.

The new features are classified by four categories:

- Generics

- Iterators

- Anonymous methods

- Partial classes

By the way, multiple inheritance is unfortunately *not* one of the new features.

Generics

Generic classes (or *Generics*), functionally similar to templates in C++, aren't really a new invention of Microsoft, but of course are new in C#. The idea is to develop universal untyped classes and let the compiler automatically create the typed version of the class whenever it's required.

A small example will demonstrate a type of problem that is solved by the use of Generics. The following lines show the simplified definition of a list similar to the ArrayList class:

```
public class MyList
{
   public void Add(object obj)
   {
      // ...
   }

   object this[int index]
   {
      get { /* ... */ }
   }
}
```

Any untyped object can be added to the list and be read. While adding an untyped object is possible in a direct manner thanks to polymorphism, there has to be an explicit type conversion on a read access. The untyped declaration of the list results in two problems. The compiler has no chance to verify the content of the list and the necessary type conversions. Type failures will be recognized only at run time—or maybe never recognized at all.

You can solve both problems by using typed classes. In this particular case, you just need two specialized lists to accept instances of MyClass's respective integer values. The base class library provides an abstract base class, CollectionBase in the System.Collections namespace, that will enable you to create typed collections easily. You have to implement the body for the different methods and the indexer. Internally, the objects are stored in an untyped ArrayList, and calls are forwarded to this class. For reference types, this approach works very well, although a new class has to be explicitly developed for each data type. However, collections for value types created in this way are inefficient, because the data needs to be (un)boxed to be stored in the ArrayList internally.

The solution for problems like this is the use of generic classes. A blueprint of the class is created just once. Instead of using a particular data type or object, a specific placeholder is added. You'll find the syntax of a generic class in C# version 2.0 in Listing 1-1.

Listing 1-1. Creating a Generic Class in C#

```
public class MyList<ItemType>
{
   public void Add(ItemType obj)
   {
      // ...
   }

   public ItemType this[int index]
   {
      get { return ItemType.default; }
   }
}
```

A custom labeled data type is defined in angle brackets behind the class name according to the general guidelines—somewhat like a parameter. Within the scope of the class, the specified data type can be used without any restrictions, as if it really existed.

> **NOTE** *Are you wondering what the* default *property used in Listing 1-1 is about? This virtual property returns the default value depending on the generic type used. For reference types, this is* null*; and for value types, this is whatever defined—for example,* 0.

The desired data type has to be specified explicitly only on use. Here again, you'll need the angle brackets—for both the declaration of the variable and for the instantiation of the class (see Listing 1-2).

Listing 1-2. Using Generics in C#

```
MyList<MyClass> myList = new MyList<MyClass>();
MyClass myClass = new MyClass();
myList.Add(myClass);
MyClass myClass2 = myList[0];
```

Using Generics, no type conversion is required when reading from the collection. Please note that the class is limited to the specified data type (and derived classes). But this is an advantage, because the compiler is now able to detect illegal assignments. This way the lines in Listing 1-3 will be marked as faulty at design time and not at run time.

Listing 1-3. Generics Type-Safe Capability

```
MyList<MyClass> myList = new MyList<MyClass>();
MyClass myClass = new MyClass();
myList.Add(myClass);
int myValue = myList[0]; // --> Compiler error
```

The code doesn't need any modifications to use the list template shown in the example with other types of data. If the collection has been implemented natively based on Generics, you may use value types without boxing and unboxing. In fact, Listing 1-4 shows a significant advantage in terms of performance compared to the integer list discussed earlier.

Listing 1-4. Generics Working with Value Types

```
MyList<int> myList = new MyList<int>();
myList.Add(3);
int myValue = myList[0];
```

Internally, generic classes aren't a feature of the language-dependent compiler but of the Intermediate Language. In the context of Just-in-Time (JIT) compilation, the Intermediate Language expects to receive the desired data type at run time. In regard to value types, the run-time environment generates a specialized class for each type. Concerning int and long, two separate classes are created based on the same model. This is the only way in which the different types can be used in a native (and optimized) way. The usage of reference types, however, is different from the preceding description. Such types consist by definition of a uniform-sized pointer (a reference) on a memory block. Consequently, it isn't necessary to create internal type-optimized versions of the class. This is even better, because exactly the same class, created by the JIT compiler, can be used for all reference types. This way the compilation gets faster and consumes fewer resources.

More Options with the Power of Generics

The previously described list requires exactly one variable data type. Depending on the nature of the class, the supply of placeholders may vary. A practical example is a dictionary that can be typed individually on both the key and the value.

In this case, the new C# version allows multiple placeholders. They have to be specified in angle brackets, separated by commas. The handling of the generic class is the same as described previously, whereas Listing 1-5 shows clearly that the indexer and the returned value can be used in a typed way.

Listing 1-5. Using Generics to Allow More Than One Unknown Type

```
public class MyDictionary<KeyType, ValueType>
{
    public void Add(KeyType key, ValueType value)
    {
        // ...
    }

    public ValueType this[KeyType key]
    {
        get { return ValueType.default; }
    }
}
```

Although using Generics is type safe, you don't have type-safe access while developing the class itself. Because the type with which the generic class is used later is absolutely unknown, it's internally assumed to be `object`. Specific members of the data type can only be accessed after an explicit and therefore unsafe conversion. Possible failures will only be detected at run time. The example in Listing 1-6 shows that an exception will be thrown if the type passed to the `KeyType` placeholder doesn't support the `IComparable` interface.

Listing 1-6. Lack of Type Safety Internally for Generics

```
// MyList
public class MyDictionary<KeyType, ValueType>
{
    public void Add(KeyType key, ValueType value)
    {
        switch(((IComparable) key).CompareTo(123))
        {
            case 0:
                // ...
                break;
        }
    }
}
```

To resolve this problem, the placeholder types can be regularized with constraints. These have to be noted after the new `where` keyword, very similar to a SQL query (see Listing 1-7).

Listing 1-7. Generics Supporting Constraints

```
// MyList
public class MyDictionary<KeyType, ValueType>
   where KeyType : IComparable
{
   public void Add(KeyType key, ValueType value)
   {
      switch (((IComparable)key).CompareTo(123))
      {
         case 0:
            // ...
            break;
      }
   }
}
```

You can also define several constraints for one as well as for several place-holder data types. The constraints have to be separated by a comma and are seen as additive, which means that all of them must comply to get acceptance from the compiler.

Generics are useful not only with classes. Structures, interfaces, and delegates as well can be declared as generic templates and be reused. On enumerations, however, Generics can't be applied. Methods are another exciting field of use for Generics. Generic methods will allow you to pass one or more data types. Listing 1-8 shows an example.

Listing 1-8. Using Generics with Methods

```
public class MyClass
{
   protected ItemType MyMethod<ItemType>(ItemType item)
   {
      return item;
   }
}
```

As you see, Generics are very important and useful if you work, for example, with any kind of collections. Because of the backwards compatibility of ASP.NET 2.0, the existing collections couldn't be modified. Instead, a new namespace named System.Collections.Generic was created. It contains a lot of generic classes, structures, and interfaces like the following:

- Dictionary<T, U>

- List<T>

- Queue<T>

- SortedDictionary<T, U>

- Stack<T>

Iterators

The easiest way to walk through the subitems of a data container is a foreach loop, as you do with collections and dictionaries. But it's possible to walk through other classes, too. For example, the string class allows you to access the contained characters of type char in the same way.

A typical example for the enumeration of a class is described in Listing 1-9. It contains a foreach loop as well as the code that the compiler processes. Internally, a while loop is used that is based on the enumerator pattern.

Listing 1-9. foreach Loops Based on an Enumerator Pattern

```
// Implementation
ArrayList list = new ArrayList();
// ...
foreach(object obj in list)
{
    DoSomething(obj);
}


// Translation through compiler
Enumerator e = list.GetEnumerator();
while(e.MoveNext())
{
    object obj = e.Current;
    DoSomething(obj);
}
```

A pattern like the IEnumerable interface has to be implemented for the class. GetEnumerator() is the only defined method, and it has to return an object that supports the IEnumerator interface. The MoveNext() and Reset() methods as well as the Current property make it possible to iterate through the class.

It's the job of the new iterators in C# 2.0 to reduce the required implementation effort. No need to work with a design pattern; just one single typed method called GetEnumerator() is sufficient. Instead of an enumerator, the particular values will be returned directly. Here the new yield keyword replaces the old return keyword. (In Beta version 1, the keyword may possibly become yield return.) The keyword returns a value iteratively, the next value in the sequence being returned each time you pass through the foreach loop. Listing 1-10 illustrates the new approach.

Listing 1-10. Using Iterators to Iterate Through a Custom Class

```
using System;
using System.Collections.Generic;

public class Names
{
    public IEnumerator<string> GetEnumerator()
    {
        yield "Smith";
        yield "Miller";
        yield "Doe";
    }
}

// Main
public class MainClass
{
    public static void Main()
    {
        Names names = new Names();

        foreach(string name in names)
        {
            Console.WriteLine(name);
        }
        Console.Read();
    }
}
```

You can easily guess what the sample does. The three listed names will appear within the console window. By the way, you can also use this keyword in loops as shown in Listing 1-11.

Listing 1-11. Using the New Yield Keyword in Loops

```
public class Names
{
    private List<string> names = new List<string>();

    public Names()
    {
        this.names.Add("Smith");
        this.names.Add("Miller");
        this.names.Add("Doe");
    }

    public IEnumerator<string> GetEnumerator()
    {
        for(int i = 0; i < this.names.Count; i++)
        {
            yield this.names[i];
        }
    }
}
```

Under the hood, almost everything remains unaffected. The C# compiler converts the new implementation into the well-known enumerator pattern. Actually, this kind of iteration is a convenience feature for the hard-pressed developer. It avoids unnecessary coding and keeps the source code short.

New and therefore absolutely necessary to mention is the capability to make any method enumerable. The method has to return a value defined as IEnumerable and use the yield keyword to return each single value. This will look somewhat like the following listing:

```
public IEnumerable GetSomeValues(int start, int stop)
{
    for (int i = start; i <= stop; i++)
    {
        yield i;
    }
}
```

...

```
foreach (int i in mc.GetSomeValues(0, 10))
{
    Console.WriteLine(i);
}
```

Anonymous Methods

Anonymous methods are another improvement of the next generation of C#. They allow you to declare methods in the context of their use and without naming them.

Listing 1-12 demonstrates the use of anonymous methods within an ASP.NET page. During Page_Load an anonymous event-handling method is assigned to a Button control. The method will change the text of the Label control, which is also placed on the page.

Listing 1-12. Assigning and Handling Events Right Away

```
void Page_Load (object sender, System.EventArgs e)
{
    this.Button1.Click += delegate(object dlgSender, EventArgs dlgE)
    {
        Label1.Text = "Yeah, you clicked the button!";
    };
}
```

What's new is that you can abandon an explicit notation of the event-handling method—as long as it's useful! Just put the code after the assignment of the delegate. Open a new scope after the delegate keyword by using a brace, enter the desired actions, and close the scope with another brace. Then you finish the whole statement with a semicolon.

Unlike what is being demonstrated in the previous example, you can use more than one line of code, of course. In doing so, you have access to the two common event parameters that have to be defined explicitly as you assign the delegate. Please notice that I've renamed these parameters to avoid a conflict with the ones for the Page_Load event.

Even if it looks somewhat unusual at first sight, it's possible to use the local variables of the outer scope within the anonymous method. According to this, the lines in Listing 1-13 are correct, although they aren't arranged very clearly.

Listing 1-13. Accessing Variables Declared in the Upper Scope

```
void Page_Load (object sender, System.EventArgs e)
{
    string text = "Yeah, you clicked the button!";

    this.Button1.Click += delegate(object dlgSender, EventArgs dlgE)
    {
        Label1.Text = text;
    };
}
```

Anonymous methods may be used with more than one event or even in a completely different way. If you want to, you can reference the delegate in a variable and handle it as usual, as Listing 1-14 shows.

Listing 1-14. Using the Delegate As Usual

```
void Page_Load (object sender, System.EventArgs e)
{
    EventHandler handler = delegate(object dlgSender, EventArgs dlgE)
    {
        Label1.Text = "Yeah, you clicked the button!";
    };
    this.Button1.Click += handler;
    this.Button2.Click += handler;
}
```

Internally, the C# compiler converts the anonymously implemented method into a class including a uniquely named method. The created delegate now points to this procedure. In real life, the usage of anonymous methods is particularly of interest with regard to smaller event-handling methods. For the sake of clarity, you should not overuse this method, particularly in combination with longer routines.

Another area you could apply such methods might be multithreading. Until now, an explicit method was required to start a new thread. In this particular case, the anonymous counterpart can provide even more clarity because the context becomes more obvious. In Listing 1-15, an approach based on a console application is exemplified. In this case, the dynamic method is directly passed in the constructor of the Thread class. This looks really funny, but it actually works!

Listing 1-15. The Entry Code for the Second Thread Passed As an Anonymous Method

```
using System;
using System.Threading;

namespace MyLittleConsoleApp
{
    public class MainClass
    {
        [STAThread]
        static void Main()
        {
            Thread myThread = new Thread(delegate()
            {
                for(int i = 0; i < 20; i++)
                {
                    Console.WriteLine("Working thread ...");
                    Thread.Sleep(500);
                }
            });
            myThread.Start();
            for (int i = 0; i < 10; i++)
            {
                Console.WriteLine("In main.");
                Thread.Sleep(1000);
            }
            Console.Read();
        }
    }
}
```

Partial Classes

The fourth main new feature of C# version 2.0 allows you to split a particular class into two or more separate files. For this purpose, every part of the class is marked with the new modifier partial. The compiler looks for the marked parts and merges them into one complete implementation. You'll see no difference at run time. The assembly of the code parts requires all elements be in the same project and a parallel compilation. In addition, the classes have to match logically and must be identical regarding their modifiers, supported interfaces, and so on. Attributes assigned at class level are handled automatically (see Listing 1-16).

Listing 1-16. One Class Split into Several Files Using the New Partial Keyword

```csharp
// foo1.cs
using System;

public partial class Foo
{
    public void SomeMethod()
    {
    }
}

// foo2.cs
using System;

public partial class Foo
{
    public void SomeOtherMethod()
    {
    }
}
```

The main reasons to implement such a feature can primarily be found in RAD development environments like Visual Studio .NET. OK, in some special cases it may be useful to split a large class into several files. But this surely won't be the general rule. One aspect you may find interesting is splitting files in conjunction with automatic code generation, as in Visual Studio .NET for example. Instead of mixing generated and written code and differentiating it later on, two separate files can now be used. More details about this topic will follow in Chapter 2.

What's New in VB .NET?

This book is based on C#, but it's always helpful to think outside of the box. Some changes have also been made to the favorite language of many developers. The first issue involved providing missing features to make VB .NET finally measure up to C#. For example, a configuration file, vbc.rsp, has been established, and it allows you to define standard parameters parallel to the C# compiler (csc.rsp). More new features are as follows:

- XML documentation (Yeah, that rocks!)

- Generics

- Operator overloading (Ever used it?)

- Partial classes

- New data types

- New keywords

XML Documentation

Until now, direct source code documentation was reserved for C# developers. With the assistance of tools like VB.DOC, it was possible to integrate comments in Visual Basic .NET, too; however, this was sort of challenging, especially because no compiler or IntelliSense support was available. This will change with the eighth version of Visual Basic. From now on, code comment functionality is supported directly. This results in a simplified way to write comments and also ensures that references within the documentation are being validated.

The comments have to start with the familiar comment character (') followed by an @ symbol to make sure that the compiler will recognize them (see Listing 1-17 and Figure 1-12). After that, you can use the same XML tags as in C#. The compiler provides the new /doc option and generates the XML data, which is necessary for tools like NDoc.

Listing 1-17. Using XML Documentation in VB .NET

```
Imports Microsoft.VisualBasic

'@ <summary>That's my little foo class</summary>
Public Class Foo

    '@ <summary>These methods return the text passed as parameter</summary>
    '@ <param name="Text">Text to be returned</param>
    '@ <returns>Returns the string passed as
       <paramref name="Text"/> parameter</returns>
    Public Function ReturnSomeString(ByVal Text As String) As String
        Return Text
    End Function

End Class
```

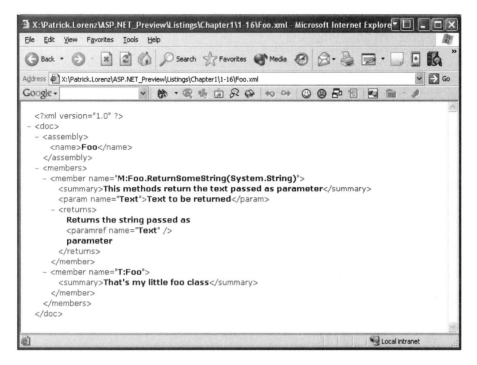

Figure 1-12. VB .NET now supports XML documentation.

At present, additional changes to the syntax are being considered. Possibly three apostrophe signs will be used in the final version of VB .NET 2.0 to mark comments. This would be similar to the approach of C#.

Generics

The new version of Visual Basic .NET supports generic data types in the same way as C#, but—surprise!—with a slightly different syntax. In VB .NET, this involves the new Of keyword, which has to be specified at the definition of generic classes. You also need the keyword whenever you use the generic type. Constraints are defined through the As keyword, which you already know from another context. Listing 1-18 demonstrates the realization of the Listings 1-1 and 1-2 shown earlier in the world of VB .NET.

Listing 1-18. Making VB .NET "Generics Enabled"

```vb
Imports System

Public Class MyList(Of ItemType As IComparable)

    Public Sub Add(ByVal Obj As ItemType)
    End Sub

    Default Public ReadOnly Property Items(ByVal Index As Integer) As ItemType
        Get
            Return Nothing
        End Get
    End Property

End Class

Public Class Foo
    Implements IComparable

    Public Function CompareTo(ByVal obj As Object) As Integer _
                    Implements System.IComparable.CompareTo
        Return 0
    End Function
End Class

Public Class MainClass

    Public Shared Sub Main()
        Dim List As MyList(Of Foo) = New MyList(Of Foo)
        List.Add(New Foo)
        Dim AnotherFoo As Foo = List(0)

        Console.Read()
    End Sub

End Class
```

Operator Overloading

Like C#, VB .NET now supports operator overloading. Although this feature is
rarely used with custom classes in the real world, it's nevertheless fun to work
with it. A small example appears in Listing 1-19. Several overloaded operators are
defined to compare, add, and subtract two instances of points in the structure.

Listing 1-19. Point Structure Allows Arithmetic and Comparison Operations

```
Imports System

Public Structure Point

    Public X As Integer
    Public Y As Integer

    Public Shared Operator +(ByVal p1 As Point, ByVal p2 As Point) As Point
        Dim p As Point = New Point
        p.X = p1.X + p2.X
        p.Y = p1.Y + p2.Y
        Return p
    End Operator

    Public Shared Operator -(ByVal p1 As Point, ByVal p2 As Point) As Point
        Dim p As Point = New Point
        p.X = p1.X - p2.X
        p.Y = p1.Y - p2.Y
        Return p
    End Operator

    Public Shared Operator =(ByVal p1 As Point, ByVal p2 As Point) As Boolean
        Return ((p1.X = p2.X) AndAlso (p1.Y = p2.Y))
    End Operator

    Public Shared Operator <>(ByVal p1 As Point, ByVal p2 As Point) As Boolean
        Return ((p1.X <> p2.X) OrElse (p1.Y <> p2.Y))
    End Operator

End Structure
```

Any operators are implemented as methods and are static by definition. Furthermore, they have to exist in pairs. Possible pairs are

- = and <>

- < and >

- >= and <=

- IsTrue and IsFalse

The operators And, Or, Not, and Xor are supported as well. Also, type conversions can be executed by such custom operators. Two new keywords are available to separate implicit (and therefore free of loss) conversion from explicit conversion: Widening and Narrowing. In Listing 1-20, you find two structures, Point2D and Point3D. Both classes allow conversion among each other, implicitly in one direction and explicitly in the other. Custom type conversions are implemented using the CType operator.

Listing 1-20. Widening and Narrowing Conversion Operations

```
Imports System

Public Structure Point2D

    Public X As Integer
    Public Y As Integer

End Structure

Public Structure Point3D

    Public X As Integer
    Public Y As Integer
    Public Z As Integer

    Public Shared Widening Operator CType(ByVal p1 As Point2D) As Point3D
        Dim p2 As New Point3D
        p2.X = p1.X
        p2.Y = p1.Y
        Return p2
    End Operator
```

```
Public Shared Narrowing Operator CType(ByVal p1 As Point3D) As Point2D
    Dim p2 As New Point2D
    p2.X = p1.X
    p2.Y = p1.Y
    Return p2
End Operator

End Structure
```

Partial Classes

Partial classes are available not only in C#, but also in the new VB .NET version. The required new keyword is Expands (see Listing 1-21). Unlike in C#, a main class exists in VB .NET, which has to be defined as usual. Only the additional classes have to be marked with the keyword, and they don't need any modifiers. The separation in several files is supported for classes and structures, too.

Listing 1-21. Separating Code Using the New Expands Keyword

```
' foo1.vb
Public Class Foo

    Public Sub SomeMethod()
    End Sub

End Class

' foo2.vb
Expands Class Foo

    Public Sub AnotherMethod()
    End Sub

End Class
```

New Data Types

The new version of VB .NET comes with an extended pool of included data types that are now identical to the ones in C#. Please note that the following new data types aren't CLS compliant, so other languages may not be able to access them:

- SByte

- UInteger

- ULong

- UShort

New Keywords

There are more new keywords besides the ones already introduced. With one exception, they are all familiar to users of C#.

Continue allows you to close the current loop and jump into the next circle. The keyword can be used with For, Do, and While loops. In nested loops of different types, the desired loop could be specified by a suffix—for example, Continue For.

The very helpful using keyword (you may already know it from C#) is now available in VB .NET, too. Here, of course, it generally starts with a capital *U*. Using offers the definition of a dispose block. The variable defined in the header will be always disposed on leaving the scope, even in case of an unhandled exception. A frequent task that is performed is database connection, which should be returned back to the pool in any case. Another possible scenario is the use of the Font class as shown in the following listing. To enable a class to be disposed in this way, it has to implement the IDisposable interface.

```
Public Sub setbigbold(ByVal c As Control)
    Using nf As New System.Drawing.Font("Arial", 12.0F, FontStyle.Bold)
        c.Font = nf
        c.Text = "This is 12-point Arial bold"
    End Using
End Sub
```

Last but not least, another new keyword is Global. This one specifies the root namespace if naming conflicts exist with the local one—for example, Global.System.Int32.

CHAPTER 2

Introducing VS .NET for Web Developers

DO YOU ALREADY KNOW Visual Studio .NET (VS .NET)? Sure, you do! And what about Web Matrix? The new version of Visual Studio .NET for Web Developers now combines the best features of Web Matrix and good old VS .NET. Moreover, it extends the set of functions with a bunch of features that make development of web applications (called "web sites" in the new terminology) as simple as possible.

So why a completely updated development environment? There are several good reasons. Neither Web Matrix nor the current version of VS .NET has been really optimized for web site development. VS .NET was targeted to desktop development. Support of web projects was available, but especially in large projects it was annoying. For example, the Microsoft HTML editors' bad habit of defacing your code was perfectly integrated here. And although Web Matrix offered some smart new features, it wasn't appropriate for larger projects at all, because some important functions such as IntelliSense, source control, or debugging weren't available.

The new version of VS .NET fills in these gaps and provides web developers with an environment especially optimized for their needs. Here's a list of some of the features offered by the new program:

- With "project-less" development, project files are no longer necessary. The integrated development environment (IDE) gets all the required information directly out of the directory.

- Besides real IIS projects, you're now able to store data directly in the file system and access the projects via FTP and FrontPage Server Extensions.

- Thanks to the integrated web server (have a look at "Cassini"), Internet Information Services (IIS) is no longer required during development, but it's still supported, of course.

- VS .NET can handle inline source code within the ASPX file, and it offers a revised code-behind model called code-beside.

- Regardless of where editing takes place, full support of IntelliSense and debugging is available.

- The new editor makes sure that manually entered HTML source code will remain unchanged; custom formatting and designs won't be lost.

- An exchangeable validation engine allows developers to check the HTML source code against standards such as Extensible Hypertext Markup Language (XHTML). Failures are entered into the Task List.

- In the final release, the output of all server controls will be clean XHTML.

Figure 2-1 shows an integrated sample web site project being edited within VS .NET. At first sight, the differences between the old and new versions seem to be small, but after a few minutes working with the IDE you'll discover that the new environment is easier and more manageable, and offers better support than the old version.

Figure 2-1. Here's the new Visual Studio .NET at work.

Installing VS .NET

VS .NET's installation process is self-explanatory. Please note that all existing IIS applications are mapped to new Internet Server Application Programming Interface (ISAPI) extension during installation of the current Alpha. As far as I know, this will be fixed in the Beta. Existing installations of an older framework, VS .NET 2002, or VS .NET 2003 don't cause any problems. Currently I use all three versions on one machine.

After you install VS .NET, a new group, Microsoft Visual Studio Whidbey, is available in your Start menu. Start it by clicking the Microsoft Visual Studio code-name Whidbey link. The IDE's documentation is accessible via the Microsoft Visual Studio 2003 Documentation link. The IDE's documentation describes the improvements in ASP.NET and introduces the new VS .NET version. If you've installed the new .NET Framework SDK, you're able to start the voluminous reference separately via a link in the newly created Microsoft .NET Framework SDK v1.2 group.

As you can see in the group description and in the file system, the .NET Framework version is 1.2. There are historical reasons for using this version number, but the next version number will be 2.0 in the RTM version (it's probably 2.0 already in the Beta version).

NOTE *If you're using Windows Server 2003, you'll need to enable the ASP.NET 1.2 (2.0) ISAPI extension manually. Start the Internet Service Manager, choose Web Service Extensions, activate ASP.NET v1.2 ISAPI, and click Enable.*

Creating and Opening Web Sites

In this section, I cover how to create a new web site and open existing ones with the new version of VS .NET. Also, I show you how to migrate applications created with the older version of the IDE.

Creating a new web site within VS .NET has become quite easy. To do so, you can use the local IIS 5.0, 5.1, or 6.0. Alternatively, storing the web site directly in your local file system and accessing it via FrontPage Server Extensions and even via FTP is possible.

Creating a New Web Site

The New Web Site dialog box (which you access through the File menu) offers all opportunities mentioned previously, as shown in Figure 2-2. When you click the Browse button, the Choose Location dialog box appears (see Figure 2-3), from which you can select the site's storage location. If you choose File System, you can create new directories. If you choose IIS Local, you can define new applications and virtual directories at the local IIS level.

VS .NET includes several sample projects. Some of these projects are pretty extensive, and you can use them as starting points for your own web sites or to discover the new features of ASP.NET v2.0:

- The project template ASP.NET Internet Site provides a web site along with a secured area, including registration and login. It demonstrates the new data source concept in action. The required data is provided by static XML files and by an included Access database. Access also acts as the storage location for user management.

- The project template ASP.NET Intranet Site is, as its name implies, targeted to intranet applications. The template's main goal is to reveal the possibilities of personalization. The example shows the visual customization of the displayed information based on the authenticated user called Web Parts.

- The templates ASP.NET Web Site and Empty Web Site are very similar at this point. The first one creates a single page automatically; the second one doesn't.

- Last but not least, the project template ASP.NET Web Services is used to create a new web services web site. Of course, you can also add web services to any other existing project.

All of the previously described templates are available in C# and Visual Basic .NET (VB .NET) versions. This isn't a big deal, however, because the templates don't require much source code thanks to the new zero-code scenarios. Samples in J# aren't available yet.

Something different from previous approaches is that there's no special project file generated at the time of project creation. From now on, every file within the selected directories belongs to the project automatically. This approach simplifies adding new files, including references to the bin directory, and moving projects. Distributing a complete project is now a job for XCopy. If you work in a team, you'll love this new approach. Besides the project files, VS .NET still offers the old solution files.

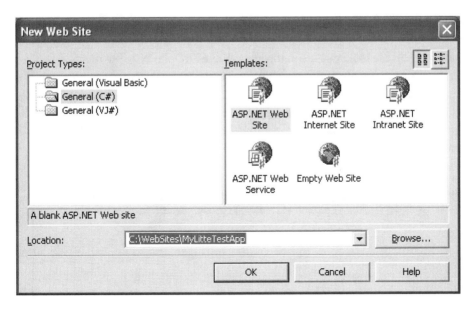

Figure 2-2. Creating a new web site is quite simple nowadays.

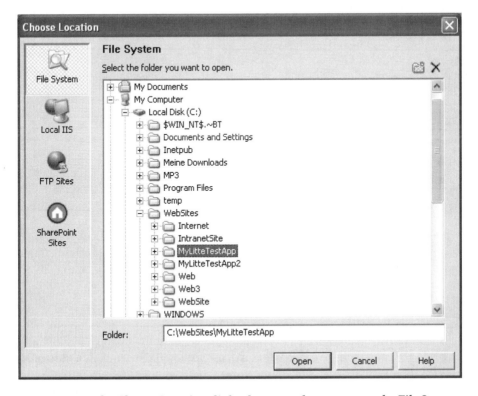

Figure 2-3. In the Choose Location dialog box, you choose among the File System, IIS Local, FTP Sites, or SharePoint Sites options.

Opening an Existing Web Site

Opening a web site is very easy too through VS .NET's Open Web Site dialog box. The Open Web Site dialog box shown in Figure 2-4 is similar to the New Web Site dialog box shown in Figure 2-1. It offers direct access to the file system, the local IIS, an FTP server, and any server offering FrontPage Server Extensions (mentioned as Share-Point Sites in the dialog box). You can also handle projects managed by Visual SourceSafe.

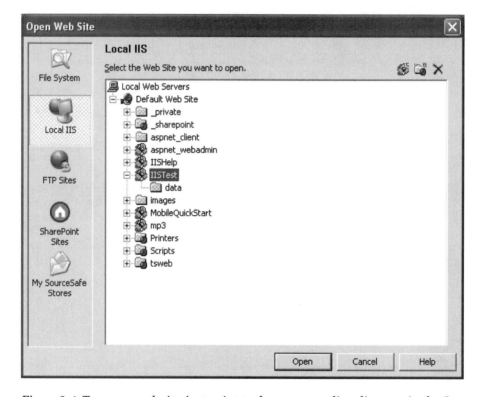

Figure 2-4. To open a web site, just point to the corresponding directory in the Open Web Site dialog box.

Migrating an Existing VS .NET 2002/2003 Web Application

Changes in the project management features are among the reasons that you need to migrate VS .NET 2002 and 2003 applications before you use them in the new version. After you confirm your intention to migrate, VS .NET performs the whole conversion without requiring further input from you. All changes are logged in the UpgradeReport.txt file. I didn't encounter any problems during my tests.

CAUTION *Keep in mind that migration works in one direction only, and the old VS .NET versions can't handle a migrated project. Make sure to create backup before you start the migration process—VS .NET doesn't create one automatically for you!*

Editing Web Sites

Now it's time to play with the new VS .NET version. Let's go! Start with a new ASP.NET Web Site project. The first thing you'll see is an almost empty ASP.NET page—only the HTML body is in there.

When you take a look at the generated page, you'll realize that the new VS .NET works without code-behind. This shouldn't upset you too much—code-behind is still supported in an updated and slightly different way. The IDE offers several views of a single file, a concept you may already be familiar with from Web Matrix. Three tab buttons allow you to switch between the different views:

- The Design button shows the visual editor.

- The Source button provides the whole file, including the server-side source code.

- The Server Code button extracts the first `<script>` block of the file and displays it.

By default, the window appears in Source mode.

To create a new page, just right-click the project node in Solution Explorer and then select Add new Item. Alternatively, you can choose the same command from the Website menu. By the way, instead of naming the newly created pages webform?.aspx, VS .NET names them default?.aspx. Makes sense, doesn't it?

Placing Server Controls

The editor now supports adding server controls in Design view as well as in Source view. Just drag the control out of the Toolbox and drop it at the desired location. The current cursor position and selection (if one exists) remain unaffected when you change the view. In both views you can rely on the Properties window to manipulate a control. Don't be surprised if you edit a tag in Source view. There is an extended version of IntelliSense at your service.

The new version of VS .NET answers the prayers of a lot of developers: It doesn't pick your manually entered HTML code to pieces as the previous versions did. Changes will be made in the particular context only—for example, if a new control is inserted. Even if you switch between the views, there will be no changes. Now go and celebrate!

If a row in the source view is modified by the environment or by the developer, it's marked in yellow next to the row number, as shown in Figure 2-5. As changes are saved, the mark changes from yellow to green.

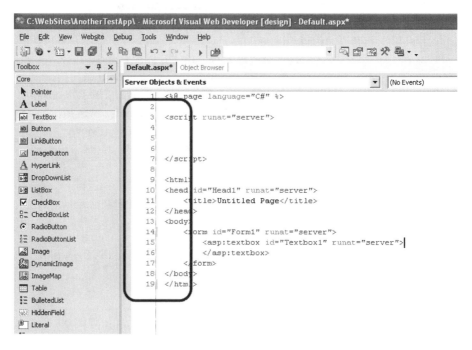

Figure 2-5. VS .NET now fully preserves your HTML code.

You'll find something new in the Toolbox, too: structure. Because the number of controls has increased dramatically, the Toolbox is split into several categories: Core, Data, Personalization, Security, Validation, Navigation, and HTML.

Editing Controls

So what about editing controls in VS .NET? It's hard to believe, but this has become much more convenient, too. With few exceptions, you don't need to edit control parameters in the HTML source code. You can change almost everything in Design view.

Smart Tags and Data Binding

Another new VS .NET feature is smart tags, which are available for all controls with assigned design-time actions—the so-called verbs. Clicking a smart tag opens a context menu with all the provided options, as shown in Figure 2-6. By the way, insiders call this *task-based editing*.

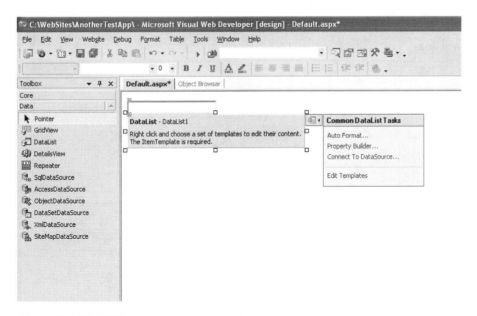

Figure 2-6. VS .NET now supports smart tags.

Smart tags are a pretty cool feature now that you can edit virtually any template in Design view. In the smart tag menu of the data control, you can choose Edit Templates. The list allows you to select one template or even a whole group of templates. Just fill the templates with some text and controls as usual. Figure 2-7 shows the new feature in action.

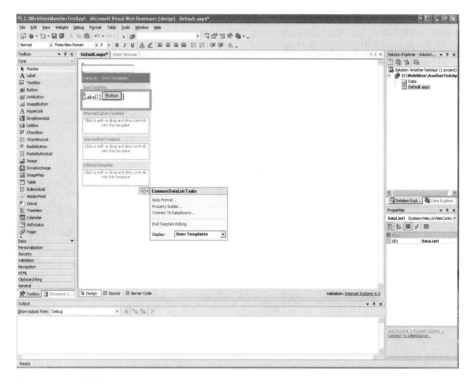

Figure 2-7. Editing templates is much easier now.

Don't worry about specifying the data-binding expression in the HTML source code, which can be challenging sometimes. Each and every control in a template features an extended smart tag menu. Select Edit DataBindings and a dialog box pops up that allows you to enter or edit the binding. As Figure 2-8 shows, you can either bind selected properties to a data source or enter an expression to be evaluated as usual.

If you look closely at Figure 2-8, you should be able to figure out which expression I've used for data binding. The syntax has been significantly shortened and therefore simplified compared to the old versions. Until now the syntax looked like this:

```
<%# DataBinder.Eval(Container.DataItem, "MyField") %>
```

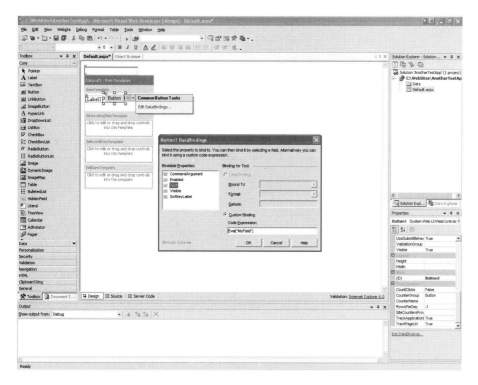

Figure 2-8. You can assign data bindings easily using this dialog box.

Using the new syntax, the same result is achieved with fewer characters:

```
<%# Eval("MyField") %>
```

This was made possible through the integration of a new protected method called Eval in the Page class. It's nice to know that you can still use an overloaded implementation of this method by passing an additional format string:

```
<%# Eval("MyDateField", "{0:d}") %>
```

Note that in the preceding dialog box, you aren't required to put the data binding in brackets.

In addition to using Eval, you may also use the new method XPath, as long as the bound data is XML:

```
<%# XPath ("orders/order/customer/@id") %>
```

You can, of course, also pass a format instruction as a second parameter.

Enhanced Table-Editing Support

Improved support for HTML tables is yet another enhancement in VS .NET. You add a table using the Table menu, and though the subsequent editing of single cells hasn't changed in a major way, it has become easier to manage, as shown in Figure 2-9. Here are some of the improvements:

- A border is displayed around the current row, making it easier to see the row you're editing.

- You can use the Tab key to switch between cells.

- You can select rows, columns, and cells by holding down the Ctrl key, even if the elements you're selecting aren't connected.

- You can change the properties of all selected items in one shot.

- You can connect cells.

- You can move tables more easily using the mouse.

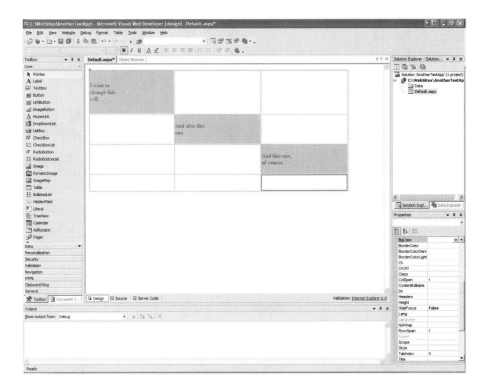

Figure 2-9. The table editing features have been slightly improved.

User Controls

If you like the way Web Matrix (since version 0.6) supports user controls, you'll be pleasantly surprised to discover that VS .NET supports them in the same way. Instead of displaying a meaningless gray box, VS .NET now shows the content of a control. Starting with the Beta version, the VS .NET IDE will display the content of user controls while you edit a page. The current Alpha version, however, still uses the gray box. And more bad news about the Alpha version: Although it provides a Properties window to edit properties, you can't use it because it's a still a bit buggy at the moment. But both will be improved in the Beta version.

With these two extensions, user controls have become more attractive, haven't they?

Enhanced Support for Control Developers

The next improvement relates to custom controls. At least this is the plan of the ASP.NET team. Some of the possible improvements are enrichment of task-based editing, addition of in-place editing, and access to the development environment, including an active source document, directives, and so on. For now, these are only plans—none has been implemented in the current Alpha version.

Validating HTML Source Code

VS .NET comes with some new features related to HTML source code validation. The current validation schema for each ASPX page is displayed at the lower right of the status bar. Just click the schema and the Options dialog box will appear, in which you can choose among several alternatives, for example, XHTML 1.0 Strict, XHTML 1.0 Transitional, Internet Explorer 6.0, and so on. Errors appear in the Task List provided by VS .NET and are also marked directly in the source code. A tool tip shows a description of the problem.

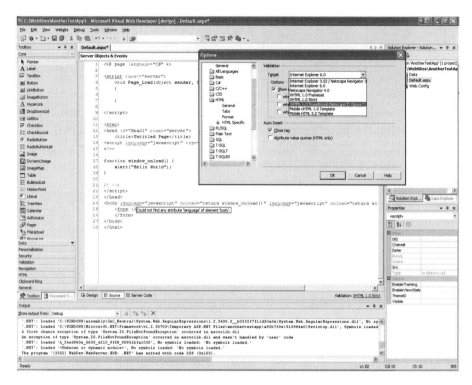

Figure 2-10. Select the validation schema you want to target.

Creating Events Handlers

So what has happened to the event-handling method creation process? It has been simplified. Though the automatic generation of the code body of a standard event by double-click onto the desired control in Design view isn't new (but it's still a nice feature, of course!), VB .NET developers can now use the Properties window to create an event-handling method. C# developers know how to do this already.

All languages provide two drop-down lists in HTML view and Source view, as shown in Figure 2-11. In one list you can select the control, and in the other you can choose the event. If you do so, the method body is automatically generated.

As you can see, everything is fine on the server side. Now what about on the client side? Support is available there too. If you select Source view, the left list contains the group Client Objects & Events. As the group's name suggests, you get access to objects such as window and document that are offered by a client-side script language (JavaScript, for example). After you select an object, the supported events are displayed in the right list. Creating the related event-handling method within a client-side script block is a matter of one mouse-click. Figure 2-12 shows this with window_onload.

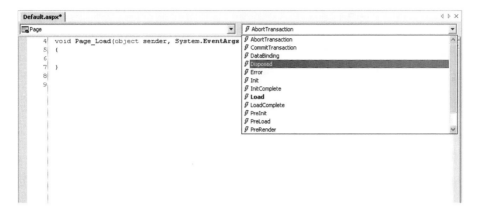

Figure 2-11. Just select the event you need to handle.

TIP *The objects and events listed in Source view may vary depending on the selected validation target.*

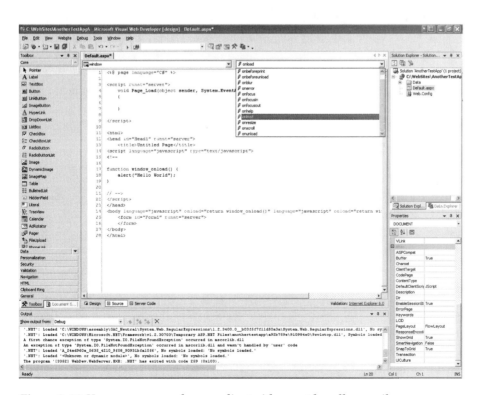

Figure 2-12. You can now apply even client-side event handlers easily.

Using IntelliSense

Compared to previous versions, in the new version of VS .NET the IntelliSense capabilities are highly enhanced. In the final release, the helpful window will be always at your service:

- On editing server code in HTML view

- On editing server code in Source view

- On editing client-side code in HTML view

- On editing server controls, HTML tags, CSS, and directives

- On editing C# or Visual Basic source code files

- On editing ASMX files (from the Beta version on)

- On editing ASHX files (from the Beta version on)

As in VS .NET 2003, preselection of frequently used class members and support for VB .NET while implementing interfaces are in the function set.

I really like IntelliSense's support for client-side scripts in the new version of VS .NET (see Figure 2-13). According to the selected validation schema (see the "Validating HTML Source Code" section for more information), all available objects and their members are listed. Sound good? Then enjoy creating client-side functions!

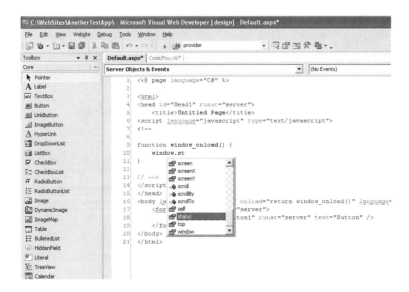

Figure 2-13. IntelliSense now supports client-side scripting.

Testing and Debugging

If you built your web application with VS .NET, you can test and debug it right inside the development environment. In edit mode press the F5 key to start your application in debug mode and press Ctrl+F5 if you don't want to use the debugger. The current page will be displayed within the standard browser.

Any application stored at the local IIS level will be used as server. Whenever you save a project in the local file system, the integrated web server, which looks somewhat like the familiar Cassini server, will be started. The final VS .NET release will likely offer you the choice to select one or both directly.

> **TIP** *So far, web projects in VS .NET aren't compiled explicitly but implicitly. The main benefit of implicit compilation is that it's possible to have a browser window open in parallel to the VS .NET window. You can edit the code, save it, and then just refresh your browser window. As I said, no explicit compilation is required—that makes development a lot easier, doesn't it?*

Please note that any page of the project, including dependent files, will be compiled at the first request dynamically (see Figure 2-14). Failures may be detected by calling each page. Another method is to compile the whole application at once by using this URL: http://<Host>:<Port>/<App>/precompile.axd. I cover precompilation further later on in the chapter.

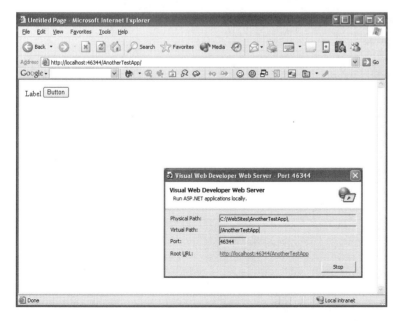

Figure 2-14. You no longer need IIS to run your project—just click and go for it.

Comfortable debugging doesn't depend on the chosen server. As usual, pressing F9 or clicking the gray area next to the row number will set or delete a breakpoint. Pressing Ctrl+Shift+F9 will remove all breakpoints at once after confirmation. Additionally, the following functions are available:

- F10: Step over

- F11: Step into

- Ctrl+F10: Run to cursor

TIP *When you start a project by pressing F5, the IDE generates a* web.config *file automatically after a confirmation if one doesn't already exist. This* web.config *file will contain the known* compilation *tag.*

Debugging in VS .NET is quite smart and intuitive. Regardless of whether the code lives in the source code file or in the ASPX file, the compiler will jump to the right position. Another nice feature is the option to change the value of a variable right in the tool tip while debugging, as shown in Figure 2-15.

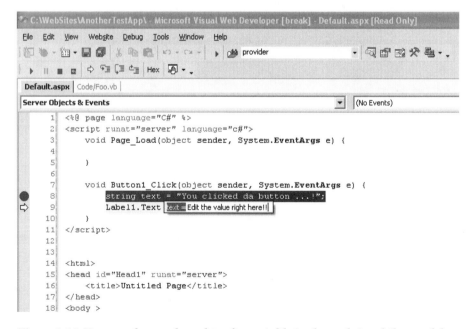

Figure 2-15. You can change the value of a variable in the tool tip while you debug.

Now I'd like to introduce the Object Inspector in VB .NET to you (see Figure 2-16). An enhanced tool tip shows all properties of an object, and you can open the sub-objects step by step. Stop dreaming: Changing the source code at run time as you can in client applications still doesn't work in web applications. But it is possible (in all languages) to edit the source code while you're debugging. The changes will take effect on the next request or postback.

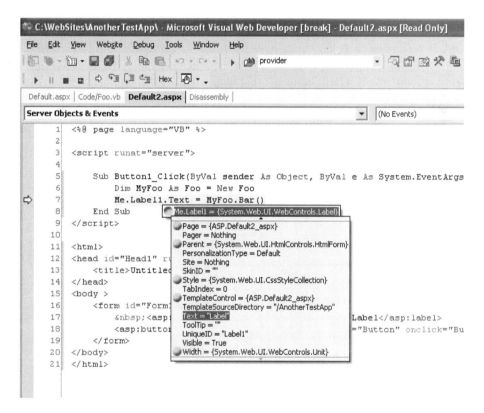

Figure 2-16. VB .NET allows a detailed view into every object.

Code-Beside/Code Separation

Code-behind was a very useful and comfortable feature for web developers. But I have some bad news: Code-behind is dead. Hey, don't worry—you'll use the new code-beside model instead.

Code-behind was smart, but from an object-based view it was far from perfect. The designed ASPX page was derived from a class that was generated in parts by the development environment. You had to declare controls in both files, and manual changes often resulted in problems. There are a lot of good reasons to move away from code-behind.

The solution is *code-beside,* which is supposed to make everything better, brighter, and of course more object oriented. This is what the ASP.NET team promises. Instead of using the class derivation as it was up to now, the design file and the source code file are created as partial classes that will be merged by the compiler (I describe partial classes in Chapter 1). This approach means that there's no automatically generated source code *at all.* Both files work hand in hand, and you can assign events directly in the server control tags.

To add a new code-beside page, right-click the project in Solution Explorer and choose Add New Item. Then select Web Form Using Code Separation in the following dialog box and click Open. Now the project contains two new files, one with the design and one with the source code. The two files are nothing new, but the source code file doesn't include any directives generated by the IDE. VS .NET has just built an empty partial class.

Figure 2-17 shows an example of code-beside. The page contains a Label control and a Button control. Clicking the Button control will assign new text to the Label control.

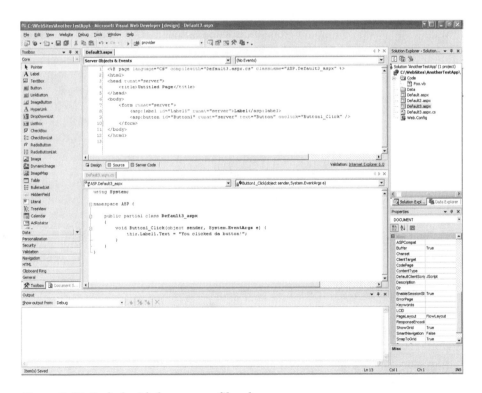

Figure 2-17. Code-beside keeps your files clean.

The old code-behind model isn't supported in the current Alpha version, but it will be supported in the Beta version. So don't worry about migrating your projects.

> **TIP** *You can use code-beside pages and single file pages within one project without any problems. VS .NET handles the files in an appropriate manner automatically, and it takes care that you get the right information while debugging. Currently, code-beside is available for pages as well as for user controls and web services.*

> **TIP** *Put source code in the code-beside file* and *in the ASPX file, and then try to debug the page. What happens? Yeah, the compiler always jumps into the correct file—well done!*

Code Directory

Earlier in the chapter I mentioned that an explicit compilation isn't required anymore. But what about your business objects, your application layer, and your data layer? Well, that's why you have the new code directory.

The code directory looks like nothing more than an ordinary folder, but it's actually quite special. It lives inside of the application root. Any source code files such as *.vb or *.cs files, but also resource files and even Web Services Description Language (WSDL) files, are saved here. Every supported file is compiled dynamically and is available instantly after you save it.

Using the Code Directory

To experience the code directory in action, you must first create a new folder with the given name "code" by right-clicking the project and choosing New Folder from the context menu. The folder shows its special meaning at once. The second step is to add a C# source code file, such as the Foo.cs file in Listing 2-1, to the folder, attach the method Bar, and save the new file.

Listing 2-1. Adding the Foo *Class to a Code Directory*

```
using System;

/// <summary>
/// Summary description for Foo
/// </summary>
public class Foo
{
    public void Bar()
    {
    }
}
```

You can use the class in your project without compilation. Even the IntelliSense window knows the class, as shown in Figure 2-18. In addition, full debugging support is available for the file. This means that you're able to step into every single method.

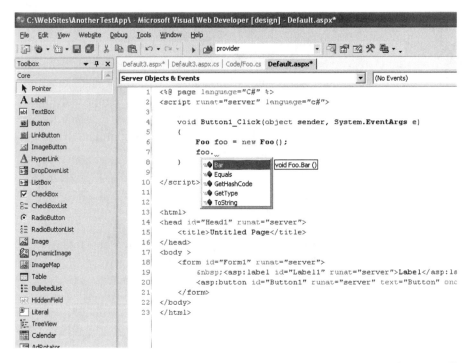

Figure 2-18. Any known file types placed within the code directory are dynamically compiled.

> **TIP** *For better structuring of your source code, it's advisable to spread the classes in subdirectories of the code folder, especially if you work with large projects. The files in subfolders will be dynamically compiled as well.*

In comparison with the previous approach, the code directory offers enhanced possibilities of teamwork, which is a significant advantage. In this new model, a team member no longer has to check out a project file to add or remove files. Changes become effective on a global basis very easily.

Multilanguage and Multitype Support

With ASP.NET you're no longer limited to one language per web site. You can now mix different .NET languages whenever you want. Does it make sense to write one page in C#, a second in VB .NET, and a third in J#? I don't know, but at least it's possible!

Another option is to mix different languages using the code directory. The Foo class written in C# and shown in Listing 2-1 works fine with VB .NET pages. This includes full IntelliSense support. But be aware that debugging isn't fully supported in such a scenario, so you can't jump from your VB .NET page to the C# source code. This is currently a major strike against using different languages. However, this will presumably be fixed within the Beta version.

As I mentioned previously, you can store many different file types in the code directory. Besides the programming languages' source code files, the following types are supported:

- RESX

- RESOURCES

- WSDL

- XSD

This list can be individually extended by a provider model. Corresponding abstract base classes are available in the System.Web.Compilation namespace. Just let your custom provider inherit from a base class and then assign the desired file extensions to it in the machine.config or web.config file.

What Happened to the Bin Directory?

Not much, it's still alive. But I wouldn't mention it if there hadn't been some changes. Because web projects are no longer compiled explicitly, there is no single project dynamic link library (DLL) anymore besides the already mentioned pre-compilation DLL. But external components are referenced in the bin directory further on.

To include a DLL in VS .NET, you just have to copy the bin directory. As a result, the contained classes are automatically available, with IntelliSense support, of course.

Precompilation

Usually an ASP.NET page, including all dependent source code files, is automatically compiled on the first request. This once-compiled version is used until the page or one of its dependencies changes. Besides this approach, version 2.0 offers precompilation. In this approach, all the pages and all related files are compiled explicitly and at once.

There are two different kinds of precompiling: in-place precompilation and precompilation for deployment. The following sections describe these precompilation types in detail.

In-Place Precompilation

You execute *in-place precompilation* by calling the following URL: `http://<Host>:<Port>/<App>/precompile.axd`. Direct integration of this functionality in VS .NET is being planned. So far, so good, but what is it worth? It has two advantages:

- The first request of each page gets accelerated because it's completely compiled already. From the second request on, there's no gain in speed.

- You can detect and fix all compilation errors at once.

Precompilation does more for you than previous versions of VS .NET did. The ASPX files are converted to classes and stored as DLLs in the cache directory together with any code-beside. Only static pages and (graphic) resources are taken out of the directory of the web site afterward.

> **NOTE** *After the first in-place precompilation, any changes are included incrementally. This kind of compilation makes sense even if there are only small changes.*

Precompilation for Deployment

The other type of precompilation is targeted for a different purpose. It allows you to distribute an entire compiled web site compiled as DLLs. In contrast to previous versions of VS. NET, the compiled version includes ASPX pages, ASCX files, and so on with the design, because they've been converted to classes and compiled too.

You can copy the result of this compilation to your server by using XCopy or you can ship it to your customers. After that, it isn't possible for the customer to change the application or any of the pages. (A perfect model for software licensing!)

Start the compilation with a new command-line application called spnet_compiler.exe. You'll find it in the `<windir>\Microsoft.NET\Framework\ <FrameworkVersion>` directory.

To compile a web site stored in the file system, just pass the path of the project and a target folder in which the compiled version of the site will be stored:

```
aspnet_compiler -v / -p <source> <target>
```

In later versions, the parameter `-v /` may not be required. It's just a workaround in the current Alpha. You can use it to define a virtual directory that will be used for absolute links.

Have a look at the result of the compilation and you'll see that it has almost the same structure as your web site (see Figure 2-19). Here you can recognize your ASPX files among other things. But they're used as marks only, and they contain just a message and no design. The documentation consists of an overview of different files and file types. Files with the extension `.compile` are important; they're necessary to establish the allocation between pages and the generated assemblies.

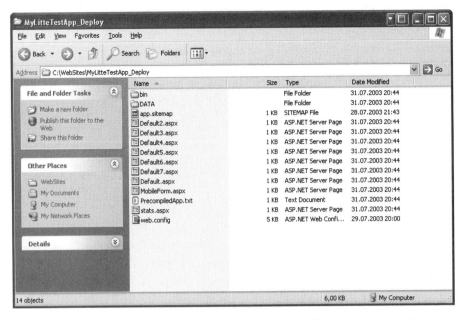

Figure 2-19. The precompilation tool creates a marker file for each page of your site.

To transfer the web site to a server, copy the whole folder. Please don't delete any of the files—they're all required for execution.

Deploying Web Sites

Deployment is much easier with the help of the previously described precompilation. A new tool named Web Copy, starting with the Beta version, will help you to easily copy and synchronize projects, for example with FTP. The corresponding command Publish has already been integrated in the Website menu, but it isn't functioning yet.

Customizing the IDE

The new version of VS .NET has a highly customizable development environment. In particular, you can configure the text editors to fit your individual needs. Figure 2-20 shows a part of the Options dialog box. It allows you, for example, to specify in detail if a line break is inserted before an angle bracket in C#, how parameters should be arranged, and much more.

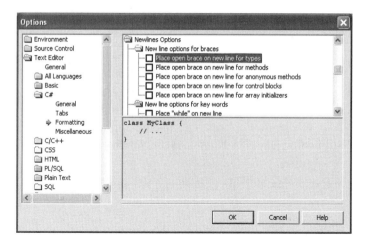

Figure 2-20. You can customize virtually any editor behavior.

For your convenience, you can save your complete settings as an XML file and copy it to a different system. This way, it's possible to enforce companywide coding guidelines. Just select Import/Export Settings from the Tools menu. Figure 2-21 shows the Import/Export Settings dialog box.

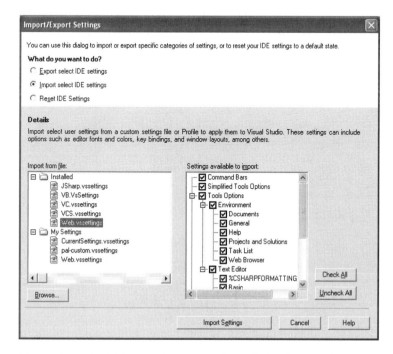

Figure 2-21. In the Import/Export Settings dialog box you back up, share, and reset your individual IDE settings.

Summary

This chapter covered a lot of enhancements in VS .NET, but even more are planned for the final release. In particular, the community features from Web Matrix will surely be taken into consideration more than in the current Alpha version. I hope you've enjoyed this little guided tour through the new development environment. The VS .NET IDE offers a number of interesting improvements, such as better integration of teamwork-related features, and it simplifies the creation of simple and even complex web sites.

CHAPTER 3

Enhanced Data Controls

THE FIRST VERSION OF ASP.NET established a useful set of data-bound controls. Visualizing and editing data became a lot easier with the support of such controls, one of the most important of which was the DataGrid control. Unfortunately, this control had its drawbacks, too. Although the DataGrid offered some built-in hooks for sorting, paging, and editing of data, you had to implement these features manually.

The new version of ASP.NET, version 2.0, follows a different approach. It solves many of the problems you may have had previously with ASP.NET and offers standard functionalities completely out of the box. Now you can sort, page, and edit any data source (and much more)—in most cases without typing a single line of code. That's fun!

It's All About Data Sources

The new features of ASP.NET 2.0 are based on a set of so-called Data Source controls. They handle the communication between data sources and controls, which is used for presentation in an abstract and generic way. Because the Data Source controls themselves don't have any visualization of their own, they are displayed as a gray box in the IDE.

If required, every Data Source control provides a view of the data. A view makes it possible to display and sort data. Depending on the data source, you can even edit the data. Other advantages of Data Source controls are automatic data binding (no call of the DataBind() method required), dramatic reduction of the amount of source code needed, and extended support at design time. Nevertheless, ASP.NET still has the flexibility that you know from version 1.x.

Available Data Source Controls

The following six Data Source controls are currently shipped with ASP.NET 2.0:

- SqlDataSource: Accesses SQL Server, OLE DB, ODBC, Oracle, and other database systems for which a custom .NET Data Provider exists (possible providers: MySQL, Firebird, etc.)

- AccessDataSource: Enables you to work easily with Microsoft Access databases by specifying a filename

- DataSetDataSource: Used with data sets

- ObjectDataSource: Lets you visualize classes/objects directly

- XmlDataSource: Used for XML files and documents

- SiteMapDataSource: Recalls the new site map data structure

Although the first four sources can handle flat data structures with one layer only, the latter two are able to process hierarchies of any depth.

Because of their open structure, you can easily implement your own Data Source controls and visualize them by using existing controls. Microsoft came up with the following potential controls:

- WebServiceDataSource

- IndexServerDataSource

- SharePointDataSource

- SqlXmlDataSource

- ExcelDataSource

- FileSystemDataSource (Dave Sussman implemented such a data source)

And there's many more.

Data Source Controls can be used with all Data Controls, the new ones and those you may know already from ASP.NET 1.x:

- AdRotator

- BulletedList

- DropDownList

- ListBox

- CheckBoxList

- RadioButtonList

- Repeater

- DataList

- DataGrid (still included for compatibility reasons)

- GridView (aka SmartGrid)

- DetailsView

- TreeView

Except for the last one, all controls are designed for flat data structures. The new TreeView control, however, accepts hierarchical sources, too. Makes sense for a TreeView, doesn't it?

Using Data Source Controls

Display data using the new Data Source controls is mere child's play. The development environment will support you step by step:

1. Place a GridView control on a new web page. Choose the Connect To DataSource command in the Task List of the control.

2. In the dialog box that appears, first select <New DataSource>, select Sql-DataSource below that, and click the Create button.

3. An assistant appears that allows you to choose either an existing connection to your local SQL Server (or MSDE) or to create a new one. Please select your nearest Northwind database sample.

4. Confirm your choice and enter the following SQL statement in the field shown in Figure 3-1:

    ```
    SELECT CustomerID, CompanyName, ContactName FROM Customers
    ```

5. Confirm this and the subsequent dialog boxes until the Set Control Properties dialog box appears. Activate the Allow Paging and Allow Sorting options and click the Finish button.

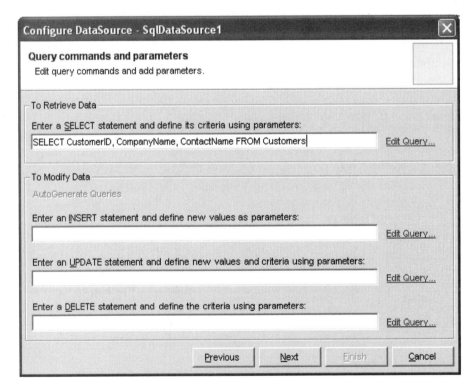

Figure 3-1. This wizard helps you create queries.

That's all, you're done! Now you can start the page by pressing the F5 key. The content of the customer table is displayed in the browser, and you also have the capability of sorting by different columns, as shown in Figure 3-2. Thanks to paging, everything is clearly arranged. And remember, you didn't write a single line of code!

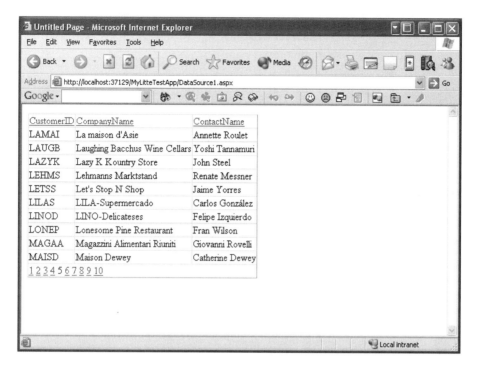

Figure 3-2. Are you ready for another zero-code-scenario?

Looking Under the Hood

You probably expect that the assistant in the previous example has generated a large and complex piece of code—but far from it. In Listing 3-1, you'll find the complete page responsible for displaying the customer data.

Listing 3-1. The Easy-to-Understand Wizard-Generated Source Code

```
<%@ page language="VB" %>

<html>
<head runat="server">
   <title>Untitled Page</title>
</head>
<body>
   <form runat="server">
      <asp:gridview id="GridView1" runat="server" allowpaging="True"
                  datasourceid="SqlDataSource1" allowsorting="True"
                  autogeneratecolumns="False">
         <columnfields>
```

```
            <asp:boundfield sortexpression="CustomerID" datafield="CustomerID"
                            readonly="True"
                            headertext="CustomerID">
            </asp:boundfield>
            <asp:boundfield sortexpression="CompanyName" datafield="CompanyName"
                            headertext="CompanyName">
            </asp:boundfield>
            <asp:boundfield sortexpression="ContactName"
                            datafield="ContactName" headertext="ContactName">
            </asp:boundfield>
        </columnfields>
    </asp:gridview>
    <asp:sqldatasource id="SqlDataSource1" runat="server" selectcommand="SELECT
        CustomerID, CompanyName, ContactName FROM Customers"
        providername="System.Data.OleDb"
        connectionstring="Provider=SQLOLEDB.1;Initial Catalog=Northwind;
        Data Source=.;Integrated Security=SSPI">
    </asp:sqldatasource>
  </form>
</body>
</html>
```

Two things are important to know about this page. First, it contains a Grid-View control. The single columns and fields are noted as separate subelements, similar to the DataGrid. Alternatively, it's still possible to have automatic generation at run time (AutoGenerateColumns property). In the example, the DataSourceID property is set to SqlDataSource1, thereby establishing a connection to the Data Source control with that particular ID.

Second, a SqlDataSource control is also placed on this page. It takes care of the connection to the database. By using the properties that I've been explained, you can specify the ADO.NET Data Provider, the connection string, and the select query. Everything else is handled automatically.

Introducing the New GridView Control

The GridView control is the official successor to the popular DataGrid control of ASP.NET version 1.x. While the DataGrid control is still supported for compatibility reasons, it isn't listed in the Toolbox anymore. So don't use it in any new projects. Anyway, why go with the old control if the newer GridView offers the same features and a good deal more? In particular, it works excellently with the new Data Source Provider concept.

> **NOTE** *In some documentation or in Microsoft examples, you'll probably encounter something called a SmartGrid control. No, it's not a new, tricky control; it's just another name for the GridView control. The name hasn't been finalized, because of an obvious conflict with the product name of a third-party vendor.*

The function set of the control includes the following:

- Binding to any flat or hierarchical (first level only) Data Source controls

- Built-in sorting

- Selection of data records

- Capability to edit and delete data records

- Support of multiple key fields

- Support of multiple fields to create hyperlinks

- Visual adjustability by Themes and Styles

- Adaptive rendering to different (mobile) devices

- Specification of a background picture

Displaying Data

The previous example demonstrated how easy it is to bind a data source to the GridView control. Instead of using the wizard, you can drag the data that you want displayed right out of the Data Explorer. For that purpose, open a new connection, choose a table, and select the desired rows. After that, drag the columns onto an empty page. Visual Studio .NET creates a GridView control and an appropriate SqlDataSource automatically. Press F5 and the data is displayed in the browser immediately.

If you have selected a table like Northwind's Customers table or similar, the returned list will be very long. To decrease the view, enable the AllowPaging property. As usual, you can specify how many records should be displayed at one time and how the pagers, like the ones you'd find on Google, should look. A new feature enables you to assign your own pictures to a pager. You want to see more? Well, enable the `AllowSorting` property, then. By the way, both properties are available in the Task List of the control. Run the revised example—paging and sorting work immediately (see Figure 3-3).

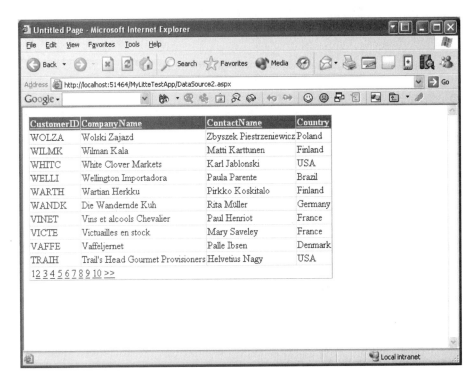

Figure 3-3. The GridView control supports sorting and paging out of the box.

Defining Fields

Similar to the existing DataGrid control, with GridView you have the choice to generate columns you intend to display at run time (by using `AutoGenerateColumns`) or to specify them manually. According to the latest vocabulary, the columns are now called `Fields` or `ColumnFields`.

You define columns through a clearly organized dialog box that is a little bit tiny. You can reach this Fields dialog box via the Edit Columns command in the Task List or the `ColumnFields` property of the control. Figure 3-4 shows the Fields dialog box, which allows you to add, delete, and move fields. A Properties grid enables you to edit the properties of each field separately. If the schema of the data source is known, all available fields will be displayed. Reload the schema by using the Refresh Schema link when necessary.

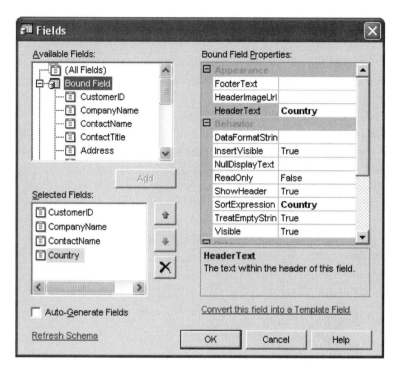

Figure 3-4. You can easily define the displayed fields.

Currently you have the following field types to choose from:

- BoundField: Displays a database field

- CheckBoxField: Displays logic values

- ButtonField: Includes LinkButton controls

- HyperLinkField: Includes HyperLink controls

- CommandField: Enables the use of several integrated commands like select, delete, or edit

- TemplateField: Defines individually designed columns

The different column types behave almost the same as those you know from the DataGrid. But some new properties like TreatEmptyStringAsNull and NullDisplayText are provided. In the latter, you can specify text that will be displayed if the related column contains no value.

Using Templates

As in the older versions of ASP.NET, in ASP.NET 2.0 an individual template can be defined for each field. And existing fields can also be converted to a template (using the link Convert this field into a Template Field).

What is new is the possibility to design these templates visually (as shown in Figure 3-5), like I explained while introducing the controls in VS .NET. Assigning a data binding to a particular control within a template is very easy. Open the Data-Bindings dialog box by using the Task List, and it will show all available data fields after refreshing the schema (see Figure 3-6).

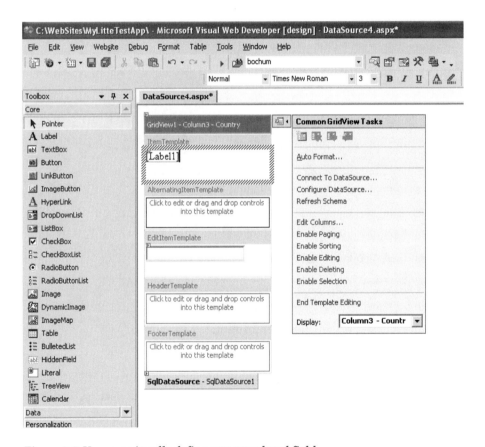

Figure 3-5. You can visually define any templated field.

> **TIP** *Currently the dialog box uses the old* `DataBinder.Eval` *expression if you select manual data binding. Just replace it with the new and shorter* `Eval`.

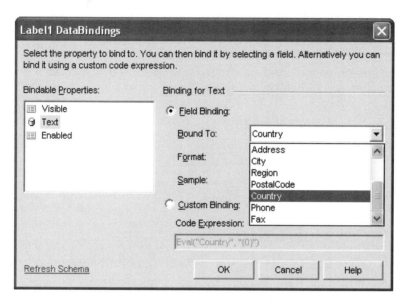

Figure 3-6. Assign a data binding by selecting the corresponding data field.

Besides the individually created fields, the GridView control offers two integrated templates, `PagerTemplate` and `NullTemplate`. The latter is used if the assigned data source returns an empty list of data records. In this case, you may want to provide a message to the user. Append the following suffix to the SELECT query to try this out:

```
WHERE 1=0
```

> **TIP** *To simply return text if no data records have been passed back, just use the* `NullText` *property. You don't have to change your template in that case.*

Deleting Data

Deleting data records isn't more difficult than displaying them. Activate the AutoGenerateDeleteButton property and open the page by using F5 in the browser window. Has anything changed? Right, the table now contains some Delete links that allow you to remove customers from the Northwind database. This works as long as it doesn't violate any related integrity rules of the database.

It works because the development environment did a good job of auto-generating queries while you selected and dragged the columns to display. It has generated not only a SELECT statement, but also a DELETE statement:

```
<asp:sqldatasource id="SqlDataSource1" runat="server"
    providername="System.Data.OleDb"
    connectionstring="..."
    selectcommand="..."
    deletecommand="DELETE FROM Customers WHERE (Customers.CustomerID = ?)"
    ...
</asp:sqldatasource>
```

As you see, a regular DELETE query has been defined, and it only expects a key field of the table to be passed. Here the query contains a question mark because the OLE DB Data Provider is used, whereas the SQL Server Providers allow named parameters.

The key field has to be assigned in the GridView control. Therefore, you pass the field name—CustomerID in this case—to the DataKeyNames property. Separate field names by commas if more than one column is defined as a primary key in your table.

```
<asp:gridview id="GridView1" runat="server"
    autogeneratecolumns="False"
    datasourceid="SqlDataSource1"
    allowpaging="True"
    allowsorting="True"
    autogeneratedeletebutton="True"
      datakeynames="CustomerID">
    ...
</asp:gridview>
```

You want to create the Delete LinkButton controls yourself instead of using the AutoGenerateDeleteButton property to generate link buttons like the ones shown in Figure 3-7? OK, simply add a Button or LinkButton control and specify Delete as the CommandName property.

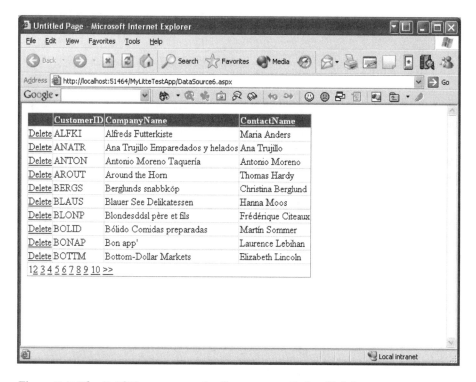

Figure 3-7. The GridView automatically generates Delete link buttons.

Many users prefer a confirmation before finally deleting a data record (see Figure 3-8). This is a matter of three easy steps:

1. Create a new `CommandField` column and activate `ShowDeleteButton`.

2. Convert the column to a `TemplateField` column.

3. Change to HTML view and assign a client-side method to the click event of the generated `LinkLabel`:

```
<asp:templatefield>
   <itemtemplate>
      <asp:linkbutton id="LinkButton1" runat="server"
          causesvalidation="False" commandname="Delete"
          text="Delete"
          onclientclick="return confirm('Are you sure you want ' +
                'to delete this record?')">
      </asp:linkbutton>
   </itemtemplate>
</asp:templatefield>
```

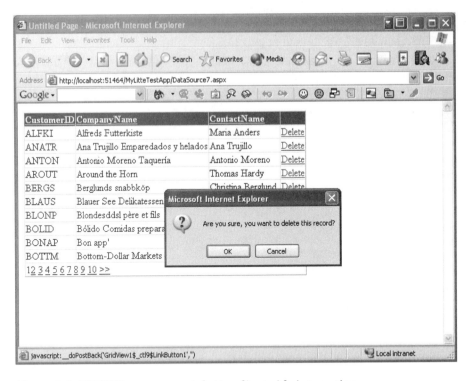

Figure 3-8. ASP.NET now supports better client-side integration.

Editing Data

You probably expect editing of data to be child's play—for example, simply displaying and item and deleting it. So, you'll be happy to hear that you can easily edit data with GridView.

The GridView control already contains all functions necessary to edit data. And this is, not surprisingly, based on the abstract generic approach of the data source concept. For this purpose, it uses the assigned source to edit data records. That means you'll have to add an additional query to the SqlDataSource control, which you saw used in the previous example.

In case you've chosen the Data Explorer in the development environment, it will have generated all the required commands already. Of course, this will work for simple queries only. Just check the AutoGenerateEditButton option, hit the F5 key, and start editing (see Figure 3-9).

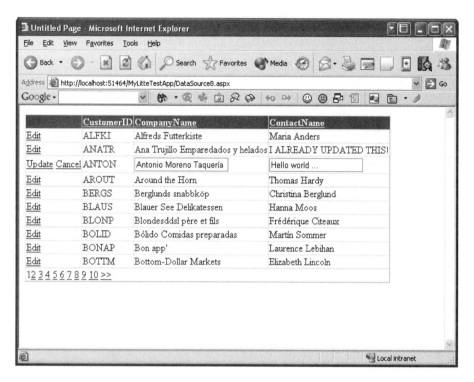

Figure 3-9. Gosh! Everything you need to edit data already ships with ASP.NET version 2.0.

The listing that follows shows the extended SqlDataSource control. Here the required SQL query has been assigned to the `UpdateCommand` property. Every single field is passed as an unnamed parameter.

```
<asp:sqldatasource id="SqlDataSource1" runat="server"
    providername="System.Data.OleDb"
    connectionstring="..."
    selectcommand="..."
    deletecommand="..."
    updatecommand="UPDATE Customers SET CompanyName = ?, ContactName = ?
                             WHERE (Customers.CustomerID = ?)">
</asp:sqldatasource>
```

Because this example uses OLE DB, and thereby includes unnamed parameters, the order of the parameters is important. The selection in the GridView control determines the order. In this case, three fields are displayed: CustomerID, CompanyName, and ContactName. Because the primary key, CustomerID, is marked as read-only, it becomes the last parameter that is passed (see Listing 3-2).

Listing 3-2. The Read-Only Marked Field Passed as the Last Parameter

```
<asp:gridview id="GridView1" runat="server" autogeneratecolumns="False"
              datasourceid="SqlDataSource1"
   ...
   <columnfields>
     <asp:boundfield nulldisplaytext="D"
                     sortexpression="CustomerID" datafield="CustomerID"
                     readonly="True" headertext="CustomerID">
     </asp:boundfield>
     <asp:boundfield sortexpression="CompanyName"
                     datafield="CompanyName" headertext="CompanyName">
     </asp:boundfield>
     <asp:boundfield sortexpression="ContactName"
                     datafield="ContactName" headertext="ContactName">
     </asp:boundfield>
   </columnfields>
   ...
</asp:gridview>
```

Using Parameters

In real life, a requirement that developers and customers frequently ask for is the visualization of Master/Detail data records. A classic example of this can be reproduced by using the Northwind database. Try to display customers and their orders hierarchically. To create a view like this has become quite easy in ASP.NET 2.0. All you need are two GridView controls and an adequate data source.

Figure 3-10 demonstrates a possible result of this kind of view.

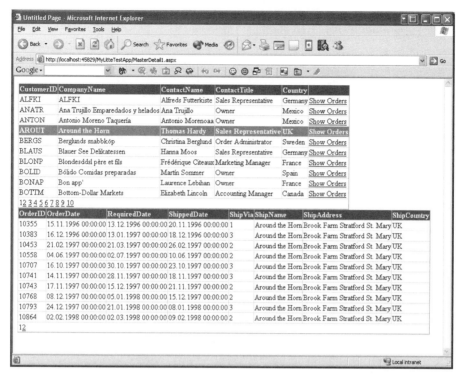

Figure 3-10. Showing Master/Detail records is a must-have feature!

It takes just a few steps to get there:

1. Drag the desired columns of the Customers table from the Data Explorer to your page. A GridView that includes an appropriate SqlDataSource is generated automatically. Add a Command column to the existing columns and set its command to `Select`.

2. Drag the columns of the Orders table below those of the Customers table. Here the GridView and the SqlDataSource are also being created without your assistance.

3. Open the Task List of the second GridView control, click the Configure DataSource button, then the Next, button, and finally the Edit Query button to modify the `SELECT` query.

4. Add the following WHERE clause to the SELECT statement and click the Infer Parameters button (see Figure 3-11):

   WHERE CustomerID=?

5. A new entry is generated in the Parameters list. Select the new one and choose Control as the source. Specify GridView1 as ControlID and SelectedValue as PropertyName.

6. Confirm your changes when asked, close the wizard, and hit F5 to start the page. Now if you select a customer, you'll get a list of all of the orders for that customer right away.

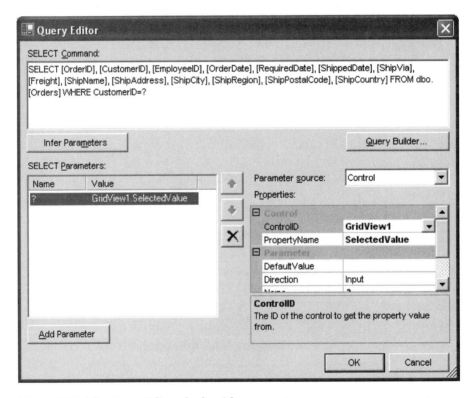

Figure 3-11. The Query Editor deals with parameters.

The Query Editor dialog box in Figure 3-11 allows you to edit the control parameters easily even for complex scenarios. It provides a way to define any named or unnamed parameters and to directly get their values. Here is a list of the supported sources:

- `Control` to query a property of any control on the current page

- `Cookie` for a temporarily or persistently saved cookie

- `Form` for a (hidden) form field

- `QueryString` for a value that is contained in the URL

- `Session` for a session variable

Optionally, you can specify a default value and a data type for every parameter. Usually the Object type will be adequate.

Here's how the parameters are listed in the source code:

```
<asp:sqldatasource id="SqlDataSource2" runat="server"
   ...
   <selectparameters>
      <asp:controlparameter name="?"
          propertyname="SelectedValue" controlid="GridView1">
      </asp:controlparameter>
   </selectparameters>
</asp:sqldatasource>
```

Caching Data

With the exception of the SiteMapDataSource controls, all the Data Source controls provide built-in caching. Depending on the type of data, this feature can be very helpful and it will increase the performance of your application.

If you would like to try caching, then activate the `EnableCaching` property and assign the desired time span in seconds to `CacheDuration`. The `CacheExpirationPolicy` property gives you the choice to use either absolute or sliding caching. The default is `Absolute`. While you work with `Sliding`, the caching duration is set back to the initial value on every request.

```
<asp:sqldatasource id="SqlDataSource1" runat="server"
   ...
   enablecaching="True"
   cacheduration="60">
</asp:sqldatasource>
```

> **NOTE** *Please notice that caching with the SqlDataSource control will only work if the option* DataSourceMode *is set to* DataSet, *which is the default value. This property allows you to define how the data is accessed internally.* DataReader *is the second possible value.*

> **TIP** *SqlDataSource supports the new SQL Server Cache Invalidation feature described in Chapter 11, which covers the enhanced Page Framework. If you want to use it, you must assign the name of the database (which is defined in the* web.config *file) followed by a colon and the name of the table on which the caching will depend to the* SqlCacheDependancy *property.*

Enhancing Control Capabilities

An important advantage of the DataGrid control was its extensibility. If the built-in mechanisms were not suitable for a particular requirement, you could easily step into the process by using the ItemCreated and the ItemDataBound events.

The GridView control offers two analogous events: RowCreated and RowDataBound. Because most of the common functions are completely integrated now, a number of additional events have been implemented that provide some new ways to customize operations. Many functions fire two events, one before execution (these end in " . . .ing") and one after execution (these end in ". . . ed"):

- PageIndexChanged

- PageIndexChanging

- RowCancellingEdit

- RowCommand

- RowDeleted

- RowDeleting

- RowEditing

- RowUpdated

- RowUpdating

- SelectedIndexChanged

- SelectedIndexChanging

- Sorted

- Sorting

Introducing the New DetailsView Control

With the DetailsView control, the ASP.NET team introduces another data-bound control to developers. And this one comes with a lot of built-in features to display and edit data, too. In contrast to GridView, DetailsView is designed to show only one data record at a time. Usually this will be a vertical list of all available fields.

Displaying, Editing, and Deleting Records

To prepare the DetailsView for use isn't a big deal. Take the previous examples and replace the GridView control with a DetailsView control and that's it. Thanks to paging, you can find and select the data record you want as shown in Figure 3-12, and then edit or even delete it.

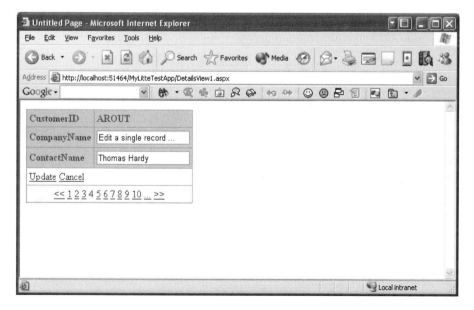

Figure 3-12. The DetailsView control displays a single record at once.

Most of the auto-generated source code is easy to understand (see Listing 3-3). For your convenience, I have removed all style formatting.

Listing 3-3. Displaying Data with the DetailsView Control

```
<%@ page language="VB" %>

<html>
<head runat="server">
    <title>Untitled Page</title>
</head>
<body>
    <form runat="server">
        <asp:detailsview id="DetailsView1" runat="server"
            allowpaging="True"
            datasourceid="SqlDataSource1"
            datakeynames="CustomerID">

            <rowfields>
                <asp:commandfield showdeletebutton="True" showinsertbutton="True"
                  showeditbutton="True">
                </asp:commandfield>
            </rowfields>

        </asp:detailsview>

        <asp:sqldatasource id="SqlDataSource1" runat="server"
            connectionstring="..."
            providername="System.Data.OleDb"
            selectcommand="SELECT CustomerID, CompanyName, ContactName
                FROM dbo.[Customers]"
            updatecommand="UPDATE Customers SET CompanyName = ?, ContactName = ?
                WHERE (Customers.CustomerID = ?)">
            deletecommand="DELETE FROM Customers WHERE
                (Customers.CustomerID = ?)"
            insertcommand="INSERT INTO Customers(CustomerID, CompanyName,
                ContactName) VALUES (?, ?, ?)"
        </asp:sqldatasource>
    </form>
</body>
</html>
```

In this case, the fields to display are auto-generated because the `AutoGenerateRows` property is enabled by default. It's also possible to define these fields manually, thereby enabling you to specify which ones the user is allowed to edit and which ones the user can't change. The Edit Fields dialog box, shown in Figure 3-13, is all you need to make this type of modification. This dialog box provides the same field types as GridView.

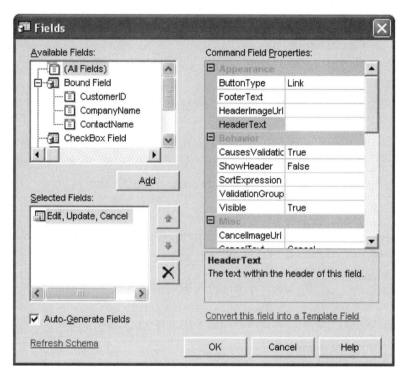

Figure 3-13. You can define what users should see and what they shouldn't.

Inserting New Records

A characteristic of the DetailsView control is the possibility to create a new data record and store it in the assigned data source. The example that you've seen previously already offers this feature. Click the New button, enter the required values, and confirm by clicking the Insert link button—the new record will be inserted as shown in Figure 3-14.

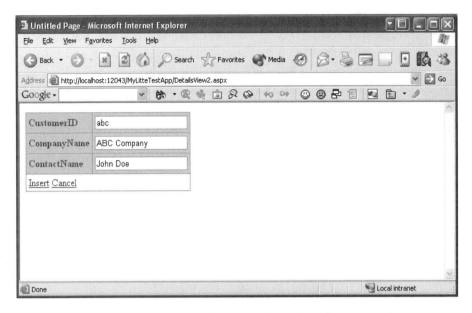

Figure 3-14. The DetailsView control supports insertion of new records.

And again, the SqlDataSource control provides an appropriate query to which the parameters of the new record have to be passed in the order of the input fields:

```
<asp:sqldatasource id="SqlDataSource1" runat="server"
   ...
   insertcommand="INSERT INTO Customers(CustomerID, CompanyName, ContactName)
      VALUES (?, ?, ?)"
</asp:sqldatasource>
```

If the database itself takes care of the ID—which will often be the case—that particular field can be deactivated so you can edit the user data.

```
<asp:detailsview id="DetailsView1" runat="server"
   allowpaging="True"
   datasourceid="SqlDataSource1"
   datakeynames="CustomerID"
   gridlines="Both"
      autogeneraterows="False">
   <rowfields>
      <asp:boundfield insertvisible="False" sortexpression="CustomerID"
         datafield="CustomerID"
         headertext="CustomerID">
```

```
        </asp:boundfield>
        <asp:boundfield sortexpression="CompanyName"
            datafield="CompanyName" headertext="CompanyName">
        </asp:boundfield>
        <asp:boundfield sortexpression="ContactName" datafield="ContactName"
            headertext="ContactName">
        </asp:boundfield>
        <asp:commandfield showdeletebutton="True" showinsertbutton="True"
            showeditbutton="True">
        </asp:commandfield>
    </rowfields>
</asp:detailsview>
```

Working with Templates—Yes, You Can!

The DetailsView control offers two possibilities for using templates. The first is to include one or more elements of type `TemplateField` analogous to those in the GridView control. The alternative is to use a template to freely design the whole display range. This approach is almost equivalent to the familiar Repeater and DataList controls.

The following template types are provided by the control. These can be modified visually by using the new design-time support of VS .NET:

- `ItemTemplate`

- `AlternatingItemTemplate`

- `EditItemTemplate`

- `InsertItemTemplate`

- `HeaderTemplate`

- `NullTemplate`

- `PagerTemplate`

What I really like is the fact that the templates and the fields, which are automatically generated, can be used together. For instance, the control in Listing 3-4 provides an individually designed view of the data, whereas edit mode is completely generated by the control itself, as you can see in Figure 3-15.

Listing 3-4. Defining an ItemTemplate

```
<asp:detailsview id="DetailsView1" runat="server" ...>
   <itemtemplate>
      Company:
      <asp:label id="Label1" runat="server"
         text='<%# Eval("CompanyName") %>'></asp:label>
      <br />
      Contact:
      <asp:label id="Label2" runat="server"
          text='<%# Eval("ContactName") %>'></asp:label>
      <br />
      <asp:linkbutton id="Linkbutton1" runat="server"
         commandname="Edit">Edit</asp:linkbutton>
   </itemtemplate>
   ...
</asp:detailsview>
```

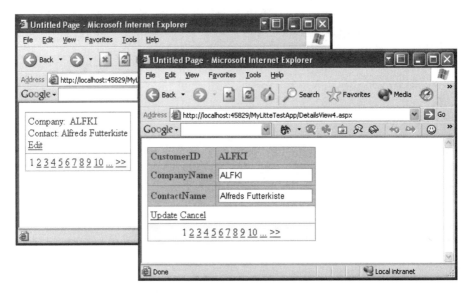

Figure 3-15. You even can mix a custom template with auto-generated fields.

Combining GridView and DetailsView

Both of the new Data Controls, GridView and the DetailsView, complement one another very well. So it's a great idea to use them together. In Chapter 2, I presented an appropriate example. By now you surely can imagine what is under the hood:

- One GridView control

- One DetailsView control

- Two SqlDataSource controls

- And a little bit of source code (hey, it's the first time!)

The GridView control is responsible for the visualization of the Customers table. The currently selected item is also displayed in the DetailsView control below the GridView control. Within the DetailsView control, the data record can be modified or deleted. And it allows you to create new customers, of course.

The connection between the two controls is defined by the SqlDataSource parameters, which I've explained before. Editing, deleting, and inserting new data records is realized by known mechanisms, as you can see in Listing 3-5.

Listing 3-5. GridView and DetailsView Working Hand in Hand

```
<%@ page language="C#" %>

<html>
<head runat="server">
    <title>Untitled Page</title>
</head>
<body>
    <form runat="server">
        <asp:gridview id="GridView1" runat="server"
            allowpaging="True"
            datasourceid="SqlDataSource1"
            allowsorting="True"
            autogeneratecolumns="False"
            datakeynames="CustomerID">
            <columnfields>
                <asp:boundfield sortexpression="CustomerID"
                    datafield="CustomerID" readonly="True"
                    headertext="CustomerID">
                </asp:boundfield>
                <asp:boundfield sortexpression="CompanyName"
                    datafield="CompanyName"
                    headertext="CompanyName">
                </asp:boundfield>
                <asp:boundfield sortexpression="ContactName"
                    datafield="ContactName"
                    headertext="ContactName">
```

```
            </asp:boundfield>
            <asp:commandfield showselectbutton="True">
            </asp:commandfield>
        </columnfields>
    </asp:gridview>

    <asp:sqldatasource id="SqlDataSource1" runat="server"
        ...
    </asp:sqldatasource> 

    <asp:sqldatasource id="SqlDataSource2" runat="server"
        ...
        <selectparameters>
            <asp:controlparameter propertyname="SelectedValue"
               controlid="GridView1">
            </asp:controlparameter>
        </selectparameters>
    </asp:sqldatasource>

     <asp:detailsview id="DetailsView1" runat="server"
         datasourceid="SqlDataSource2"
         autogeneraterows="False"
         datakeynames="CustomerID">
         <rowfields>
             <asp:boundfield sortexpression="CustomerID" datafield="CustomerID"
                 readonly="True"
                 headertext="CustomerID">
             </asp:boundfield>
             <asp:boundfield sortexpression="CompanyName"
                 datafield="CompanyName"
                 headertext="CompanyName">
             </asp:boundfield>
             <asp:boundfield sortexpression="ContactName"
                 datafield="ContactName"
                 headertext="ContactName">
             </asp:boundfield>
             <asp:commandfield showdeletebutton="True" showinsertbutton="True"
                showeditbutton="True">
             </asp:commandfield>
         </rowfields>
     </asp:detailsview>
    </form>
</body>
</html>
```

To get this example running, a little piece of source code is necessary (my apologies for that). After modifying the data pool in the DetailsView control, you have to inform GridView to reload the data. Calling the `DataBind()` method in the `ItemInserted`, `ItemUpdated`, and `ItemDeleted` event is all you have to do. Within the `Page_Load` event you may want to use the new anonymous methods of C# for that. Figure 3-16 shows the sample in the browser window.

```
void Page_Load(object sender, System.EventArgs e)
{
    DetailsViewStatusEventHandler handler =
        delegate { this.GridView1.DataBind(); };
    this.DetailsView1.ItemInserted += handler;
    this.DetailsView1.ItemUpdated += handler;
    this.DetailsView1.ItemDeleted += handler;
}
```

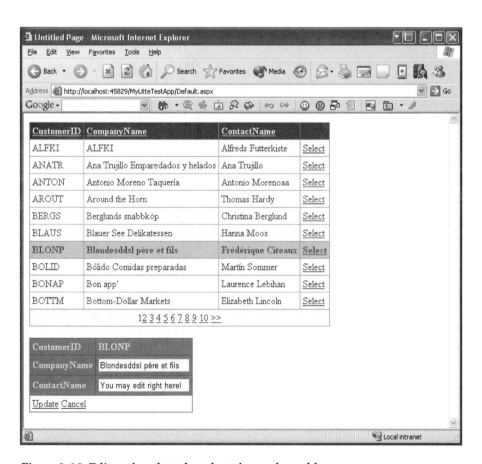

Figure 3-16. Edit and update the selected record or add a new one.

Introducing the New TreeView Control

Unlike what you probably thought at first, the new TreeView control has nothing to do with the IE Web Control. It does *not* use the related IE behavior. The control has been newly developed and is especially targeted at the new data source concept.

Here is a list of the most important features of this control:

- Allows connection to any data source that supports the IHierarchicalDataSource interface (already included: XmlDataSource and SiteMapDataSource)

- Enables site navigation similar to MSDN Online

- Displays the nodes as text or hyperlinks

- Provides access to the object model at run time

- Allows node population at client side, if supported by the browser (currently Internet Explorer version 5.0 or higher and Netscape version 6.0 or higher)

- Displays CheckBox controls

- Includes adjustable visualization via templates, styles, pictures, and Themes

- Allows adaptive rendering to different target systems and browsers

Using Static Data

The easiest way to populate a TreeView control is to assign the tree items statically. Drag a new control to your page and choose the Edit Nodes command in the Task List. The dialog box that appears, which should look like the one you see in Figure 3-17, allows you to create tree nodes and add them to the hierarchy of the tree. Use the Properties grid to specify the properties of the elements. This includes the text label, an internal value, an optional navigation URL, the display status, and much more.

Figure 3-17. You can create, edit, and move your static tree nodes.

The created items are added to the HTML source code as separate subcontrols:

```
<asp:treeview id="TreeView1" runat="server">
   <nodes>
      <asp:treenode value="My Root Element" expanded="True" text="My Root Element">
         <asp:treenode value="My Child Element" text="My Child Element">
         </asp:treenode>
         <asp:treenode checked="True" value="Another Child" expanded="True"
            showcheckbox="False"
            selectaction="SelectExpand" selected="True" text="Another Child">
            <asp:treenode value="A Childs Child"
               selectaction="None" text="A Childs Child">
            </asp:treenode>
         </asp:treenode>
      </asp:treenode>
   </nodes>
</asp:treeview>
```

Hold on, before running this example in the browser by hitting F5, you should take care of an appropriate visualization. Select Auto Format in the Task List of the control and choose your favorite standard format. I chose MSDN. Figure 3-18 shows the result.

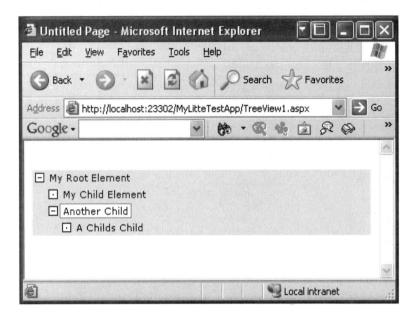

Figure 3-18. The newly created tree nodes are displayed in an MSDN-like style.

Using XmlDataSource

You can use the XmlDataSource control to display flat or hierarchical XML data. Either assign a XML block to it or—as you'll probably want to do more often—a local XML file. The TreeView control allows you to present any hierarchically structured data.

In Listing 3-6, the books.xml XML file, which serves as the data source, contains a catalogue of a few books.

Listing 3-6. books.xml

```
<?xml version="1.0" standalone="yes"?>
<bookstore>
  <genre name="fiction">
    <book ISBN="10-000000-001">
      <title>The Iliad and The Odyssey</title>
```

```
      <price>12.95</price>
      <comments>
        <userComment rating="4">
            Best translation I've read.
        </userComment>
        <userComment rating="2">
            I like other versions better.
        </userComment>
      </comments>
    </book>
    <book ISBN="10-000000-999">
      <title>Anthology of World Literature</title>
      <price>24.95</price>
      <comments>
        <userComment rating="3">
          Needs more modern literature.
        </userComment>
        <userComment rating="4">
          Excellent overview of world literature.
        </userComment>
      </comments>
    </book>
  </genre>
  <genre name="nonfiction">
    <book ISBN="11-000000-002">
      <title>Computer Dictionary</title>
      <price>24.95</price>
      <comments>
        <userComment rating="3">A valuable resource.</userComment>
      </comments>
    </book>
    <book ISBN="11-000000-003">
      <title>Cooking on a Budget</title>
      <price>23.95</price>
      <comments>
        <userComment rating="4">Delicious!</userComment>
      </comments>
    </book>
  </genre>
</bookstore>
```

After creating the file, you can place a new TreeView control on your page. Now choose the Connect To DataSource command in the Task List. Select the books.xml file as the new XmlDataSource. If desired, you can apply one of the built-in format templates I explained previously. Then hit F5 and see what's happening in your browser window.

Figure 3-19 shows the result, which looks pretty professional, but I guess you may have expected the data in a different shape.

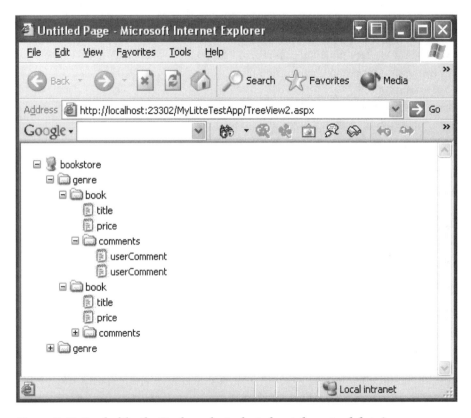

Figure 3-19. Looks like the Explorer, but what about the actual data?

To achieve the right visualization (see Figure 3-20), you'll have to tell the control how it should look. Use the Edit Bindings dialog box for this purpose. The structure of the XML file is already given.

- Select the option Auto-Generate Bindings.

- Add an empty binding and set the Text property to My Bookstore.

- Select genre, add it, and set its TextField property to name.

- Repeat this for book and set the TextField property to isbn here.

- Run the example by pressing F5.

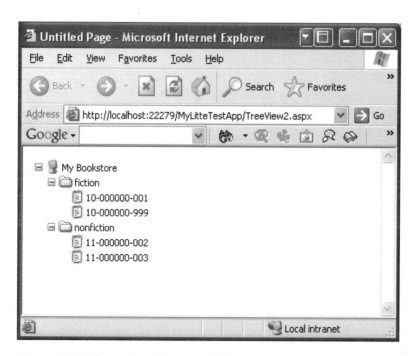

Figure 3-20. Oh, that's really better, I think.

You can find the generated HTML source code in Listing 3-7. As you see, there is no programming code at all—again a zero-code scenario.

Listing 3-7. Displaying Trees Without Any Coding

```
<%@ page language="VB" %>

<html>
<head runat="server">
    <title>Untitled Page</title>
</head>
<body>
    <form runat="server">
        <asp:treeview id="TreeView1" runat="server"
            datasourceid="XmlDataSource1"
            imageset="XP_Explorer"
            autogeneratebindings="False">

            <bindings>
                <asp:treenodebinding value="My Bookstore"
                    depth="0" text="My Bookstore">
                </asp:treenodebinding>
                <asp:treenodebinding datamember="genre" textfield="name" depth="1">
                </asp:treenodebinding>
                <asp:treenodebinding datamember="book" textfield="isbn" depth="2">
                </asp:treenodebinding>
            </bindings>
        </asp:treeview>
        <asp:xmldatasource id="XmlDataSource1" runat="server" datafile="Books.xml">
        </asp:xmldatasource>
    </form>
</body>
</html>
```

And of course, the XmlDataSource control offers many more features than you've seen so far. For example, you have the option to assign a schema file (XSD file), a transformation file (XSL file) or an XPath expression to the corresponding properties. If the XML file is displayed without transformation, you even have write access. Caching also belongs to the functions set.

Using Client-Side Population—You'll Love It!

I'm sure that you know MSDN Online. The navigation of this web site is based on a tree. Because the tree has a lot of subentries, the subtrees are loaded on demand without causing a postback for the whole page. This feature is called *client-side population* and is being offered by the new ASP.NET TreeView control. Another nice example of this is the visualization of the structure of the local file system on the server. Come on, I'll show you how it works:

1. Create a new page and place a TreeView control on it.

2. Use the Auto Format command in the Task List to select the standard formatting template XP File Explorer.

3. Open the Edit Nodes dialog box and create a new root node. Call it Drive C:\. Set the Value property to c:\. Now set the SelectAction property to SelectExpand and enable PopulateOnDemand.

4. Create a method to handle the TreeNodePopulate event and append the following source code to it:

```
void TreeView1_TreeNodePopulate(object sender,
    System.Web.UI.WebControls.TreeNodeEventArgs e)
{
    if (e.Node.ChildNodes.Count == 0)
    {
        this.LoadChildNodes(e.Node);
    }
}


private void LoadChildNodes(TreeNode node)
{
    DirectoryInfo directory;
    if (node.ValuePath.Length == 0)
    {
        directory = new DirectoryInfo(node.Value);
    }
    else
    {
        directory = new DirectoryInfo(node.ValuePath);
    }
    foreach(DirectoryInfo subDirectory in directory.GetDirectories())
    {
```

```
            TreeNode subNode = new TreeNode(subDirectory.Name);
            subNode.PopulateOnDemand = true;
            subNode.SelectAction = TreeNodeSelectAction.SelectExpand;
            node.ChildNodes.Add(subNode);
        }
    }
```

That's it! Use F5 to run the page and experience the directory explorer in action. Every time you open a folder, the contained subfolders are loaded, as shown in Figure 3-21.

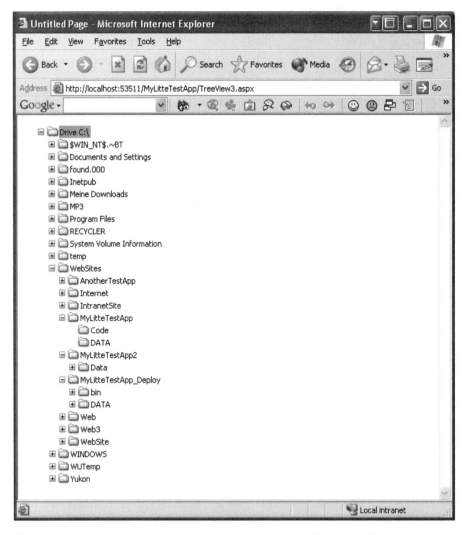

Figure 3-21. Nested directories are populated dynamically if you click the parent.

Actually this isn't a zero-code scenario, but it's just a tiny and understandable piece of code that is needed for this example. Within the `TreeNodePopulate` event the current node is checked as to whether it already contains subnodes. If not, those are loaded using the `LoadChildNodes` method.

This method queries the value of the selected node or, if available, of the `ValuePath` property. The latter returns a list of all values from the current node up to the root. In this case, the result is the current path. By using the `DirectoryInfo` class in the `System.IO` namespace, you can read the subfolders and pass them as subnodes to the TreeView control.

You'll better understand this example by using the debugger; just place a breakpoint in the `LoadChildNodes` method.

> **NOTE** *The dynamical loading of the TreeView control is based on the new Client Callback feature, which I'll explain later in the book. It's supported by Internet Explorer version 5.0 (or higher) and Netscape version 6.0 (or higher) and uses XmlHttp.*

Working with ObjectDataSource

ObjectDataSource is really a fun feature, in addition to being very useful. Instead of getting the data from any type of data storage, as would be the case with other DataSource controls, it simply uses business objects (classes that just store your application data). This is even more interesting if you work with the new Object-Spaces feature set included with Microsoft Visual Studio Whidbey Mobile Control through which objects are stored directly in the database.

Displaying Business Objects

So what do you need first of all to display business objects? Yes, some business objects! I've already created two for holding personal information in Listing 3-8: the `Person` class, with the `Id`, `Firstname`, and `Lastname` properties; and the `PersonCollection` class, which is based on Generics.

Listing 3-8. The Person and PersonCollection Classes

```csharp
// Person.cs
using System;

public class Person
{

    private int id;
    private string firstname;
    private string lastname;

    public Person(int id, string firstname, string lastname)
    {
        this.id = id;
        this.firstname = firstname;
        this.lastname = lastname;
    }

    public int Id
    {
        get { return this.id; }
        set { this.id = value; }
    }

    public string Firstname
    {
        get { return this.firstname; }
        set { this.firstname = value; }
    }

    public string Lastname
    {
        get { return this.lastname; }
        set { this.lastname = value; }
    }
}

// PersonCollection.cs
using System;
using System.Collections.Generic;

public class PersonCollection : List<Person>
{
```

```
public void Remove(int id)
{
    Person person = this.FindPersonById(id);
    if (person != null)
    {
        base.Remove(person);
    }
}

public Person FindPersonById(int id)
{
    foreach (Person person in this)
    {
        if (person.Id.Equals(id))
        {
            return person;
        }
    }
    return null;
}
}
```

The ObjectDataSource control expects to receive a qualified name of a class, which is responsible for processing the objects. Usually this is a class of your business layer. The first step of the implementation of a `PersonManager` class is shown in Listing 3-9. The `SelectPersons()` method creates a new `PersonCollection`, fills it with data, and returns it afterwards. The data is also stored in application scope. On consecutive calls, the data will be read from there.

Listing 3-9. Handling Application Logic with the PersonManager Class

```
using System;
using System.Web;

public class PersonManager
{

    private const string personsKey = "persons";

    public PersonCollection SelectPersons()
    {
        HttpContext context = HttpContext.Current;
```

```
if (context.Application[personsKey] == null)
{
    PersonCollection persons = new PersonCollection();
    persons.Add(new Person(0, "Patrick", "Lorenz"));
    persons.Add(new Person(1, "Micha", "Brunnhuber"));
    persons.Add(new Person(2, "Thomas", "Ballmeier"));
    persons.Add(new Person(3, "Marc", "Höppner"));
    context.Application[personsKey] = persons;
}

return (context.Application[personsKey] as PersonCollection);
    }
}
```

OK, that's enough preparation. Now let's get to the meat. Add a GridView control to a new page and create a new ObjectDataSource control by using the wizard. Modify the properties of the new source and assign `PersonManager` to `TypeName` and `SelectPersons` to `SelectMethod`. Ready, steady, go! Hit the F5 key and the result should look like what you see in Figure 3-22.

Figure 3-22. You can connect business objects directly to any Data Control.

> **TIP** *Of course, the data source, or rather the GridView control, allows you to define explicitly the properties that will be visualized including their order. Just disable the automatic column generation and define them manually, as usual.*

Using Parameters

The use of the ObjectDataSource control combined with parameters is pretty interesting. You can assign them to the data source and specify the data type to use as shown earlier and demonstrated in Figure 3-23. Here, I'll talk about SelectParameters.

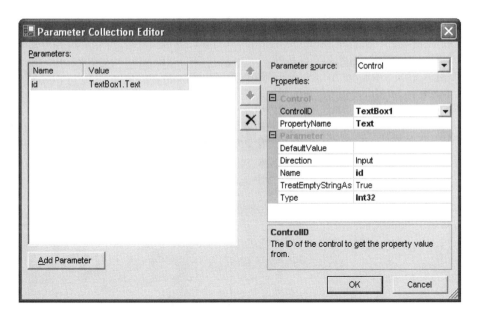

Figure 3-23. Use parameters to select what data you want displayed.

The defined parameters are passed to the select method. Unique names are required, and the data types must match. Overloading isn't supported. Be careful in the current Alpha version, which is case sensitive (this may change in the final release).

For this example, I have written a new method called SelectPerson (singular) which expects an ID as parameter (see Listing 3-10). The returned object is of type Person and gets bound to a DetailsView control. The ID is entered into a TextBox control, which serves as the source for the parameter. Figure 3-24 shows how to use it.

Listing 3-10. Ensuring Parameter Names Match

```
// PersonManager.cs
using System;
using System.Web;

public class PersonManager
{
    private const string personsKey = "persons";

    public PersonCollection SelectPersons()
    {
        HttpContext context = HttpContext.Current;

        if (context.Application[personsKey] == null)
        {
            PersonCollection persons = new PersonCollection();
            persons.Add(new Person(0, "Patrick", "Lorenz"));
            persons.Add(new Person(1, "Micha", "Brunnhuber"));
            persons.Add(new Person(2, "Thomas", "Ballmeier"));
            persons.Add(new Person(3, "Marc", "Höppner"));
            context.Application[personsKey] = persons;
        }

        return (context.Application[personsKey] as PersonCollection);
    }

    public Person SelectPerson(int id)
    {
        return this.SelectPersons().FindPersonById(id);
    }
}

// ObjectDataSource2.aspx
<%@ page language="C#" %>

<html>
<head runat="server">
    <title>Untitled Page</title>
</head>
```

```
<body>
    <form runat="server">
        ID:  
        <asp:textbox id="TextBox1" runat="server" width="32px">0</asp:textbox>
        <asp:button id="Button1" runat="server" text="Show Person" />
        <br />
        <br />
        <asp:detailsview id="DetailsView1" runat="server"
            datasourceid="ObjectDataSource1">
        </asp:detailsview>
        <asp:objectdatasource id="ObjectDataSource1" runat="server"
            typename="PersonManager"
            selectmethod="SelectPerson">
            <selectparameters>
                <asp:controlparameter name="id"
                    propertyname="Text"
                    type="Int32"
                    controlid="TextBox1">
                </asp:controlparameter>
            </selectparameters>
        </asp:objectdatasource>

    </form>
</body>
</html>
```

Figure 3-24. Enter a valid ID to display the corresponding Person object.

Editing a SelectMethod and Deleting Business Objects

The features of the ObjectDataSource control don't stop at the visualization of data. It also provides editing and even deleting capabilities, if your business object allows this (see Figure 3-25). All you have to do is to add two more methods, Update and DeletePerson, as shown in Listing 3-11, and you're almost done. To get this example running, you have to assign the additional methods to the ObjectData-Source control and set the DataKeyNames property of the GridView control to Id.

Listing 3-11. Altering PersonManager to Support Editing and Deleting of Records in Memory

```
// PersonManager.cs
using System;
using System.Web;

public class PersonManager
{
    private const string personsKey = "persons";

    ...

    public void DeletePerson(int Id)
    {
        HttpContext context = HttpContext.Current;
        PersonCollection persons =
            (context.Application[personsKey] as PersonCollection);

        persons.Remove(Id);
    }
}

// ObjectDataSource3.aspx
<%@ page language="C#" %>

<html>
<head id="Head1" runat="server">
    <title>Untitled Page</title>
</head>
<body>
    <form id="Form1" runat="server">
        <asp:gridview id="GridView1" runat="server"
            datasourceid="ObjectDataSource1"
```

```
            autogeneratecolumns="False"
            datakeynames="Id">
            <columnfields>
                <asp:boundfield datafield="Id" readonly="True" headertext="ID">
                </asp:boundfield>
                <asp:boundfield datafield="Firstname" headertext="Firstname">
                </asp:boundfield>
                <asp:boundfield datafield="Lastname" headertext="Lastname">
                </asp:boundfield>
                <asp:commandfield showeditbutton="True">
                </asp:commandfield>
                <asp:commandfield showdeletebutton="True">
                </asp:commandfield>
            </columnfields>
        </asp:gridview>

        <asp:objectdatasource id="ObjectDataSource1" runat="server"
            typename="PersonManager"
            selectmethod="SelectPersons"
            updatemethod="Update"
            deletemethod="DeletePerson">
        </asp:objectdatasource>

    </form>
</body>
</html>
```

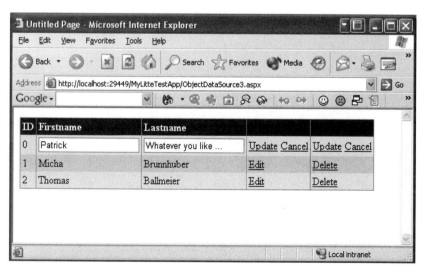

Figure 3-25. You can edit and delete your business object in a very direct manner.

Adding Data to Business Objects

Last but not least, I should show you how to insert new data records. One solution is to use a combination of a GridView control and a DetailsView control as discussed previously. Because all parameters are returned as strings by the input fields, it's crucial to specify the adequate data types while defining the parameters.

Only a few changes are necessary. You need an additional DetailsView control, which you have to bind to the existing data source. The rest is done by the `Insert` method in the `PersonManager` class (see Listing 3-12). Inserting the record for a new person is shown in Figure 3-26.

Listing 3-12. Adding a New Person to the Collection

```
// PersonManager.cs
using System;
using System.Web;

public class PersonManager
{
    private const string personsKey = "persons";

    ...

    public void Insert(int Id, string Firstname, string Lastname)
    {
        HttpContext context = HttpContext.Current;
        PersonCollection persons =
            (context.Application[personsKey] as PersonCollection);

        persons.Add(new Person(Id, Firstname, Lastname));
    }
}

// ObjectDataSource4.aspx
    ...

    <asp:objectdatasource
        id="ObjectDataSource1"
        runat="server"
        typename="PersonManager"
        selectmethod="SelectPersons"
        deletemethod="DeletePerson"
        updatemethod="Update"
        insertmethod="Insert">
        <insertparameters>
```

```
                    <asp:parameter name="Id" type="Int32"></asp:parameter>
              </insertparameters>
        </asp:objectdatasource>

        <asp:detailsview id="DetailsView1"
              runat="server"
              datasourceid="ObjectDataSource1"
              defaultmode="Insert"
              autogeneraterows="False"
              datakeynames="Id">

              <rowfields>
                    <asp:boundfield datafield="Id" headertext="ID:">
                    </asp:boundfield>
                    <asp:boundfield datafield="Firstname" headertext="Fn:">
                    </asp:boundfield>
                    <asp:boundfield datafield="Lastname" headertext="Ln:">
                    </asp:boundfield>
                    <asp:commandfield showinsertbutton="True">
                    </asp:commandfield>
              </rowfields>
        </asp:detailsview>

</form>
</body>
</html>
```

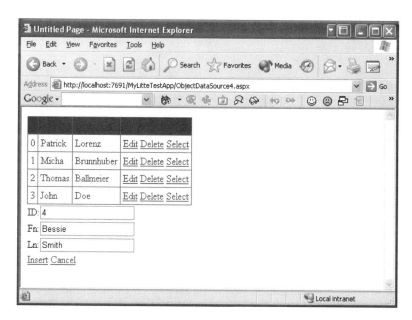

Figure 3-26. Of course, inserting new records is now supported as well.

Summary

Wow, that's a lot of new stuff, right? The new concepts introduced in this chapter will totally change the way you handle data within ASP.NET. Thanks to Data Source controls, it's so much simpler now to connect a page with a database. One of the biggest benefits is that you can easily build your own providers to access your custom data sources as well.

CHAPTER 4

Working with Master Pages

THE MASTER PAGES FUNCTIONALITY goes by many names, one of which is "page templating." All of these expressions have the same meaning. They refer to the central deposit of site layouts, including the navigation, which will then automatically be transferred to single Content Pages. From now on, you have to make changes to the general layout in just one place. Those changes will become effective on all corresponding pages that use the Master Page you changed. Sounds like a standard requirement for approximately 100% of all web sites, don't you agree? Right!

The 1.0 and 1.1 versions of ASP.NET didn't offer the Master Pages functionality. That was a good reason for many developers to implement their own approaches. These approaches went from the static output of HTML tags to the implementation of user controls to the drilling of page life cycles. The latter offered the greatest flexibility and was my favorite too. I have to admit, however, that it wasn't an ideal solution.

With version 2.0, ASP.NET offers its own and fully integrated support for Master Pages for the first time. You develop one or several layouts as Master Pages and allocate them to single Content Pages. In combination with VS .NET, you can now design the Content Pages visually within the Master Pages context and fill one or several defined placeholders.

Creating a New Master Page

Please create a new and empty web site before you start with a new Master Page. Then choose Add New Item from the Website menu and establish a new element from the type MasterPage with the name MasterPage1.master. All Master Pages have this special ending, which helps you avoid starting the page directly within the browser.

In the result, you get a new page that includes a control of type ContentPlaceHolder. This is a regular control, which means that you can integrate it as usual into the HTML layout of the page. Now I would like to show you a table to which I've added some text. I also placed the control in one of the cells, as you can see in Figure 4-1.

Figure 4-1. Design your site any way you want!

Have a look at the source code of the page in Listing 4-1 and you can see that the structure of the Master Page is compatible with a normal web site. The ContentPlaceHolder control is positioned just like a normal server control. There is still one difference, however: the @Master directive. In this case, it replaces the @Page directive and enables you to place default values for several attributes. If you set attribute values for @Master and don't overwrite them in your @Page directive, you adopt them. This shows clearly that the setting of the page has priority.

Listing 4-1. The Master Page Source Code

```
<%@ master language="C#" %>

<script runat="server">

</script>

<html>
<head runat="server">
```

```
        <title>Untitled Page</title>
    </head>
    <body>
        <form runat="server">
            <table id="Table1" cellspacing="1" cellpadding="1" width="100%" border="1">
                <tr>
                    <td colspan="2">                    .
                        <h1>My Little Company</h1>
                    </td>
                </tr>
                <tr>
                    <td>Navigation?</td>
                    <td>
                        <asp:contentplaceholder
                            id="ContentPlaceHolder1"
                            runat="server">
                        </asp:contentplaceholder>
                    </td>
                </tr>
                <tr>
                    <td>
                    </td>
                    <td>
                    </td>
                </tr>
            </table>
        </form>
    </body>
</html>
```

Creating a New Content Page

After you've successfully completed the template, you really get into it! You can start with the actual page and its individual content. To do so, you simply use the Add New Item command to add a new page of type ContentPage, and name it ContentPage1.aspx. As soon as you've finished, the dialog box shown in Figure 4-2 appears. Here you can choose the desired Master Page if you have more than one. In this example, I just have the one I created earlier.

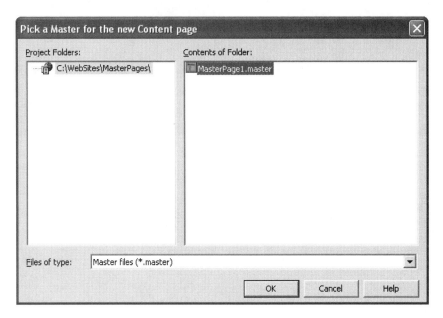

Figure 4-2. Select which Master Page to use.

The new page is now shown in Source view. The content is a bit poor and consists of just one line. The chosen Master Page is referenced by the @Page directive:

```
<%@ page language="C#" master="~/MasterPage1.master" %>
```

A change to the Design view uncovers the real capabilities of the new developing environment, VS .NET. The new Content Page is shown in the context of the Master Page, which has been placed in the background with the help of alpha blending. The ContentPlaceHolder control is active and can be filled with content, as Figure 4-3 shows.

Instead of the text shown in the example, you can obviously place other controls in the placeholder. In this respect, you have no limitations! You can even use user controls and any source code on the server side or client side without any changes. Let's have a look at the HTML source code to see what's going on inside. The text is being saved within a Content control, which is linked with the ContentPlaceHolder control in the Master Page by the property ContentPlaceHolderId:

```
<%@ page language="C#" master="~/MasterPage1.master" %>
<asp:content id="Content1"
    contentplaceholderid="ContentPlaceHolder1"
    runat="server">
You can visually edit your content page right within the master ... cool stuff!
</asp:content>
```

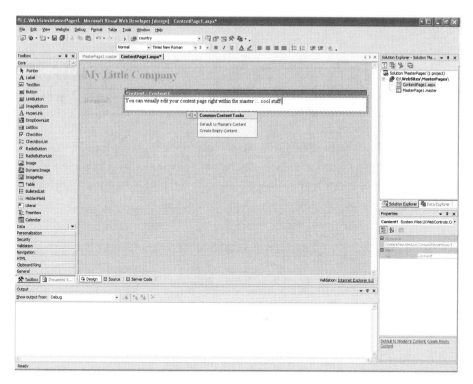

Figure 4-3. You can visually edit your Content Pages.

CAUTION *Please be aware you may only place content within the Content controls. You can't place objects outside the areas defined by the Master Page. This includes standard HTML tags such as* <html>, <head>, *and* <body>, *which are already included in the Master Page. You can change these only in the corresponding Master Page itself.*

Having edited your first Content Page, you may relax for a while and then add as many pages as you'd like. Any changes in the Master Page will become effective at once and automatically on all related pages.

TIP *Instead of defining individual Master Pages with the* @Page *directive for each page, you may act more globally and define an undocumented attribute in the* web.config *file:*

```
<pages
    master="~/MasterPage.master"
/>
```

Using Multiple Content Regions and Default Content

Depending upon the requirements for each individual project, it can be interesting to define several placeholders to ensure high flexibility in the design of each individual page. The system has no limits in this respect, and you can place an unlimited number of ContentPlaceHolder controls on a page and fill them later on with content.

The option to place standard content feels quite comfortable (see Figure 4-4). You can, for example, fill the area of the footer with remarks about the copyright. Normally, this text is shown. Additionally, you have the option to replace text individually on some chosen subpages.

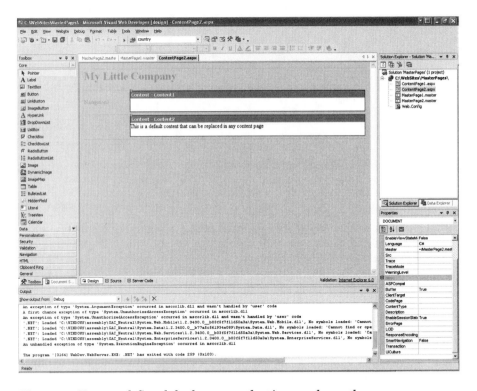

Figure 4-4. You can define default content that is spread over the pages.

CAUTION *Please be aware that standard content is always being overwritten by any page content you put inside the placeholder. You have no choice about endorsing the existing content. Therefore, you must decide between the use of standard or individual content.*

> **TIP** *If you've already placed content and you want to replace it later on with standard content, you just use the command Default To Master's Content from the Task List of the particular Content control.*

Master Pages Under the Hood

You may ask how these Master Pages really work. In this context, it's quite interesting to have a look at the control tree of generated pages. As you can see in Figure 4-5, the Master Page is being created as an independent control directly below the page itself. You can recognize the ContentPlaceHolder controls as well. They directly contain the objects that are being placed either in the Content Page or as default content in the Master Page.

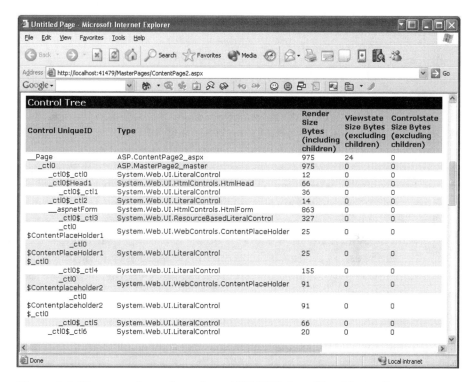

Figure 4-5. The control tree shows how ASP.NET is handling Master Pages.

If you want to work with events within the Master Page and/or the Content Page, you should watch out for the correct sequence:

1. Master Page child controls initialization.

2. Content Page child controls initialization.

3. Master page initialization.

4. Content Page initialization.

5. Content Page load.

6. Master Page load.

7. Master Page child controls load.

8. Content Page child controls load.

Dynamically Using Master Pages

The dynamic use of Master Pages is a very exciting idea. Depending on individual parameters you may, for example, show the same pages with different designs. Another idea is to format content in different ways to show a printable version.

Unfortunately—and this has led to many controversial discussions in non-public Alpha forums—Master Pages *cannot* be defined dynamically at present. The reason is that Master Pages are already being integrated in the page during its dynamic compilation and they are fixed within each page.

At present, the ASP.NET team is checking on the feasibility of including dynamic Master Pages as a feature. If this is the case, the corresponding functionality could already be implemented into the Beta version. Until then, the team recommends the "misuse" of Device Filters as a workaround. The following listing shows how this works.

Two `Master` attributes will be placed within the `@Page` directive of the Content Page. One is the standard value, and the other is device specific. Additionally, the `TestDeviceFilter` method, which is normally used for the evaluation of the Device Filter, has to be overwritten. The alternative Master Page will be switched on if the word "print" is part of the query string.

```
<%@ page language="C#" master="~/main.master"
    printcontent:master="~/print.master" %>

<script runat="server" language="c#">

  public override bool TestDeviceFilter(string deviceFilterName)
  {

    if (deviceFilterName.Equals("printcontent"))
    {
        if (this.Request.QueryString["print"] != null)
        {
            return true;
        }
    }
    return base.TestDeviceFilter(deviceFilterName);
  }

</script>
<asp:content id="Content1"
    contentplaceholderid="ContentPlaceHolder1"
    runat="server">

    Test Test Test Test Test Test Test Test
    Test Test Test Test Test Test Test Test
    Test Test<br />
    <br />

    <asp:hyperlink id="HyperLink1" runat="server"
        navigateurl="Default.aspx?print=1">
        Print me!
    </asp:hyperlink>
</asp:content>
```

> **TIP** *If you intend to use this type of approach, I recommend you derive a central class from the page, provide it with functionality, and derive the single pages from this class.*

> **TIP** *Naturally, you can use the device-specific application of Master Pages in its original sense in different devices (PDA, Pocket PC, mobile device, etc.) with different templates.*

Accessing Master Page at Run Time

The ASP.NET Framework offers the possibility to access Master Pages programmatically during run time. You can use this as a basis for individual enhancements and changes. The Content Page offers the Master property, which is marked as protected. This way, you get an instance on the individual Master Page, from which you get access to the public properties and methods.

The assignment of an individual page title is a typical example for the application. The files in Listing 4-3 show this using a Literal control placed on the Master Page. The text is assigned through a custom and public property, HtmlTitle, which passes the text to the label.

Listing 4-3. Access Any Public Members Through the Master Properties

```
// MasterPage3.master
<%@ master language="C#" %>

<script runat="server">

    public string HtmlTitle
    {
        get { return this.LT_HtmlTitle.Text; }
        set { this.LT_HtmlTitle.Text = value; }
    }

</script>

<html>
<head runat="server">
    <title><ASP:Literal id="LT_HtmlTitle" runat="server" /></title>
</head>
<body>
    <form runat="server">
        <asp:contentplaceholder id="ContentPlaceHolder1" runat="server">
        </asp:contentplaceholder>
    </form>
```

```
</body>
</html>

// ContentPage3.aspx
<%@ page language="C#" master="~/MasterPage3.master" %>

<script runat="server" language="c#">

    void Page_Load(object sender, System.EventArgs e)
    {
        this.Master.HtmlTitle = "Hello World!";
    }

</script>
```

If you intend to define meta tags dynamically, I recommend you use the page's Header object, which implements IPageHeader. The object gives access to meta tags, external CSS files, and any style sheets defined globally on that page. The approach shown in Listing 4-4 works well in Master Pages, Content Pages, and normal pages.

Listing 4-4. Assigning Custom Meta Tags

```
<%@ page language="C#" master="~/MasterPage4.master" %>
<script runat="server" language="c#">

void Page_Load(object sender, System.EventArgs e)
{
    this.Master.HtmlTitle = "Hello World!";
    this.Header.Metadata.Add("Author", "Patrick A. Lorenz");
}

</script>
```

Nested Master Pages

It's possible to nest Master Pages, though this will certainly be an exception rather than a rule. To do so, you can define an additional (parent) Master Page for an existing Master Page and so on. This approach is very useful for times when you want to modify a comprehensive layout and use it for different areas of your web site.

The example in Listing 4-5 comes from the online help. You can already use this example in the Alpha version. The IDE, however, is still facing some difficulties with regard to nesting Master Pages that will probably be corrected in the Beta version. Figure 4-6 shows the nested Master Pages in action.

Listing 4-5. Nesting Master Pages

```
// MasterMasterPage5.master (Parent Master)
<%@ Master Language="C#" %>

<html>
<body>
<form id="Form1" runat=server>
   <h1>Parent Master</h1>
   <p>
   <font color=red>This is Parent-master content.</font>
   </P>
<asp:contentplaceholder id="MainContent" runat=server/>
</form>
</html>
</body>

// MasterPage5.master (Child Master)
<%@ master language="C#" master="~/MasterMasterPage5.master" %>

<asp:content id="Content1" contentplaceholderid="MainContent" runat="server">
   <asp:panel runat="server" id="panelMain" backcolor="lightyellow">
   <h2>Child master</h2>
      <asp:panel runat="server" id="panel1" backcolor="lightblue">
        <p>This is childmaster content.</p>
        <asp:contentplaceholder id="Content1" runat="server" />
      </asp:panel>
      <asp:panel runat="server" id="panel2" backcolor="pink">
        <p>This is childmaster content.</p>
        <asp:contentplaceholder id="Content2" runat="server" />
      </asp:panel>
   </asp:panel>
</asp:content>

// ContentPage5.aspx
<%@ page language="C#" master="~/MasterPage5.master" %>
```

```
<asp:content id="Content1" contentplaceholderid="Content1" runat=server>
    <asp:label runat="server" id="Label1"
        text="Child label1" font-bold=true/>
    <br>
</asp:content>
<asp:content id="Content2" contentplaceholderid="Content2" runat=server>
    <asp:label runat="server" id="Label2"
        text="Child label2" font-bold=true/>
</asp:content>
```

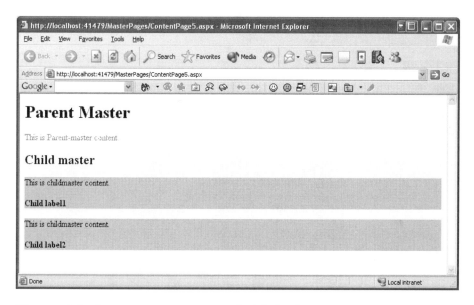

Figure 4-6. Both master pages are merged with the Content Page.

Master Pages and User Controls

At first glance, it seems to be strange, but it's actually possible to combine user controls and Master Pages without limitations and with the aim of reusing existing layouts. Therefore, the @Control directive offers a "master" attribute similar to @Page.

The sample in Listing 4-6 shows such an approach in combination with Master Pages, a user control, and a page putting it all together. The Master Page contains a table with two ContentPlaceHolder controls in it. Those are filled through the user control. As you can see from Figure 4-7, all elements are displayed correctly. Of course, you could also think about adding a Master Page for the page itself.

Listing 4-6. Combining User Controls and Master Pages

```
// UCMaster.master
<%@ master language="C#" %>

<table id="Table1" bordercolor="black" cellspacing="1" cellpadding="1" width="100%"
    border="2">
    <tr>
        <td>
            <asp:contentplaceholder id="ContentPlaceHolder1" runat="server">
            </asp:contentplaceholder>
        </td>
        <td>
        </td>
        <td>
        </td>
    </tr>
    <tr>
        <td>
        </td>
        <td>This is my Master Page!</td>
        <td>
        </td>
    </tr>
    <tr>
        <td>
        </td>
        <td>
        </td>
        <td>
            <asp:contentplaceholder id="ContentPlaceHolder2" runat="server">
            </asp:contentplaceholder>
        </td>
    </tr>
</table>

// UCMaster.ascx
<%@ control language="C#" classname="UCMaster" master="~/UCMaster.master" %>

<asp:content id="Content1"
    contentplaceholderid="ContentPlaceHolder1"
    runat="server">
    This is my User Control
</asp:content>
```

```
<asp:content id="Content2"
    contentplaceholderid="ContentPlaceHolder2"
    runat="server">
    This is my User Control, too
</asp:content>

// UCMaster.aspx
<%@ page language="C#" %>
<%@ register tagprefix="uc1" tagname="UCMaster" src="~/UCMaster.ascx" %>

<script runat="server">

</script>

<html>
<head runat="server">
    <title>Untitled Page</title>
</head>
<body>
    <form runat="server">
        <p>This text is embedded in the page itself.</p>
        <uc1:ucmaster id="UCMaster1" runat="server"></uc1:ucmaster>
        <p>This text is again embedded in the page.</p>
    </form>
</body>
</html>
```

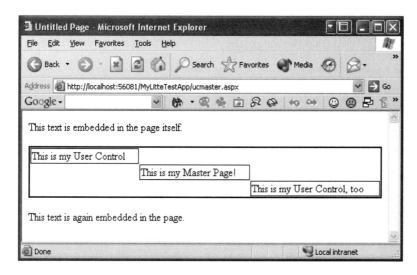

Figure 4-7. Gosh—it works!

Summary

Master Pages are a frequently asked-about feature—a "must-have." The seamless visual integration in VS .NET makes it quite easy to take advantage of this new feature. Additionally, you can access your Master Pages through a type-safe property that is dynamically added to the Page class. The one missing function is the capability to switch Master Pages at run time.

CHAPTER 5

Integrating Site Navigation

BE HONEST, NOW: Did you ever make a web site without navigation? OK, maybe apart from one or two little test projects. Anyway, any web site that consists of more than two or three pages needs navigation.

The second version of ASP.NET offers special features for implementing navigation elements. In this chapter I present these new features to you.

Defining a Site Map

ASP.NET's integrated support for defining a site map is based on an XML file named app.sitemap, which is placed in the root directory of the application. The structure of the file complies with a specific schema:

```
<siteMap>
    <siteMapNode title="" description="" url="">
        <siteMapNode .../>
    </siteMap>
</siteMap>
```

Every single siteMapNode element included in this schema can be nested and results in the hierarchy of the navigation. The documentation presents one example for such a hierarchy, which Listing 5-1 shows.

Listing 5-1. App.sitemap Contains an XML-Formatted Site Map Hierarchy

```
<?xml version="1.0" encoding="utf-8" ?>
<siteMap>
    <siteMapNode title="Home" description="Home" url="default.aspx" >
        <siteMapNode title="Products" description="Our products"
            url="Products.aspx">
            <siteMapNode title="Hardware" description="Hardware choices"
                url="navigation1.aspx" />
```

```
            <siteMapNode title="Software" description="Software choices"
                url="Software.aspx" />
        </siteMapNode>
        <siteMapNode title="Services" description="Services we offer"
            url="Services.aspx">
            <siteMapNode title="Training" description="Training classes"
                url="Training.aspx" />
            <siteMapNode title="Consulting" description="Consulting services"
                url="Consulting.aspx" />
            <siteMapNode title="Support" description="Supports plans"
                url="Support.aspx" />
        </siteMapNode>
    </siteMapNode>
</siteMap>
```

The two areas, "Products" and "Services," are placed below "Home" and have some submenus themselves. Please note that the structures being used here don't have to correspond with the physical structure of your files and directories. But it can be quite easy to define the navigation by the file structure and vice versa. Particularly with large projects, you'll get a much better overview this way.

Apart from the attributes title, url, and description, you may additionally allocate keywords to a list of keywords for each individual page. Multiple keywords are separated by commas. If you intend to give only limited access to a page, or rather the navigation item itself, you must pass the permitted roles to the attribute roles. Don't forget to use commas to separate the roles. I explain the use of the new user management features later in Chapter 6. By the way, you may place any individual attributes here as well.

If you want to allocate this (or a different) navigation to your application, you should keep on reading. Add a new XML file with the previously mentioned name, app.sitemap, to your project and copy the content shown in Listing 5-1 into it.

Using the TreeView Control for Navigation

Naturally, the TreeView control is predestined to show hierarchical site map navigation. To implement such navigation automatically in all pages, I recommend you use Master Pages, as described in the last chapter.

This is how it works:

1. Place a new TreeView control at the position of your choice within the page or the Master Page.

2. Choose the Connect To DataSource command from the task list and create a new source of type SiteMapDataSource.

3. Set the `InitialExpandDepth` property of the TreeView control to 2.

4. Start the web site by pressing F5.

The SiteMapDataSource control reads the data automatically out of the aforementioned XML file and makes it available for the TreeView control. Your browser should now look like Figure 5-1 if you didn't make any other changes.

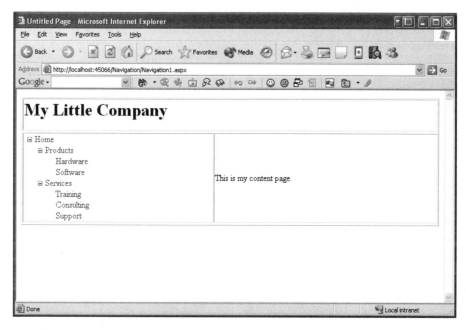

Figure 5-1. You can use the TreeView control to display any kind of hierarchical site map.

The required HTML source code for this example is quite short and looks like this:

```
<asp:treeview id="TreeView1" runat="server"
    font-underline="False"
    datasourceid="SiteMapDataSource1"
    initialexpanddepth="2">
    <parentnodestyle font-underline="False">
    </parentnodestyle>
```

```
        <leafnodestyle font-underline="False">
        </leafnodestyle>
        <nodestyle font-underline="False">
        </nodestyle>
        <rootnodestyle font-underline="False">
        </rootnodestyle>
</asp:treeview>
<asp:sitemapdatasource id="SiteMapDataSource1" runat="server">
</asp:sitemapdatasource>
```

> **NOTE** *The page used in this section's example is called* navigation1.aspx. *This page has been applied as the destination for the site map entry Home ➤ Products ➤ Hardware. Some other entries comply with files used in later examples in this chapter.*

Creating a Split Navigation System

The SqlDataSource control offers several properties to adapt the site's navigation. You can specify, for example, that the entries should start from root, from the active element, or from the active element's parent. Alternatively, you can define the level to be shown directly (zero based).

The following example (see Listing 5-2) is an enhancement of the previous example. This time, however, the three main points are shown in a horizontal navigation bar. This is accomplished through a DataList control that has a separate SqlDataSource control assigned to it. Now the TreeView shows only the navigation points from the second level on, naturally depending on the actual position of the site.

Listing 5-2. A Different Way to Create a Real-World Navigation System

```
<table id="Table1" cellspacing="1" cellpadding="1" width="100%" border="1">
    <tr>
        <td colspan="2">
            <h1>My Little Company</h1>
        </td>
    </tr>

    <tr>
        <td colspan="2">
```

```
        <asp:datalist id="DataList1" runat="server"
            repeatdirection="Horizontal"
            datasourceid="SiteMapDataSource2">
            <itemtemplate>
                <asp:hyperlink
                    id="HyperLink1"
                    runat="server"
                    navigateurl='<%# Eval("url") %>'
                    text='<%# Eval("title") %>'>
                </asp:hyperlink>
            </itemtemplate>
        </asp:datalist>
        <asp:sitemapdatasource id="SiteMapDataSource2"
            runat="server"
            sitemapviewtype="Flat"
            flatdepth="2">
        </asp:sitemapdatasource>
    </td>
</tr>

<tr>
    <td valign="top">
        <asp:treeview id="TreeView1" runat="server"
            datasourceid="SiteMapDataSource1"
            initialexpanddepth="2" >
        </asp:treeview>
        <asp:sitemapdatasource id="SiteMapDataSource1"
            runat="server"
            startingdepth="1">
        </asp:sitemapdatasource>
    </td>
    <td>
        <asp:contentplaceholder id="ContentPlaceHolder1" runat="server">
        </asp:contentplaceholder>
    </td>
</tr>
<tr>
    <td>
    </td>
    <td>
    </td>
</tr>
</table>
```

Listing 5-2 shows the source code of the page and two SqlDataSource controls with different parameters. The properties in use are `SiteMapViewType` and `FlatDepth` for the main navigation, and `StartingDepth` for the area navigation. Figure 5-2 shows the result.

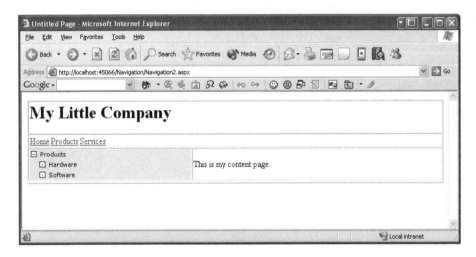

Figure 5-2. The main navigation and area navigation are split.

Introducing Breadcrumb Navigation

Do you know what breadcrumbs are? No, I'm not talking about the means by which Hansel and Gretel found their way out of the forest and back home, but that's where this expression may originally come from. In the context of web development, *breadcrumbs* refer to the display of the page's position in the navigation hierarchy.

ASP.NET 2.0 offers a control that specially addresses the positioning display. This control is called SiteMapPath and you can easily position it on the page without assigning a data source. In this case, the application of Master Pages makes absolute sense as well:

```
You are here:
<asp:sitemappath id="SiteMapPath1" runat="server">
</asp:sitemappath>
```

Based on the previous example, Figure 5-3 shows the application of this new control.

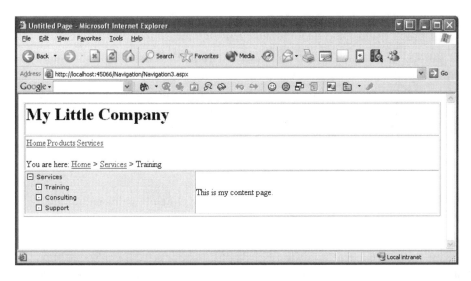

Figure 5-3. The new SiteMapPath control offers your visitors a way to see where they actually are.

Customizing the SiteMapPath Control

The SiteMapPath control is a prime example for adaptability. With the help of various properties, you can define how the current position is shown. With the Path-Separator property, for example, you can indicate the separator, and with the RenderCurrentNodeAsLink property you may define if the current page can be accessed by a link. You can even show a tool tip with a description of each individual element of the navigation. You may customize all the areas visually with styles, of course.

If all of these ways to influence the behavior of the control aren't enough for you, the following individual templates may be appropriate:

- NodeTemplate

- CurrentNodeTemplate

- RootNodeTemplate

- PathSeparatorTemplate

Still not satisfied? Then take the two events ItemCreated and ItemDataBound and do whatever you want with them.

Using a Rich Dynamic HTML Menu Control

The ASP.NET team plans to ship an important dynamic HTML (DHTML) menu control with the final version 2.0. In a similar way as the SiteMapPath control, this control will pull data out of the active `SiteMap` provider. The current ASP.NET Alpha version, however, doesn't include this control. Stay tuned!

Working with the SiteMap API

The SiteMapPath control and most likely the menu control (which will be available later on) won't need an explicit data source to show the navigation. Why? The controls use an application programming interface (API) that is available for your direct use as well. The basis of this API is the `SiteMap` class from the `System.Web` namespace. The class gives you access to the node (`CurrentNode`) and root node (`RootNode`) via four static properties, among other things. Actually, the SiteMap-DataSource control uses these properties to give other data controls access to the navigation data.

In addition to the `SiteMap` class, it's worth mentioning the `SiteMapNode` class. This class represents a single element of the navigation. It knows various properties and methods to query the attributes of an entry about which `ParentNode`, `ChildNodes`, or the previous, the next, or even all nodes on the same level can be found. Via the `IsDescendantOf()` method, you can find out whether the element is derived from the second `SiteMapNode` that was passed over as a parameter.

Accessing the Current Navigation Node

Listing 5-3 shows the use of the `SiteMap` class. The title of the active navigation entry (`SiteMapNode`) is retrieved within the `Page_Load` method of the Master Page, and then it's reused as HTML title of the page.

Listing 5-3. Complete API for Accessing the Site Navigation

```
<%@ master language="C#" %>

<script runat="server">

    void Page_Load(object sender, System.EventArgs e)
    {
        if (SiteMap.CurrentNode != null)
        {
```

```
            this.LT_HtmlTitle.Text = SiteMap.CurrentNode.Title;
        }
    }

</script>

<html>
<head id="Head1" runat="server">
    <title><ASP:Literal id="LT_HtmlTitle" runat="server"/></title>
</head>
...
```

Using Custom Attributes

If the page title doesn't have to be identical to the navigation entry (as in the previous example), or if you want to allocate individual data to the single entries, that's fine. For example:

```
<siteMapNode title="Support"
    description="Supports plans"
    url="navigation5.aspx"
    pagetitle="Here's a custom page title"
/>
```

You can include as much data as you want by putting it in the app.sitemap file. With the Attributes collection of the SiteMapNode class you can access the data very comfortably at run time. Following this idea, the next example shows the output of a page title, assuming that you've added one to the file:

```
<%@ master language="C#" %>

<script runat="server">

    void Page_Load(object sender, System.EventArgs e)
    {
        SiteMapNode currentNode = SiteMap.CurrentNode;
        if (currentNode != null)
        {
            if (currentNode.Attributes["pagetitle"] != null)
            {
                this.LT_HtmlTitle.Text = currentNode.Attributes["pagetitle"];
            }
```

```
        else
        {
            this.LT_HtmlTitle.Text = currentNode.Title;
        }
    }
}

</script>

<html>
<head id="Head1" runat="server">
    <title><ASP:Literal id="LT_HtmlTitle" runat="server"/></title>
</head>
...
```

Enhancing the Provider Model

Like many other new features of ASP.NET, the navigation is based on a *provider model.* Here, you may use individual sources of data as, for example, a database to build up your navigation. The data generally doesn't have to come out of the app.sitemap file.

If you want to build a new provider, you must first create a class that implements the ISiteMapProvider interface. This interface defines three methods and four properties that are used by the SiteMap class to form the desired object model.

You can find an example of how to implement an individual provider in the documentation for the aforementioned interface.

Summary

The new navigation system offers you a flexible and extensible way to provide your web site users with a comfortable navigation. You can easily use the new configuration file to define the site structure and the new controls to display it. Also, you can create your own custom SiteMap provider, for example, if your site map is generated dynamically from a database.

CHAPTER 6

Managing Users

WITH THE FIRST VERSION OF ASP.NET, you already had the option to authenticate users against several services. This served as the basis for allowing individual users access to specific areas of a web site. For intranet solutions, you could rely on Windows Authentication integrated by IIS. In the case of public web sites for the Internet, you could use Forms Authentication. The latter offered the possibility to place user-specific data in the web.config configuration file. Additionally, custom systems could be used to check user data against a database, for example. If your application required individual roles in this context, the situation started to get a little bit complicated.

The possibilities the ASP.NET version 2.0 provides go far beyond that. Now you have two complete built-in systems at your service: Membership Management and Role Management. These systems take the place of the authentication and authorization features of previous ASP.NET versions. Used in combination, both systems offer a completely generic and openly designed framework for the administration of users and roles—independent of the data store being used.

The Membership Management system offers the following features, among other things:

- Creation of new users

- Storage of user data like name, login, password, and so on in the SQL Server, Microsoft Access, or any other data source of your choice by individual membership providers

- Administration of passwords, including storage, verification, resetting, expiration, and so on, as well as web controls for passwords that have been forgotten

- Authentication of users via specific web controls or individually with the help of the Membership Management API

- Provision of unique user IDs for authenticated users as a basis for individual authorizations and personalization

- Optional allocation of unique IDs for nonauthenticated and anonymous users to attach information to them within the scope of personalization, for example

Additionally, the following functions are just two of the many being integrated via the Role Management system:

- Administration of roles, including a Role Management API to add or to delete them

- Storage of roles in an encrypted cookie

Setting Up User Management

First, you have to make some settings in the web.config configuration file before you can benefit from the user management features of ASP.NET. In addition, you need a database for storing users and roles. Instead of doing this job manually, you may use the new Web Site Administration tool I introduced you to in Chapter 1.

Using the ASP.NET Web Site Administration Tool

The Web Site Administration tool is offered to developers and administrators for setting up and configuring their applications. The tool should make the direct use of the web.config configuration file dispensable in many scenarios. It also can be expanded for custom purposes. At present, this new tool is still under construction. The administration of users and roles, however, is already integrated—which is good for us!

If you want to add user management to your new web site, you must open the configuration tool with the command ASP.NET Configuration from the Website menu in Visual Studio .NET. To save the project in your local IIS, you must enter the following address into your browser:

```
http://localhost/<application>/webadmin.axd
```

Click the Security option on the index page and make sure the Security Setup Wizard radio button is selected. Then click the Next button, which appears in the lower right of this page. The assistant that appears will aid you in performing the whole job of configuration in six steps:

1. The first page of the assistant will give you some initial information.

2. In the second step, you can specify whether your web site is going to be used for Internet or intranet purposes. Depending on your selection, the user administration of ASP.NET or the Windows Authentication feature will be used. For the purposes of this example, I've chosen an Internet web site.

3. With the help of the wizard, you may automatically create a database at this point in the process. You have the choice between Microsoft Access or SQL Server. If you choose the first option, you must enter **aspnetdb** in both the Database Name and the File Name fields. Now you are asked to choose which data you want stored as shown in Figure 6-1. After this, the database will be configured. You have a choice of saving passwords as a one-way hash or as text; the latter option enables you to later send a password to a user if necessary.

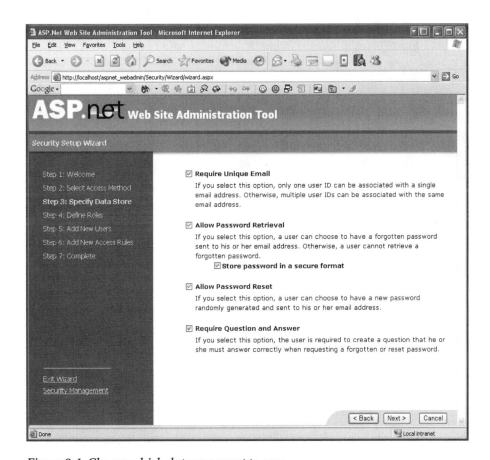

Figure 6-1. Choose which data you want to save.

4. Figure 6-2 shows the fourth step of the wizard. You can decide if you want to use roles in general. If so, you can create them right here—just fill in the New Role Name field and click the Add Role button. You may change or add new roles at a later date, of course.

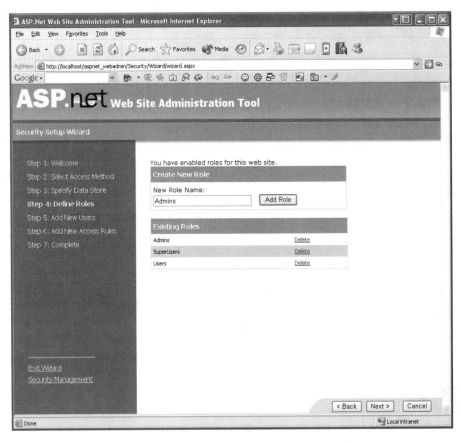

Figure 6-2. You can define as many custom roles as you like.

5. Having finished specifying roles, you may now add an administrative user in the fifth step. Please put off the creation of additional users to a later time for this example. The dialog box shown in Figure 6-3 will appear differently depending on the options you have chosen in the third step. The combination of a question and an answer can be used to reset a forgotten password, as offered by many web sites today. If you activate the option Send Password, users will receive a small e-mail with their user data and passwords, which by default looks like this:

```
From: <Hoster>
Subject: Account Information
To: <lorenz@pgk.de>

Your account name is: lorenz@pgk.de.
   Your password is: ***************.
```

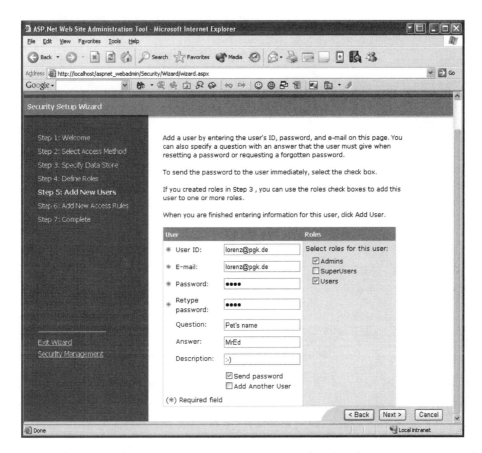

Figure 6-3. Here you can create one or more users and assign them to one or more of the created roles.

6. In the last step of the wizard, things are getting interesting. You can decide in a very sophisticated way which role and/or which user should have access or not to each directory, as shown in Figure 6-4. By doing so, the corresponding web.config file(s) will be created or modified for each folder.

> **NOTE** *Please be aware that at present the configuration of access authorization is only possible when using Internet Information Services. It isn't yet possible in combination with the integrated web server of the IDE.*

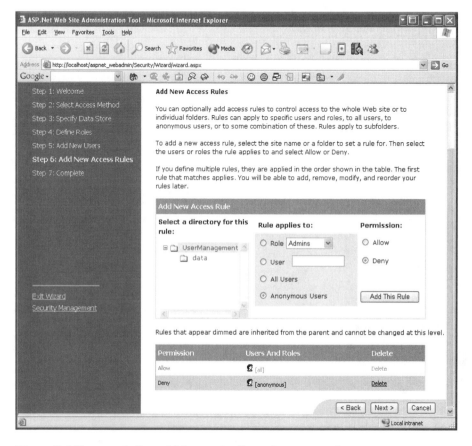

Figure 6-4. You can define which user is allowed to access what content.

That's it! Now your page is protected! The results that the assistant produces are one or several adapted `web.config` files within the various directories of your web site. Additionally, a subfolder named `data` is created containing a preconfigured Microsoft Access database with the name of your choice (for example, `aspnetdb.mdb`). This database includes all data involving users and roles and can take on additional data (for example, data associated with personalization) later on.

Setting Up the Web Site

Figure 6-5 shows the Solution Explorer containing the web site structure I've chosen. As you can see, there are two protected areas: one for any authenticated user and one just for administrators. Each directory has a web.config file with the specified access rights. These are placed within <authorization> tags as shown.

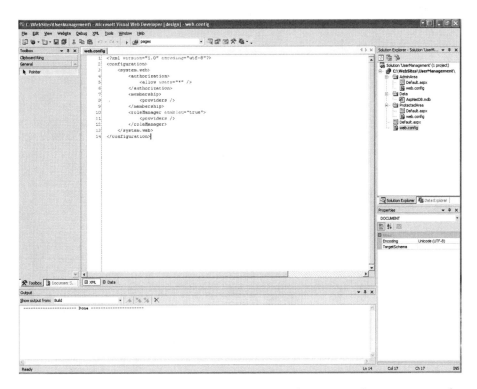

Figure 6-5. The new web site contains two protected areas, one for any users and one for administrators only.

Figure 6-5 shows the web.config file of the root directory of the application as well. Here access is allowed for all users. Additionally, Membership Management and Role Management have been activated explicitly.

Updating the Configuration

Of course, you can change the configuration, roles, users, and user rights anytime afterward initial setup. Simply start the ASP.NET Web Site Administration tool and click the Security tab. Then, you select the Security Management radio button option and click Next. Now you get a screen with three different areas: Users, Roles, and Permissions (see Figure 6-6). You can use the options associated with each area to make changes similar to the way you used the previously shown Security Setup Wizard.

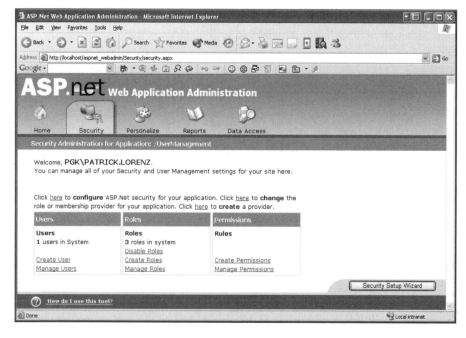

Figure 6-6. Just start the new administration tool to update the configuration.

Introducing the New Security Web Controls

With ASP.NET 1.x, you had to take care of the interaction between users and your custom user management all by yourself. Now there is good news ahead! With the new version, you'll get support from a couple of web controls:

- Login provides a login form that you can use as is or adapt by using styles. You can even design it to suit your needs with a template.

- PasswordRecovery is adaptable in a similar way and allows you to reset and/or send a password that was forgotten.

- LoginStatus provides a Login or Logout link depending on the actual status of authentication.

- LoginName outputs the login name.

- LoginView handles an expandable set of templates. Whether these are shown depends on the authentication status or the assigned roles of the user.

I've adapted the previously shown structure for the use of Master Pages to provide a good basis for further examples. All of the three pages you've seen so far are based on this template. The Master Page consists of a table with a Content-PlaceHolder control, three links, and a LoginName and LoginStatus control in the upper-right side. In combination with a single content page, default.aspx from the root directory of the application, the entire page now looks as shown in Figure 6-7. As you can see, the Login link button appears in the upper-right side.

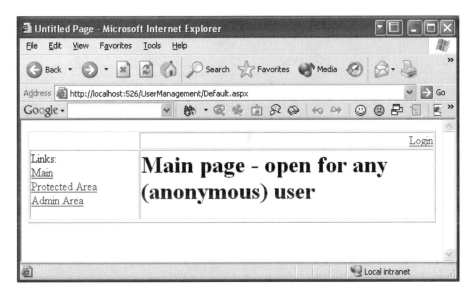

Figure 6-7. The main page is accessible even for anonymous users like me.

Login Control

The Login control has one simple task: It takes data from a user who isn't authenticated yet, makes a validation, and depending on that validation, confirms the authentication or denies it.

I've created a new page, login.aspx, in the root area of the application to demonstrate the control. As in previous versions, one page with this name is used by default to log on the user. This page is also shown if users try to access a page for which they have to be authenticated, for example. Naturally, the created page uses the previously defined Master Page. In addition, I've included the Login control (see Listing 6-1).

Listing 6-1. Providing a Rich Login Surface Without Writing a Line of Code Through the Login Control

```
<%@ page language="C#" master="~/MasterPage.master" %>

<asp:content id="Content1"
    contentplaceholderid="ContentPlaceHolder1" runat="server">

    <asp:login id="Login1" runat="server"
        font-names="Verdana"
        font-size="10pt"
        borderwidth="1px"
        bordercolor="#999999"
        borderstyle="Solid"
        backcolor="#FFFFCC"

        instructiontext="Please enter your user name and password to log in"
        remembermeset="True"
    >

        <titletextstyle font-bold="True" forecolor="#FFFFFF" backcolor="#333399">
        </titletextstyle>
    </asp:login>

</asp:content>
```

Through the Task List, the control offers the option Auto Format, with which you can choose between various standard formats, similar to other controls. I decided to go for Classic for this example.

This control offers real Plug and Play capability. If you've been following along with this example, and you start your web site and click the Login link button, you can already start using the control to log in. Using the correct user data, you get access to the protected pages (see Figure 6-8). Check it out!

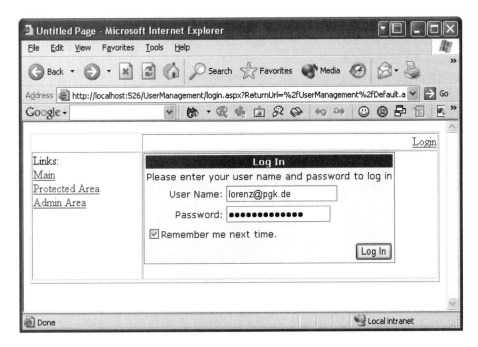

Figure 6-8. The Login control includes everything you need for a user to log in to your web site.

Customizing the Login Control

You can adapt your Login control to make it unique to your site, not like login features on other web sites. A whole range of different formatting properties and styles is at your service for this purpose. The Submit button, for example, can be defined either as a regular button, a link button, or an image button. Additionally, you can define whether the input fields should be displayed horizontally or vertically and whether the text should be shown above or beside the fields. Naturally, you may adapt all the text, for example, to localize it.

Functional changes are possible without any difficulty. Using the `DisplayRememberMe` property, you can define whether the possibility of a permanent login should be offered to the user via a CheckBox control. With `RememberMeSet`, you can define the initial value of the CheckBox control. The behavior in the case of errors and many other situations may be handled individually.

If these options are not enough for you to make the modifications you desire, you can use templates instead, an example of which is shown in Figure 6-9. You can avoid a lot of manual work by converting the actual configured state with the help of the Task List into a template, and then working on the template afterward. The functionality of the control stays as it is, as long as you haven't changed the defined IDs of the controls.

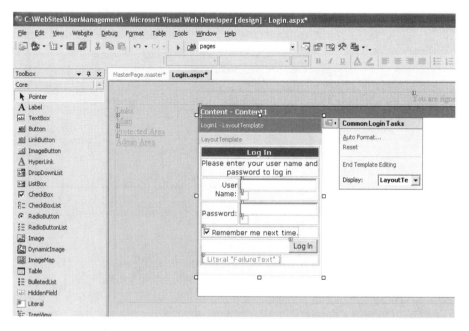

Figure 6-9. Customizing included—the Login control supports templating.

It is obvious that using a template results in more source code. It's getting much clearer, however, how the control is working on the inside. Listing 6-2 offers a snippet.

Listing 6-2. Customizing the Login Control

```
<%@ page language="C#" master="~/MasterPage.master" %>
<script runat="server" language="c#">

</script>


<asp:content id="Content1"
    contentplaceholderid="ContentPlaceHolder1" runat="server">
    <asp:login id="Login1" runat="server"
```

```
        ...
        >


        <layouttemplate>
            <table style="FONT-SIZE: 10pt; FONT-FAMILY: Verdana" border="0">
                ...
                <tr>
                    <td align="right">User Name:</td>
                    <td>
                        <asp:textbox id="UserName" runat="server">
                        </asp:textbox>
                        <asp:requiredfieldvalidator
                            id="UserNameRequired" runat="server"
                            errormessage="User Name."
                            validationgroup="Content1$Login1_Group"
                            controltovalidate="UserName">
                                *
                        </asp:requiredfieldvalidator>
                    </td>
                </tr>
                ...
                <tr>
                    <td align="right" colspan="2">
                        <asp:button id="Button" runat="server"
                            validationgroup="Content1$Login1_Group" text="Log In"
                            commandname="Submit" />
                    </td>
                </tr>
                <tr>
                    <td style="COLOR: red" colspan="2">
                        <asp:literal id="FailureText" runat="server">
                        </asp:literal>
                    </td>
                </tr>
            </table>
        </layouttemplate>
    </asp:login>
</asp:content>
```

Consuming Events

The Login control offers four events by which you can interact with the Login process:

- BeforeLogin is raised before the authentication takes place. Here you have the capability to check the syntax of the created data, for example, and stop the login if necessary.

- AfterLogin will be raised after successful authentication and will allow you to pass through additional routines—for example, to load individual user data or to record the login.

- Authenticate can be used whenever you want to provide a customized authentication. With the help of the event arguments, you can specify whether or not the checking of user data has been successful. Normally, however, you'll implement your own mechanism for the authentication by an individual membership provider.

- LoginError is raised when the authentication stops and the user data is incorrect.

PasswordRecovery Control

One would think that users could remember their passwords. The reality, however, can be quite different! That's why it really makes sense to offer a specific control to determine forgotten passwords. Such a control exists and has the name PasswordRecovery.

The control helps users to determine their forgotten passwords. First users must enter their login name. Then the question that was typed in with the entry is shown. If they give the correct answer, their existing password will be mailed to the specified address or a new password will be created. The latter is necessary if a hash value has been stored in the database instead of the password in the form of text, and for that a recovery of the original password is impossible. This shows that the behavior of the control is changing according to the settings you've made during setup of Membership Management.

Using the PasswordRecovery Control

I've placed the control on the formerly shown login page so that you can see it in action in Listing 6-3. It really makes sense to place both controls on the same page, as shown in Figure 6-10. Alternatively, you may as well create a new page and link it with the help of a template-based Login control.

Listing 6-3. The PasswordRecovery Control in Action

```
<asp:passwordrecovery id="PasswordRecovery1"
    runat="server" font-names="Verdana"
    font-size="10pt"
    bordercolor="#999999"
    borderwidth="1px"
    borderstyle="Solid"
    backcolor="#FFFFCC">

    <titletextstyle font-bold="True"
        forecolor="White" backcolor="#333399">
    </titletextstyle>

    <maildefinition from="lorenz@pgk.de">
    </maildefinition>
</asp:passwordrecovery>
```

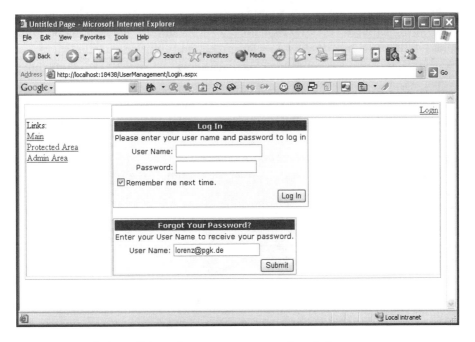

Figure 6-10. Oh dear, did you forget your password again?

If you want the control to do its job, you must enable it to send e-mails. Therefore, the following configuration is placed in the machine.config as a standard. If you've installed and activated a local SMTP service, you can leave the setting untouched. If you are using a different mail server, however, you can overwrite the data in the local web.config file.

```
<smtpMail
    serverName="localhost"
    serverPort="25">
/>
```

Additionally, you must edit the data of the password message to be sent. In the best-case scenario, it will do to assign the From property of the MailDefinition subobject to a sender's address. Here, the control will use the standard e-mail template. The result looks more or less like this:

```
From: <lorenz@pgk.de>
Subject: Password
To: <lorenz@pgk.de>

Please return to the site and log in using the following information.
User Name: lorenz@pgk.de
Password: 6BR7afTDcl
```

The e-mail doesn't look really smart yet, so you may want to make individual changes to the template. Using several properties of the MailDefinition class, you may also define a couple of things apart from the sender's address: Should a carbon copy of the e-mail be sent? Which format is going to be used (text or HTML)? Do you want to set a subject and a priority?

The option to create a message based completely upon a template is very useful. Just create a new text file in the root directory of the application and name it, for example, PasswordRecovery.txt. Now you place the desired e-mail text in the file, but without the heading lines. Then you use <%UserName%> and <%Password%> as placeholders for the username and the password. A simple template might look like this:

```
Hi there!

Your user name is <%UserName%>.
Your password is <%Password%>.

Thanks!
```

In order to use the template, you must assign the PasswordRecovery control's `MailDefinition.BodyFileName` property to the filename you've chosen.

Customizing the Control

PasswordRecovery is quite similar to the previously mentioned Login control and can be adapted thoroughly as well. Here, a couple of `Style` properties are at your service, and all the text can be adapted, of course.

The control offers three different templates that you can build up completely from scratch or use on the basis of the already integrated views:

- `UserName` is the initial view of the control, and it asks the user to type in a user name, that is, the login name.

- `Question` is used if the user must answer a question to get to the password.

- `Answer` is shown if the password has been detected successfully or has been set back and e-mailed to the user.

Consuming Events

The PasswordRecovery control implements a couple of events that you may handle to step through the control's cycle:

- `BeforeUserLookup`: Is raised before the control tries to find out the user account belonging to the specified name. You have the option to use individual tests and to cancel the process.

- `UserLookupError`: Allows you to stop the cycle in case the entered user name can't be validated.

- `BeforeAnswerLookup`: Is used before the answer entered by the user is checked. You may cancel this operation within the scope of the event.

- `AnswerLookupError`: Is raised if the entered answer isn't correct.

- `BeforeSendMail`: Is raised before an e-mail is sent to the user. With the help of the event arguments, you get access to the instance of the `MailMessage` class that is based on the template mentioned earlier. This way you can modify the message and add more data if desired.

LoginStatus and LoginName Control

LoginStatus and LoginName, though rather unspectacular, are nevertheless two quite useful controls.

LoginName shows the name of registered users regardless of which provider they were authenticated by. With the FormatString property, you have the capability to add a format description. If a user isn't authenticated, the control will not create any output to the page.

In the simplest case, LoginStatus shows either a login or a logout link, depending on the status of the authentication. With the help of various properties, both texts can be changed individually. Alternatively, you may add pictures to this control to correspond to login and logout states, similar to what is done with .NET Passport.

As you can see in the following code, I've placed both controls, LoginName and LoginStatus, on the top-right side of the Master Page so that they can be used automatically on each single page.

```
<td>
    <p align="right">
        <asp:loginname id="LoginName1"
            runat="server"
            formatstring="You are signed in as: {0}">
        </asp:loginname>
        <asp:loginstatus id="LoginStatus1" runat="server">
        </asp:loginstatus>
    </p>
</td>
```

The Login link of the LoginStatus control automatically refers to the page that is placed in the configuration (by the standard login.aspx page). You can specify a logout page, if desired, to be shown after the logout. With the LogoutAction enumerations property, you may also define whether another page will be shown after logout or if the current one will be updated.

LoginView Control

Like the LoginStatus control, which has two different views depending on the authentication process, the LoginView control itself offers automatic changeover. Here, however, you may define the shown elements individually with the help of two templates. The application for this control is in the area of conditional display of pages for anonymous and for authenticated users.

Previously, I adapted the existing Master Page a little bit to demonstrate the details. I've a feeling, however, that it isn't really ideal to display the links to the two protected areas to anonymous users. You can avoid this by using the new Login-View control as shown in Listing 6-4.

Listing 6-4. Using Two Different Templates with the LoginView Control

```
<asp:loginview id="LoginView1" runat="server">
    <anonymoustemplate>
        Links:<br />
        <asp:hyperlink runat="server"
            navigateurl="~/Default.aspx">
            Main
        </asp:hyperlink>
    </anonymoustemplate>
    <loggedintemplate>
        Links:<br />
        <asp:hyperlink runat="server"
            navigateurl="~/Default.aspx">
            Main
        </asp:hyperlink><br />

        <asp:hyperlink runat="server"
            navigateurl="~/ProtectedArea/Default.aspx">
            Protected Area
        </asp:hyperlink><br />

        <asp:hyperlink runat="server"
            navigateurl="~/AdminArea/Default.aspx">
            Admin Area
        </asp:hyperlink>
    </loggedintemplate>
</asp:loginview>
```

As you can see, two templates have been assigned to the control. Following a main behavior of the control, only one of the two templates is shown. That is why the link to the starting page is repeated in the second template. Alternatively, this link could be placed outside of the control. Figure 6-11 shows the view for anonymous (that is, unauthenticated) users.

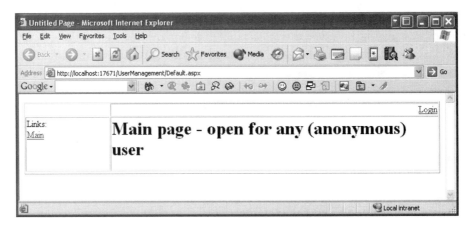

Figure 6-11. Are you looking for the protected area?

Creating Role-Based Templates

Unfortunately, the approach shown previously has one small issue. As soon as a user logs in, that user will see all the links, even those to the admin area. In reality, only a small number of people will have the right to access the administration. In cases like this one, the LoginView control enables you to create as many role-based templates as you want, and they will be displayed depending on the roles to which the users belong.

To create a new role-based template, you must select the LoginView control in the Design or Source view and choose the entry RoleGroups from the Properties grid. With the "…" button, you can open the Collection Editor, shown in Figure 6-12, and use it to create new templates based on one or several roles.

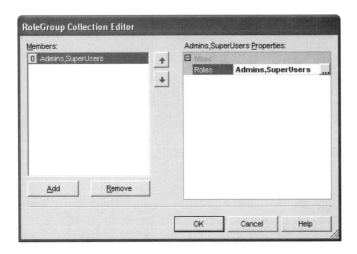

Figure 6-12. You can define custom role-based templates.

Templates created in this way can be edited visually in the Design view and filled with content as usual. With each entry in the source code, a subcontrol of the type RoleGroup will be created, to which a ContentTemplate property will be assigned (see Listing 6-5).

Listing 6-5. The Created RoleGroup Subcontrol with Assigned ContentTemplate

```
<asp:loginview id="LoginView1" runat="server">
    <anonymoustemplate>
        Links:<br />
        <asp:hyperlink runat="server"
            navigateurl="~/Default.aspx">
            Main
        </asp:hyperlink>
    </anonymoustemplate>
    <rolegroups>
        <asp:rolegroup roles="Admins,SuperUsers">
            <contenttemplate>
                Links:
                <br />
                <asp:hyperlink runat="server"
                    navigateurl="~/Default.aspx">
                    Main
                </asp:hyperlink>
                <br />
                <asp:hyperlink runat="server"
                    navigateurl="~/ProtectedArea/Default.aspx">
                    Protected Area
                </asp:hyperlink>
                <br />
                <asp:hyperlink runat="server"
                    navigateurl="~/AdminArea/Default.aspx">
                    Admin Area
                </asp:hyperlink>
            </contenttemplate>
        </asp:rolegroup>
    </rolegroups>
    <loggedintemplate>
        Links:<br />
        <asp:hyperlink runat="server"
            navigateurl="~/Default.aspx">
            Main
        </asp:hyperlink>
```

```
        <br />
        <asp:hyperlink runat="server"
            navigateurl="~/ProtectedArea/Default.aspx">
            Protected Area
        </asp:hyperlink>
    </loggedintemplate>
</asp:loginview>
```

NOTE *Please be aware that only one template is shown at any given time. The control checks the role-based templates first. The first template with a matching role membership gets the award. If none of the groups is suitable, the general* LoggedInTemplate *property will be used.*

And What About a CreateUser Control?

Now, judging by all the controls presented so far, you would logically assume there should be one that allows the independent registration of new users. Such a control is planned but not yet implemented. The Beta version of ASP.NET 2.0 is expected to offer this control. Until then, you can use the Membership Management API to create users as described later in this chapter.

Another control that is planned to be shipped with the Beta version is called ChangePassword; you can probably guess its purpose by its name.

Creating a Role-Based Navigation System

Another useful capability that the user management feature offers is to assign roles to single navigation nodes. Elements marked like this will only be shown in the navigation controls if the user is a member of one of the assigned roles, similar to what was demonstrated in the earlier examples of the LoginView control.

The allocation of roles is already possible at present with the site map configuration file app.sitemap, which was presented in Chapter 5. The specification of roles in the file looks similar to the following:

```
<?xml version="1.0" encoding="utf-8" ?>
<siteMap>
    <siteMapNode title="Home" description="Home" url="default.aspx" >
        <siteMapNode title="Admin"
            description="For admins only"
```

```
            url="admin.aspx"
            roles="Admins,SuperUsers"
        />
    </siteMapNode>
</siteMap>
```

The site navigation object model offers the deposited roles as a dictionary through the SiteMapNode.Roles property. But those roles are not being evaluated yet, so the navigation properties are shown completely unconditioned in the preceding example. This is another feature that will be available in the Beta version.

Managing Anonymous Users

With ASP.NET 2.0, anonymous users are not that anonymous anymore. Now you have the option to automatically assign an ID to unknown users. This ID will either be saved in a persistent cookie or in the URL. If a cookie is used, you can recognize the anonymous user on a later visit.

The use of a unique ID for anonymous users offers important advantages. You can save information about such users in your database, even without any login or registration information submitted from that person. This particularly applies to personalization, which I'll explain to you in the next chapter. The anonymous ID can be used automatically in that situation!

By default, the generation of an anonymous user ID is deactivated. Activation through the web.config configuration file is similar to the following:

```xml
<?xml version="1.0"?>
<configuration>
    <system.web>
        <anonymousIdentification
            enabled="true"
        />
    </system.web>
</configuration>
```

By means of additional parameters, you can specify the cookie to be used. You may as well change the expiration time, which is set to 100,000 minutes as a standard (with sliding expiration). Additionally, you may define whether the ID should be saved in a cookie or in the URL. When using the setting UseDeviceProfile, this will depend on the utilized device/browser.

Please keep in mind that the user is displayed as *not* logged on while the anonymous ID is used. Consequently, the ID *can't* be queried by the allocated IIdentity object. Instead, the ID is accessible via the AnonymousId property of the HttpRequest class. The ID is delivered as a GUID that has been transformed into the following string by the Request.AnonymousId property (see Figure 6-13):

```
... = this.Request.AnonymousId
```

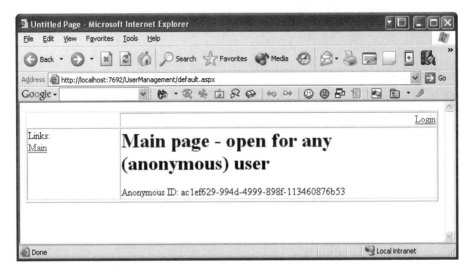

Figure 6-13. ASP.NET automatically generates an anonymous user ID.

TIP *The storage of anonymous user data will be described in detail in Chapter 7.*

Working with the Membership Management API

ASP.NET version 2.0 provides you with an API through which you can administrate your users without knowledge of the underlying membership providers. The Membership and MembershipUser classes (from the System.Web.Security namespace) form the core of the API. The first class basically offers a range of static methods to create, update, or delete users. The instance of the second class represents an individual user and gives access to that user's data.

Creating a New User

The creation of a new user is done through the overloaded Membership.CreateUser method. The overload that is recommended allows passing of the desired username, password, e-mail address, and finally status as an out parameter. If successful, an instance of the MembershipUser class or null will be returned.

I've expanded the existing example by including a new page for the registration of new users in Listing 6-6. The page basically consists of four input boxes for username, e-mail address, password, and password confirmation. Next to the input controls you can find various validation controls, a label for potential error messages, and a button. A click of this button initiates the creation of a new user based on the entered data.

Listing 6-6. Adding a Page for New User Registration

```
<%@ page language="C#" master="~/MasterPage.master" %>
<script runat="server" language="c#">

void Button1_Click(object sender, System.EventArgs e)
{
    if (this.IsValid)
    {
        MembershipCreateStatus status;
        MembershipUser user = Membership.CreateUser(this.TB_Username.Text,
            this.TB_Password.Text, this.TB_Email.Text, out status);

        switch (status)
        {
            case MembershipCreateStatus.Success:
                FormsAuthentication.RedirectFromLoginPage(user.Username, false);
                break;

            case MembershipCreateStatus.DuplicateEmail:
                this.LB_CreateError.Text = "The email address is " +
                    "already registered.";
                break;

            case MembershipCreateStatus.DuplicateUsername:
                this.LB_CreateError.Text = "The username is already registered.";
                break;

            case MembershipCreateStatus.InvalidEmail:
                this.LB_CreateError.Text = "This email address is invalid.";
```

```
                    break;

            case MembershipCreateStatus.InvalidPassword:
                this.LB_CreateError.Text = "This password is invalid.";
                break;

            case MembershipCreateStatus.UserRejected:
                this.LB_CreateError.Text = "The user was rejected " +
                    "for an unknown reason.";
                break;
        }
    }
}

</script>

<asp:content id="Content1"
    contentplaceholderid="ContentPlaceHolder1" runat="server">
    <table cellspacing="1" cellpadding="1" border="1">
        <tr>
            <td>User Name:</td>
            <td>
                <asp:textbox id="TB_Username" runat="server">
                </asp:textbox>
            </td>
            <td>
                <asp:requiredfieldvalidator
                    id="RequiredFieldValidator1"
                    runat="server"
                    controltovalidate="TB_Username"
                    setfocusonerror="True">*
                </asp:requiredfieldvalidator>
            </td>
        </tr>

        ...

        <tr>
            <td>
            </td>
            <td>
                <asp:button id="Button1"
                    runat="server"
```

```
                 text="Register New User"
                 onclick="Button1_Click" />
         </td>
         <td>

         </td>
      </tr>
   </table>
</asp:content>
```

If successful, the Membership.CreateUser method returns the newly created user in the form of an instance of the MembershipUser class. The method delivers the status of the creation as an out parameter in any case. The enumeration value allows you to determine in a sophisticated way if the creation succeeded and, if not, how it happened. If the method has not been accepted, an error message will be displayed in the Label control. If everything goes well, the user will be directly logged in by Forms Authentication. Figure 6-14 shows the newly created registration page in action.

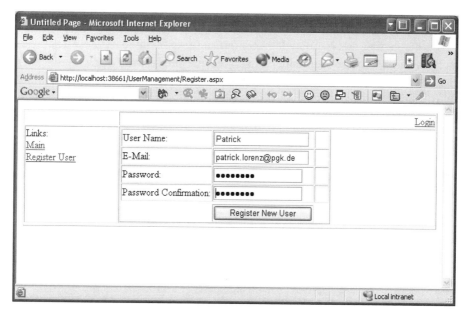

Figure 6-14. Starting with the Beta version, ASP.NET 2.0 will include a CreateUser control out of the box.

> **NOTE** *The behavior of the* CreateUser *method depends on other adjustments you've made during the configuration of Membership Management as depicted earlier in this chapter. This way you can define, for example, whether the entered e-mail address must be unique or can be used by several users.*

Validating and Accessing a User

Normally the Login control shown previously is used to authenticate users. Of course, you may handle this manually as well. The Membership class therefore offers the ValidateUser method, which when it receives a username and password returns a Boolean value. By the way, this method is used internally by the Login control as well.

```
if (Membership.ValidateUser(username, password))
{
    // ...
    // FormsAuthentication.RedirectFromLoginPage(username, false);
}
```

Please note that this method does *not* return the associated MembershipUser object. However, you can manually request this object afterward by using the GetUser() method. This method is overloaded in multiple ways and returns the actual user if called without parameters. Alternatively, you may specify the desired name explicitly. The GetAllUsers() method returns a list of all users.

The example in Listing 6-7 is used in the protected area for administrators. An abstract of all users registered in the system is shown within a GridView control. If a user is selected, that user's complete data will appear in a DetailsView control placed directly below the GridView.

Listing 6-7. Displaying Registered Users Through a GridView Control in the Protected Area

```
<asp:gridview id="GV_UserList" runat="server"
    autogeneratecolumns="False"
    datakeynames="Username"
    onselectedindexchanged="GV_UserList_SelectedIndexChanged">

    ...

    <columnfields>
        <asp:commandfield showselectbutton="True">
```

```
        </asp:commandfield>
        <asp:boundfield datafield="Username" headertext="Username">
        </asp:boundfield>
        <asp:boundfield datafield="Email" headertext="Email">
        </asp:boundfield>
        <asp:boundfield datafield="LastLoginDate" headertext="LastLoginDate">
        </asp:boundfield>
    </columnfields>
</asp:gridview><br />

<asp:detailsview id="DV_User" runat="server">
    ...
</asp:detailsview>
```

Unlike previous examples, I'm not talking about a zero-code scenario here! But the required source code is absolutely kept to a limit. It consists only of the two event handlers, Page_Load and SelectedIndexChanged, provided by the GridView control.

```
<script runat="server" language="c#">

    void Page_Load(object sender, System.EventArgs e)
    {
        this.GV_UserList.DataSource = Membership.GetAllUsers();
        this.GV_UserList.DataBind();
    }

    void GV_UserList_SelectedIndexChanged(object sender, System.EventArgs e)
    {
        string userName = (this.GV_UserList.SelectedValue as string);
        MembershipUser user = Membership.GetUser(userName);
        this.DV_User.DataSource = new MembershipUser[] { user };
        this.DV_User.DataBind();
    }

</script>
```

Both event handlers are self-explanatory. A little trick, however, is necessary to allocate the data source to the DetailsView control, which only accepts enumerable data sources. An array is quickly generated from the instance of MembershipUser.

Figure 6-15 shows the sample page in action. The DetailsView control displays the properties being offered by the `MembershipUser` class.

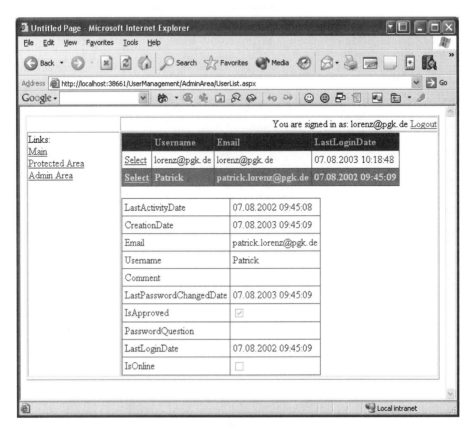

Figure 6-15. The administrator can access a list of all users, including detailed data.

Updating User Data

User data changes now and then. Therefore, it is useful to offer users the option of editing their own data. You can reflect these changes directly with the help of the properties of the `MembershipUser` class. However, many properties such as `Username` are write-protected and can't be changed.

I've added the sample page in Listing 6-8 to the protected area. By means of a parameterless overload of the `GetUser` method, the actual user will be acquired. The corresponding user data will be displayed in a label and two input boxes. Now users have the option to modify their data and store it afterward with a button click (see Figure 6-16). The event treatment of the button acquires the corresponding instance of the `MembershipUser` class again. The event values are newly assigned and stored using the `Membership.UpdateUser` method.

Listing 6-8. Acquiring the Current User Record Through GetUser

```
<%@ page language="C#" master="~/MasterPage.master" %>

<script runat="server" language="c#">

    void Page_Load(object sender, System.EventArgs e)
    {
        if (this.IsPostBack == false)
        {
            MembershipUser user = Membership.GetUser();

            this.LB_Username.Text = user.Username;
            this.TB_Email.Text = user.Email;
            this.TB_Comment.Text = user.Comment;
        }
    }

    void Button1_Click(object sender, System.EventArgs e)
    {
        if (this.IsValid)
        {
            MembershipUser user = Membership.GetUser();

            user.Email = this.TB_Email.Text;
            user.Comment = this.TB_Comment.Text;
            Membership.UpdateUser(user);
        }
    }

</script>

<asp:content id="Content1"
    contentplaceholderid="ContentPlaceHolder1"
    runat="server">

    <table cellspacing="1" cellpadding="1" border="1">
        <tr>
            <td>User Name:</td>
            <td>
                <asp:label id="LB_Username"
                    runat="server"/>
            </td>
```

```
            <td> </td>
        </tr>

        ...

        <tr>
            <td>
            </td>
            <td>
                <asp:button id="Button1"
                    runat="server"
                    text="Update User Data"
                    onclick="Button1_Click" />
            </td>
            <td>
            </td>
        </tr>
    </table>
</asp:content>
```

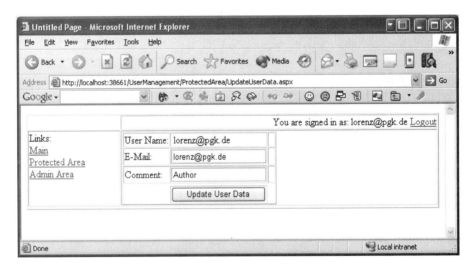

Figure 6-16. Users can update their personal data on their own.

NOTE *Are you curious about how to edit other personal data for users in this example? Again, you must exercise some patience! This will be a topic covered in the next chapter.*

> **TIP** *If you don't know the name of certain users, you can identify them through their e-mail addresses, too. Naturally, this will only work if the address is unique. The* Membership *class offers the* GetUserNameByEmail() *method for this purpose.*

Changing a User's Password

The previously mentioned example doesn't offer the capability to change the password of the user. I've enhanced the example by including three input boxes that will enable users to input the current and new password and provide a confirmation. The new password as well as the old one is transferred to the MembershipUser.ChangePassword method.

```
void Button1_Click(object sender, System.EventArgs e)
{
    if (this.IsValid)
    {
        MembershipUser user = Membership.GetUser();

        user.Email = this.TB_Email.Text;
        user.Comment = this.TB_Comment.Text;
        Membership.UpdateUser(user);

        if ((this.TB_OldPassword.Text.Length > 0) &&
                (this.TB_NewPassword.Text.Length > 0))
        {
            user.ChangePassword(this.TB_OldPassword.Text,
                this.TB_NewPassword.Text);
        }
    }
}
```

Please be aware that the ChangePassword() method always requests the old and the new password; null or an empty string won't be accepted. You have two choices if you want to skip the input of the old password.

You may use the GetPassword method to acquire the existing password. This solution turns out to be difficult because it will only work depending on the configuration of the chosen membership providers. If the passwords are being saved as hash values, readout of the password is virtually impossible.

```
if (this.TB_NewPassword.Text.Length > 0)
{
    string oldPassword = user.GetPassword();
    user.ChangePassword(oldPassword, this.TB_NewPassword.Text);
}
```

Therefore, I recommend resetting the password with ResetPassword() instead. This method delivers a new automatically generated password in return, which can be modified immediately.

```
if (this.TB_NewPassword.Text.Length > 0)
{
    string oldPassword = user.ResetPassword();
    user.ChangePassword(oldPassword, this.TB_NewPassword.Text);
}
```

Determining the Active User Count

Communities often commonly request that the number of active users be shown. In the future, you can identify this number easily with Membership.GetNumberOfUsersOnline.

With this in mind, I've adapted the Master Page of the example web site in a way that the number of active users is displayed on each page. As you can see in Figure 6-17, it would be nice to have more visitors.

```
void Page_Load(object sender, System.EventArgs e)
{
    if (this.IsPostBack == false)
    {
        Membership.ApplicationName = "test";
        this.LB_ActiveUsers.Text = Membership.GetNumberOfUsersOnline().ToString();
    }
}
```

CAUTION *In the current Alpha version, the retrieval of the active user count fails because of a bug within* AccessMembershipProvider. *This will be fixed for the Beta version.*

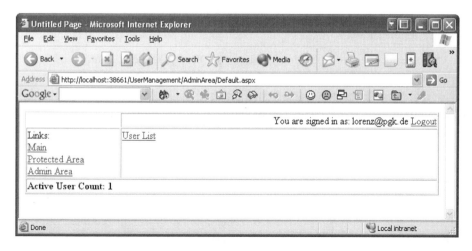

Figure 6-17. My site is looking for more visitors.

NOTE *Please note that authenticated as well as anonymous users are counted if they have been activated. For details see the "Managing Anonymous Users" section earlier in this chapter.*

Working with the Role Management API

As in the Membership Management API, the Role Management API is placed in the System.Web.Security namespace. The latter consists basically of two classes: Roles and RolePrincipal. RolePrincipal supports the IPrincipal interface and is used as the principal object for each respective request. Thus the class offers access to the roles of the current users. Instead of identifying them with each request in the database, they are placed automatically in an encoded cookie.

The Roles class can be compared with the Membership class, in that it allows you to administrate the roles and their members in the system by means of static methods. Using the Roles class, you have to bear in mind the following:

1. A Role class doesn't exist. Each role is represented and administrated only by its name (which in fact is a string).

2. There is no direct relationship with Membership Management. Therefore, the users are also administrated as a string.

Managing Roles

The various static methods of the Roles class are mostly self-explanatory, as you can see by their names: CreateRole, DeleteRole, GetAllRoles, GetUsersInRole, and GetRolesForUser. The options for adding new users and roles are very sophisticated. You can add a) a user to a role, b) a user to several roles, c) several users to one role, and d) several users to several roles. Conversely, you have four methods to delete role memberships that either accept strings or string arrays as parameters, too.

The source code shown in Listing 6-9 demonstrates simplified role administration. You can show all users attached to a role and add or delete individual members. Furthermore, it is possible to create new roles. The different routines use numerous methods offered by the Roles class. Figure 6-18 shows the page in action.

Listing 6-9. Performing Simplified Role Administration

```
void Page_Load(object sender, System.EventArgs e)
{
    if (this.IsPostBack == false)
    {
        this.UpdateRoleList(null);
    }
}


void DDL_RoleList_SelectedIndexChanged(object sender, System.EventArgs e)
{
    this.UpdateRoleMemberList();
}


void BT_RemoveRole_Click(object sender, System.EventArgs e)
{
    if (this.DDL_RoleList.SelectedIndex != -1)
    {
        Roles.DeleteRole(this.DDL_RoleList.SelectedValue);
        this.UpdateRoleList(null);
    }
}


void BT_AddRole_Click(object sender, System.EventArgs e)
{
    if (this.TB_NewRole.Text.Length > 0)
    {
        Roles.CreateRole(this.TB_NewRole.Text);
        this.UpdateRoleList(this.TB_NewRole.Text);
```

```
        }
    }

    void BT_RemoveUserFromRole_Click(object sender, System.EventArgs e)
    {
        if (this.LB_RoleUsers.SelectedIndex != -1)
        {
            Roles.RemoveUserFromRole(this.LB_RoleUsers.SelectedValue,
                this.DDL_RoleList.SelectedValue);
            this.UpdateRoleMemberList();
        }
    }

    void BT_AddUserToRole_Click(object sender, System.EventArgs e)
    {
        if (this.TB_NewUser.Text.Length > 0)
        {
            Roles.AddUserToRole(this.TB_NewUser.Text, this.DDL_RoleList.SelectedValue);
            this.UpdateRoleMemberList();
        }
    }

    private void UpdateRoleList(string role)
    {
        this.DDL_RoleList.DataSource = Roles.GetAllRoles();
        this.DDL_RoleList.DataBind();

        if (role != null)
        {
            ListItem item = this.DDL_RoleList.Items.FindByText(role);
            if (item != null)
            {
                item.Selected = true;
            }
        }
        this.UpdateRoleMemberList();
    }


    private void UpdateRoleMemberList()
    {
        string role = this.DDL_RoleList.SelectedValue;

        this.LB_RoleUsers.DataSource = Roles.GetUsersInRole(role);
        this.LB_RoleUsers.DataBind();
    }
```

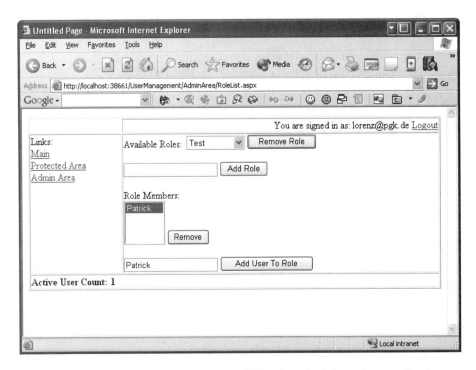

Figure 6-18. Creating an individual console for the administration won't take very long.

Switching to SQL Server Providers

In this chapter, I've used the shipped Microsoft Access file `aspnetdb.mdb` as the database for storage of membership and role data to make the example as simple as possible. This file is used by the default provider and can be recommended for smaller web sites. Additionally, all the providers are available in an alternative implementation to be used with SQL Server. You can switch between both providers in minutes. This should be done particularly for web sites that are bigger and/or highly frequented.

If you want to use SQL Server for the storage of membership and role data, you'll have to create a corresponding database first, including some tables. Instead of doing this manually, you can work more comfortable by using the shipped `aspnet_regsql.exe` tool, which you can find in this directory:

```
<windir>\Microsoft.NET\Framework\<version>
```

The program is a hybrid that you can use either as a command-line tool with various parameters (for example, "-?" for help) or as a Windows wizard, as shown in Figure 6-19. The assistant will guide you through the various steps of the implementation. At present, you must basically name the desired SQL Server. As long as you won't specifically choose an existing database or specify a new name in the ongoing process, a database called aspnetdb will be created.

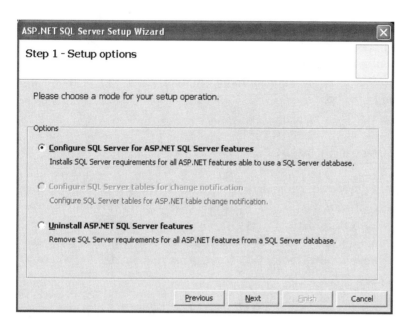

Figure 6-19. This wizard helps create a database for storing membership data and much more ASP.NET-related stuff.

After the database has been created, you can specify the new provider in the web.config configuration file. First you have to make sure that the assigned ConnectionString entry with the name localSqlServer is referring to the created database. Naturally, you may use a different name, but this results in more work because you have to reconfigure the providers in the corresponding way. Afterward you map the desired application services to the new default provider. The following example shows a complete configuration file for the use of the local SQL Server:

```
<?xml version="1.0"?>
<configuration>

    <connectionStrings>
        <add name="LocalSqlServer"
            connectionString="data source=127.0.0.1;Integrated Security=SSPI" />
```

```
        </connectionStrings>

        <system.web>
            <membership defaultProvider="AspNetSqlProvider" />
            <roleManager enabled="true" defaultProvider="AspNetSqlProvider" />
        </system.web>
    </configuration>
```

You can switch the providers for other application services in the same way to allow, for example, personalization and side counters (which I'll discuss in Chapters 7, 8, and 10 of this book.

Creating Custom Providers

A big advantage of the Membership Management and Role Management systems described in this chapter is the fact that you never directly touch the data source. You work exclusively with generic classes of the System.Web.Security namespace instead. To maintain the highest flexibility and to give you the option to integrate individual data sources, the system is based upon a provider model that you can expand as you desire.

Your new provider has only to support the IMembershipProvider IRoleProvider interfaces and be deposited in the web.config file. The members of both interfaces comply mostly with the already described APIs, because many calls are more or less handed over on a one-to-one basis to the provider.

This interface-oriented concept is currently being revised in favor of abstract classes. It's possible that there will be big changes with regard to the Beta version. For this reason, I won't include a detailed description for the implementation of custom providers.

Summary

Do you remember the ASP.NET team's goal to reduce lines of code by up to 70%? I mentioned this intention at the beginning of Chapter 1. This chapter showed how the team is going to achieve its ambition. You can now easily manage your users, roles, and security settings in most cases without a single line of code. Forget about writing the same stuff again and again!

CHAPTER 7

Personalization

ONE OF THE NICEST FEATURES **of ASP.NET 2.0** from my point of view is personalization. How often have you manually saved user-related data such as addresses, phone numbers, web site addresses, and so on? Did you ever think of persisting the shopping basket of your Web application between several visits from a particular user?

The new personalization feature is the answer for this and many other issues. Without a single line of code, you can save nearly any information relating to your application's users—even if they haven't been authenticated yet! You don't believe it? Then keep on reading!

> **TIP** *ASP.NET version 2.0 provides another type of personalization called* Page Personalization *or* Web Parts. *These topics are described in Chapter 8.*

Creating a Personalized Web Site

Personalization is activated by default and is used for all authenticated users. Before using personalization, you must specify which data you would like to save individually for each user. The definition of such a profile takes place in the <personalization> section of the web.config configuration file. As shown in the following example, you may place individual properties here, such as a nickname. In principle, you can define as many profile properties as you want by simply using the corresponding <property> tags.

```
<?xml version="1.0"?>
<configuration>
    <system.web>
        <personalization>
            <profile>
                <property name="Nickname" />
            </profile>
        </personalization>
    </system.web>
</configuration>
```

If you switch back to the source code of one of your pages after saving the configuration file, you can now call the IntelliSense window for this.Profile. You'll see that the property you defined a couple of seconds ago is already there. A corresponding typed class was generated dynamically from the defined profile, and then compiled and integrated into your web site's assembly. The local name of the class is HttpPersonalization. Its base class, called HttpPersonalizationBaseClass, is located in the framework.

You have two options to catch the current profile: either by using the object model of the current page or through the HttpContext class. In both cases, the personal data store is returned through a property called Profile (see Figure 7-1).

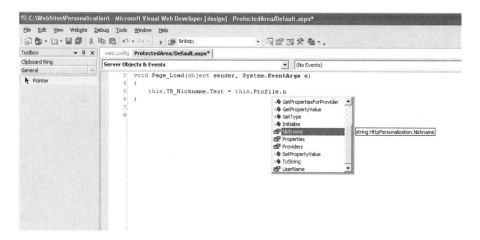

Figure 7-1. Any defined properties are available through a type-safe profile object.

Storing Data and Accessing the Profile

You may now access and start reading or writing to your defined properties without further ado. The data is saved and automatically made available with the user's next visit.

The example in Listing 7-1 is based on the user administration example of the last chapter. An input box appears in the protected area for the nickname of the authenticated user (see Figure 7-2). The name is saved to the profile with just a button click. With all subsequent calls of the page, the nickname will be read out of the profile again and assigned to the TextBox control as an initial value, even if the user closes the browser or logs on from a different computer.

Listing 7-1. Accessing the Defined Profile Object

```
<%@ page language="C#" master="~/MasterPage.master" %>

<script runat="server" language="c#">

void Page_Load(object sender, System.EventArgs e)
{
    if (this.IsPostBack == false)
    {
        this.TB_Nickname.Text = this.Profile.Nickname;
    }
}

void BT_UpdateNickname_Click(object sender, System.EventArgs e)
{
    this.Profile.Nickname = this.TB_Nickname.Text;
}

</script>

<asp:content id="Content1" contentplaceholderid="ContentPlaceHolder1"
    runat="server">

    <asp:hyperlink id="HyperLink1"
        runat="server"
        navigateurl="UpdateUserData.aspx">
        UpdateUser Data
    </asp:hyperlink>
    <br />
    <br />
    Your nickname:
    <asp:textbox id="TB_Nickname" runat="server"></asp:textbox>
    <asp:button id="BT_UpdateNickname" runat="server"
        text="Update" onclick="BT_UpdateNickname_Click" />
</asp:content>
```

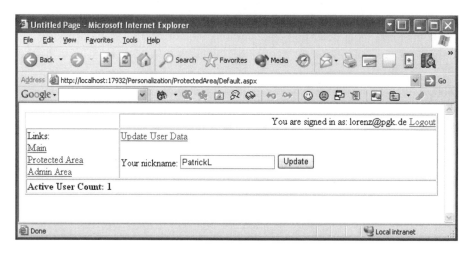

Figure 7-2. Profile data is automatically stored.

Gosh! But Where's the Profile Actually Stored?

Like many other infrastructure components of the latest version of ASP.NET, personalization is based on a provider model. ASP.NET ships with two providers, one for Microsoft Access and another for SQL Server. Although Microsoft Access is set as the default, I recommend using SQL Server, or at least it's MSDE version, for bigger projects.

In the last example, I worked with the default provider. The nickname is stored in the Microsoft Access database aspnetdb.mdb, which you already know from the previous chapter is as an instrument for saving specific data for users and roles. The profile-related information is saved in direct relation to the membership data. Figure 7-3 shows the corresponding tables in Microsoft Access. Here you can find the recently edited nickname as well.

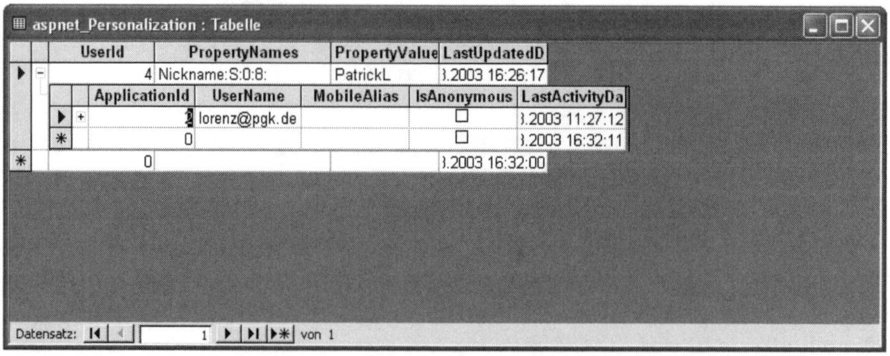

Figure 7-3. A Microsoft Access database is used to store profile data.

> **NOTE** *Instead of using the Membership Management system as shown in the present example, the personalization feature can automatically work together with any other authentication system—for example, Windows Authentication or .NET Passport. You may even use your own custom systems as long as they deliver a username via* HttpContext.Current.User.Identity.Name.

Accessing Somebody Else's Profile

Apart from access to the profile of the current user, you may also inquire about any other user. The HttpPersonalization class offers an instance method, called GetProfile(), to which the explicit user name is passed. With the help of the returned instance of HttpPersonalization, you can retrieve the data saved in the profile.

```
HttpPersonalization profile = this.Profile.GetProfile("Patrick");
string name = profile.Nickname;
```

Even write access is possible. In this case, however, changes won't merely be transferred automatically but have to be saved explicitly by calling the CommitSettings() method against the underlying data source:

```
HttpPersonalization profile = this.Profile.GetProfile("Patrick");
profile.Nickname = "Mr. Ed";
profile.CommitSettings();
```

Defining Advanced Personalization Properties

As shown in the previous examples, all properties defined for a profile are saved as a string by default. This isn't mandatory, however, because you can place almost every object in the profile as long as it's serializable in some way.

Storing Base Types

Apart from using strings, you'll frequently wish to save other standard data types. You may, for example, store the date of birth of a user as DateTime. To do so, you only have to specify the class name of the desired data type via the attribute type when defining the profile properties.

In the following example, the user's birth date and a numeric value is saved. The value shows the number of years of experience the user has working with ASP.NET.

```
<personalization>
    <profile>
        <property name="Nickname" />
        <property name="Birthday" type="System.DateTime" />
        <property name="YearsExperienceASPNET" type="int" defaultValue="1" />
    </profile>
</personalization>
```

If necessary, specify the complete class name of the data type including the corresponding namespace, such as System.DateTime in this case. If you want to use a static standard value, you can add it with the attribute defaultValue. Otherwise, the implemented standard value will be used in case of value types.

The enlarged profile can be edited by each user through a new page named editprofile.aspx. As demonstrated in Listing 7-2, access to the properties of the profile object takes place in a type-safe way according to the data type assigned in the configuration previously shown (see Figure 7-4).

Listing 7-2. Accessing the Profile Object in a Type-Safe Manner

```
<%@ page language="C#" master="~/MasterPage.master" %>

<script runat="server" language="c#">

void Page_Load(object sender, System.EventArgs e)
{
    if (this.IsPostBack == false)
    {
        this.LB_Username.Text = this.User.Identity.Name;
        this.TB_Nickname.Text = this.Profile.Nickname;
        this.TB_Birthday.Text = this.Profile.Birthday.ToShortDateString();
        this.TB_Experience.Text = this.Profile.YearsExperienceASPNET.ToString();
    }
}

void Button1_Click(object sender, System.EventArgs e)
{
    if (this.IsValid)
    {
        this.Profile.Nickname = this.TB_Nickname.Text;
```

```
        DateTime birthday;
        if (DateTime.TryParse(this.TB_Birthday.Text, out birthday))
        {
            this.Profile.Birthday = birthday;
        }

        int experience;
        if (int.TryParse(this.TB_Experience.Text, out experience))
        {
            this.Profile.YearsExperienceASPNET = experience;
        }
    }
}

</script>

<asp:content id="Content1"
    contentplaceholderid="ContentPlaceHolder1"
    runat="server">

    <table cellspacing="1" cellpadding="1" border="1">
        <tr>
            <td>User Name:</td>
            <td>
                <asp:label id="LB_Username" runat="server" />
            </td>
            <td> </td>
        </tr>
        <tr>
            <td>Nickname:</td>
            <td>
                <asp:textbox id="TB_Nickname" runat="server">
                </asp:textbox>
            </td>
            <td> </td>
        </tr>

        ...

    </table>
</asp:content>
```

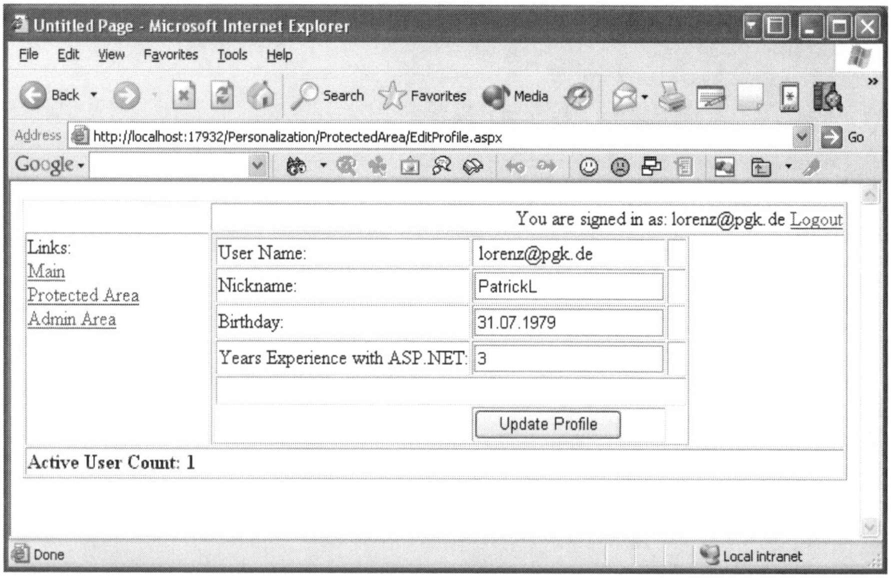

Figure 7-4. You can use any base data type for storing data in the user's profile.

Storing Complex Types

Apart from standard data types, you can store other classes from the base class library within the profile as long as they are marked as serializable (using the Serializable attribute). To define the type, you therefore have to specify the class's full name, including its namespace.

All objects are serialized as a string by default. This is quite a new concept, and an example is shown in the following snippet. As you can see, the property values are stored right by each other. The values are distinguished by their start position and length.

```
PropertyNames: UserName:S:0:7:Theme:S:7:9:
PropertyValuesString: PatrickBasicBlue
```

With reference types, however, string serialization isn't advisable. Of course, this doesn't apply for the string type itself, which is basically a reference type, too. You should choose serialization in the form of XML or binary instead. You can assign the desired setting (String, Binary, or Xml) to the serializeAs attribute.

The following example shows the allocation of a StringCollection that is serialized in the database as XML. The StringCollection is available in the profile through the property Bookmarks.

```
<personalization>
    <profile>
        <property name="Nickname" />
        <property name="Birthday" type="System.DateTime" />
        <property name="YearsExperienceASPNET" type="int" defaultValue="1"/>
        <property name="Bookmarks"
            type="System.Collections.Specialized.StringCollection"
            serializeAs="Xml"/>
    </profile>
</personalization>
```

The new Profile property of the Page and HttpContext classes is used to store personal bookmarks (aka favorites). Taking advantage of this property, the Master Page has a new LinkButton control through which the URL of the current page can be dropped into the collection. The corresponding source code looks like this:

```
void LinkButton1_Click(object sender, System.EventArgs e)
{
    HttpPersonalization profile = (HttpPersonalization) this.Context.Profile;
    profile.Bookmarks.Add(this.Request.Url.ToString());
}
```

The conversion shown in the example is necessary because the code is placed in the Master Page, which doesn't allow type-safe access to the custom profile. The HttpContext class is used instead, which redelivers the profile across the HttpPersonalizationBaseClass base class and therefore won't give access to the custom properties. After the conversion, they are at your disposal as usual.

> **NOTE** *Please be aware that all reference types are already instantiated by the personalization system using the class's default constructor. So you can directly access the object without any further checks.*

I've created a new page in the protected area to illustrate the workings of the previously shown source code. This page lists stored bookmarks and allows you to delete individual entries. The following example contains the source code of the page, and Figure 7-5 shows the action:

```
<%@ page language="C#" master="~/MasterPage.master" %>

<script runat="server" language="c#">

void Page_Load(object sender, System.EventArgs e)
{
    if (this.IsPostBack == false)
    {
        this.UpdateBookmarkList();
    }
}

void BT_DeleteBookmark_Click(object sender, System.EventArgs e)
{
    if (this.LB_Bookmarks.SelectedIndex != -1)
    {
        this.Profile.Bookmarks.RemoveAt(this.LB_Bookmarks.SelectedIndex);
        this.UpdateBookmarkList();
    }
}

private void UpdateBookmarkList()
{
    this.LB_Bookmarks.DataSource = this.Profile.Bookmarks;
    this.LB_Bookmarks.DataBind();
}

void BT_OpenBookmark_Click(object sender, System.EventArgs e)
{
    if (this.LB_Bookmarks.SelectedIndex != -1)
    {
        this.Response.Redirect(this.LB_Bookmarks.SelectedValue, true);
    }
}
```

```
</script>

<asp:content id="Content1"
    contentplaceholderid="ContentPlaceHolder1"
    runat="server">
    <asp:listbox id="LB_Bookmarks" runat="server"/>
    <br />
    <asp:button
        id="BT_OpenBookmark" runat="server"
        text="Open" onclick="BT_OpenBookmark_Click" />

    <asp:button id="BT_DeleteBookmark"
        runat="server" text="Delete"
        onclick="BT_DeleteBookmark_Click" />
</asp:content>
```

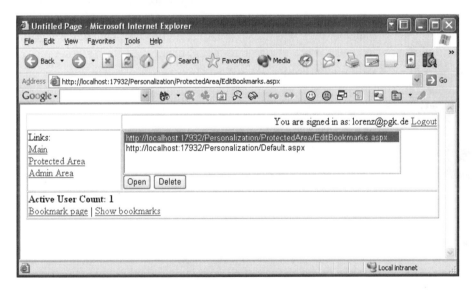

Figure 7-5. The bookmarks are stored using the StringCollection class.

Storing Custom Types

If you thought storing custom types must be doable in ASP.NET 2.0, you are right, of course! Yes, you can store any individual data in a profile. But again, this will work only under the condition that your class supports serialization.

A typical example for such a class is the shopping basket in a web application. I already gave you a glance at such an example early in this chapter. Wouldn't it be great if your customers could keep their shopping basket in between several visits until they finally place an order? I think so! And with the Profile Management system of ASP.NET 2.0, this can easily be done, as I'll demonstrate to you!

Creating a Simple Shopping Basket

The two classes Basket and BasketItem form the basis of your shopping basket. They represent the shopping basket itself as well as the single products inside of it. Basket is nothing but a derivation of the generic System.Collections.Generic.List class that has been slightly enhanced. Likewise, the second class, called BasketItem, is a simple business object prototype with four easy properties. Both classes are explicitly marked with attribute Serializable.

```
// Basket.cs
using System;

[Serializable]
public class Basket : System.Collections.Generic.List<BasketItem>
{
    public void Remove(int productId)
    {
        BasketItem item = this.FindItemByProductId(productId);
        if (item != null)
        {
            base.Remove(item);
        }
    }

    public BasketItem FindItemByProductId(int productId)
    {
        foreach (BasketItem item in this)
        {
            if (item.ProductId.Equals(productId))
            {
```

```
                    return item;
            }
        }
        return null;
    }
}

// BasketItem.cs
using System;

[Serializable]
public class BasketItem
{
    private int productId;
    private string name;
    private int count;
    private decimal unitPrice;

    public BasketItem() {}

    public BasketItem(int productId, string name, int count, decimal unitPrice)
    {
        this.productId = productId;
        this.name = name;
        this.count = count;
        this.unitPrice = unitPrice;
    }

    public int ProductId
    {
        get { return this.productId; }
        set { this.productId = value; }
    }

    public string Name
    {
        get { return this.name; }
        set { this.name = value; }
    }

    public int Count
    {
        get { return this.count; }
```

```
        set { this.count = value; }
    }

    public decimal UnitPrice
    {
        get { return this.unitPrice; }
        set { this.unitPrice = value; }
    }
}
```

The classes created and stored in the Code directory of the web site can now be included in the profile through the web.config configuration file:

```
<personalization>
    <profile>
        <property name="Basket" type="Basket" serializeAs="Xml" />
    </profile>
</personalization>
```

Done! From now on, you can save new items in the profile of the user, as this example demonstrates:

```
this.Profile.Basket.Add(new BasketItem(1, "Hello world product", 5, 12.34m));
```

The persisted shopping basket will still be available for users on their next visit.

Using the ObjectDataSource Control to Access the Basket

I've created a small page as an example to show you the flexible use of the profile object in conjunction with the new Data Controls. These are very helpful tools when it comes to the modification of the shopping basket. As with some of the Data Control examples I showed you in Chapter 3, you'll find a GridView control on this page that allows users to show, edit, and delete the current content of the shopping basket as well as a DetailsView control to add new items. The complete administration of the data is managed with an ObjectDataSource control.

```
<%@ page language="C#" master="~/MasterPage.master" %>

<asp:content id="Content1"
    contentplaceholderid="ContentPlaceHolder1"
    runat="server">
```

```
<asp:gridview id="GridView1" runat="server"
    datasourceid="ObjectDataSource1"
    autogeneratecolumns="False"
    datakeynames="ProductId">

    <columnfields>
        <asp:boundfield datafield="ProductId" readonly="True"
            headertext="Product ID">
        </asp:boundfield>
        <asp:boundfield datafield="Name" headertext="Name">
        </asp:boundfield>
        <asp:boundfield datafield="Count" headertext="Count">
        </asp:boundfield>
        <asp:boundfield datafield="UnitPrice" headertext="Unit Price">
        </asp:boundfield>
        <asp:commandfield showdeletebutton="True" showeditbutton="True">
        </asp:commandfield>
    </columnfields>

</asp:gridview>

<asp:detailsview id="DetailsView1"
    runat="server"
    datasourceid="ObjectDataSource1"
    autogeneraterows="False"
    defaultmode="Insert"
    datakeynames="ProductId">

    <rowfields>
        <asp:boundfield datafield="ProductId" readonly="True"
            headertext="Product ID">
        </asp:boundfield>
        <asp:boundfield datafield="Name" headertext="Name">
        </asp:boundfield>
        <asp:boundfield datafield="Count" headertext="Count">
        </asp:boundfield>
        <asp:boundfield datafield="UnitPrice" headertext="Unit Price">
        </asp:boundfield>
        <asp:commandfield showinsertbutton="True" showcancelbutton="False">
        </asp:commandfield>
    </rowfields>
</asp:detailsview>
```

```
<asp:objectdatasource
    id="ObjectDataSource1"
    runat="server"
    selectmethod="GetBasket"
    typename="BasketManager"
    updatemethod="Update"
    insertmethod="Insert"
    deletemethod="Delete">

    <updateparameters>
        <asp:parameter name="UnitPrice" type="Decimal">
        </asp:parameter>
        <asp:parameter name="Count" type="Int32">
        </asp:parameter>
        <asp:parameter name="ProductId" type="Int32">
        </asp:parameter>
    </updateparameters>

    <insertparameters>
        <asp:parameter name="ProductId" type="Int32">
        </asp:parameter>
        <asp:parameter name="Name" type="String">
        </asp:parameter>
        <asp:parameter name="Count" type="Int32">
        </asp:parameter>
        <asp:parameter name="UnitPrice" type="Decimal">
        </asp:parameter>
    </insertparameters>
</asp:objectdatasource>

</asp:content>
```

The communication between profile, shopping basket, and ObjectDataSource is handled by the `BasketManager` class, which offers the essential methods to select, edit, add, and delete entries. The source code of the class is shown in the following example:

```
using System;
using System.Web;
using System.Web.Personalization;

public class BasketManager
{
```

```
public Basket GetBasket()
{
    HttpPersonalizationBaseClass profile = HttpContext.Current.Profile;
    return (profile.GetPropertyValue("Basket") as Basket);
}

public void Delete(int ProductId)
{
    Basket basket = this.GetBasket();
    basket.Remove(ProductId);
}

public void Update(int ProductId, string Name, int Count, decimal UnitPrice)
{
    Basket basket = this.GetBasket();
    BasketItem item = basket.FindItemByProductId(ProductId);

    if (item != null)
    {
        item.Name = Name;
        item.Count = Count;
        item.UnitPrice = UnitPrice;
    }
}

public void Insert(int ProductId, string Name, int Count, decimal UnitPrice)
{
    Basket basket = this.GetBasket();
    basket.Add(new BasketItem(ProductId, Name, Count, UnitPrice));
}
}
```

As you can see from the preceding example and Figure 7-6, type-safe access to the profile isn't possible at present from within a separate code class. Therefore, the shopping basket has to be retrieved untyped using the GetPropertyValue() method implemented by the base class HttpPersonalizationBaseClass. Starting with the Beta version, it will presumably be possible to integrate a special namespace, ASP, by which you get access to the individual typed profile.

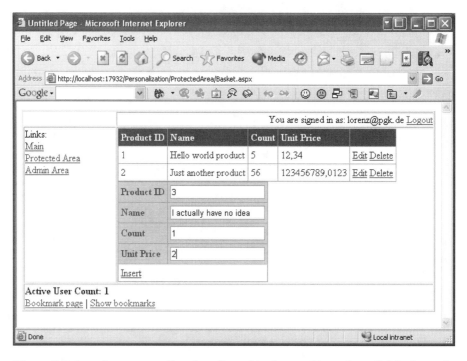

Figure 7-6. Any changes are directly reflected in the profile and available throughout the whole profile lifetime.

Using Personalization with Anonymous Users

So far, the examples for storage of profile information require an authenticated user. In the last chapter, you learned that ASP.NET 2.0 can identify anonymous users. As long as this feature is activated, you can mark custom properties of the profile so that they can be saved even if the user is anonymous.

A typical example once more is the shopping basket. The user should be able to put products into a basket without registering first. As opposed to the normal storage into a session variable, which I've used so far in this context, anonymous users will be recognized at a later visit so that their shopping basket is still available.

Activating Profile Properties for Anonymous Users

Before profile information can be saved for anonymous users, the profile properties feature has to be activated. This happens as described in the previous chapter through the web.config configuration file:

```
<?xml version="1.0"?>
<configuration>
    <system.web>
        <anonymousIdentification
            enabled="true"
        />
    </system.web>
</configuration>
```

Afterwards, for each property of the profile, you can define whether it should be stored for anonymous users or not. This has to be done with the `allowAnonymous` attribute. If the attribute isn't noted, the property won't be stored.

Based on the previous examples, it seems useful to make the shopping basket and bookmark functionality accessible to anonymous users. More personal data, such as the nickname and date of birth, are reserved for authenticated users.

```
<personalization>
    <profile>
        <property name="Nickname" />
        <property name="Birthday" type="System.DateTime" />
        <property name="YearsExperienceASPNET" type="int" defaultValue="1" />

        <property name="Bookmarks"
            type="System.Collections.Specialized.StringCollection"
            serializeAs="Xml"
            allowAnonymous="true"
        />

        <property name="Basket"
            type="Basket"
            serializeAs="Xml"
            allowAnonymous="true"
        />
    </profile>
</personalization>
```

I've copied the `basket.aspx` file to the nonprotected root directory of the web site to test its anonymous usage. As shown in Figure 7-7, users can edit their shopping basket even if they aren't authenticated (as evidenced by the Login link on the top-right side).

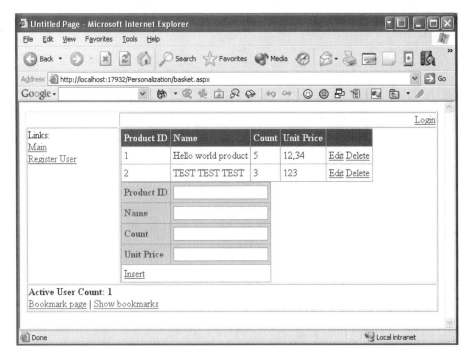

Figure 7-7. Even anonymous users can store items in their personal shopping basket.

Migrating Anonymous Profiles to Authenticated Users

Migration is a crucial feature when it comes to storing profiles of anonymous users. Think again of the shopping basket. Let's say a user is putting all sorts of things into a basket and wants to register afterwards to place the order. Naturally, the complete contents of the shopping basket mustn't get lost.

Such a migration of an anonymous profile is possible, but has to be implemented manually. This makes sense because it's the only way that the developer can make the decision about the type and the data flow of the migration.

The migration can be handled in the `MigrateAnonymous` event of the class `PersonalizationModule`. This will typically happen in the `global.asax` file, which has to be added to the web site to fulfill this purpose. As you can see in the following example, you get access to the anonymous user ID by the event arguments as well as to the new profile. With the ID, you can request the old profile and take over the contents according to your wishes. In this case, the bookmarks as well as all the entries of the shopping basket are copied, as shown in Figure 7-8.

```
<%@ application language="C#" %>

<script runat="server">

void Personalization_MigrateAnonymous(object sender,
    PersonalizationMigrateEventArgs e)
{
    HttpPersonalization oldProfile =
        ((HttpPersonalization) e.Context.Profile).GetProfile(e.AnonymousId);
    HttpPersonalization newProfile = (HttpPersonalization) e.Context.Profile;

    // Merging Bookmarks
    string[] bookmarks = new string[oldProfile.Bookmarks.Count];
    oldProfile.Bookmarks.CopyTo(bookmarks, 0);
    newProfile.Bookmarks.AddRange(bookmarks);

    // Merging Basket
    newProfile.Basket.AddRange(oldProfile.Basket);
}

</script>]
```

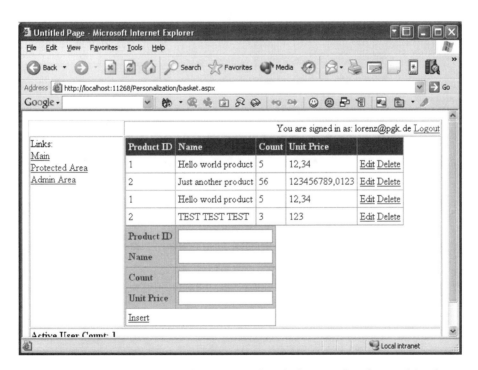

Figure 7-8. The anonymous basket is merged with the one already saved for the authenticated user.

Summary

The new personalization features of ASP.NET 2.0 help you to easily store custom information belonging to your individual users. You can add not only simple strings, but also complex data structures such as a shopping basket. Also, you can identify anonymous users throughout their current visit and even subsequent visits to your site.

CHAPTER 8

Creating Portals with Web Parts

IN CHAPTER 7, you learned about the personalization feature of ASP.NET version 2.0. *Web Parts*, internally known as the *Page Personalization* feature, are based on similar ideas. The framework behind this feature will enable users to adapt a single page of your web site individually according to their needs.

Similarly to how portals such as MSN.com work, users can choose their relevant information with Web Parts and adapt it in various ways (see Figure 8-1). Additionally, they have the option to define the position of elements on the page. Web Parts are based on the personalization system and therefore get stored individually for each user.

At first glance and even a second, Web Parts seem to be very similar to the homonymous feature of SharePoint Portal Server 2.0. The similarities, however, exist only from a visual point of view. Under the hood, these technologies have nothing to do with each other.

There are many situations in which you'll want to apply Web Parts. From a user point of view, they cover among other things the following features:

- Visual movement of displayed content

- Minimization and hiding of content

- Adding content from a catalog

- Editing form and content

- Connecting two Web Parts with each other

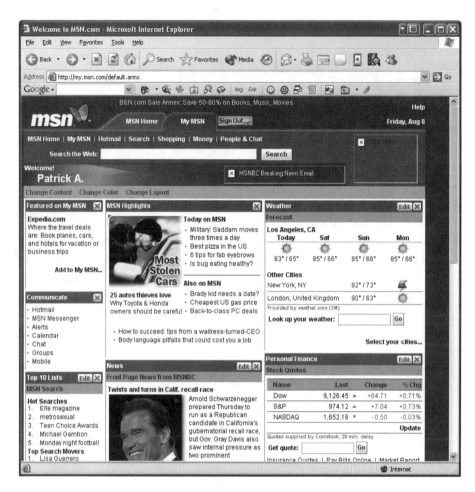

Figure 8-1. MSN.com allows authenticated visitors to customize the portal.

Understanding Web Parts

The concept of Web Parts is quite simple indeed. You can define one or several so-called Web Part Zones on your page. They do a great job of serving as placeholders and can carry one or several Web Parts containing the actual content. This way Web Parts can be shown vertically (one below the other) or horizontally (side by side) within a zone. Figure 8-2 shows differentiation based on MSN.com.

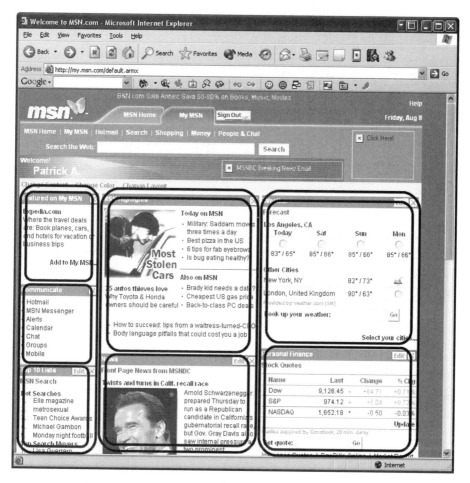

Figure 8-2. Following the ASP.NET terminology, MSN.com consists of three zones and includes several subparts.

Four Web Part Display Modes

Using the view mode of a page, users can minimize a single Web Part to a headline bar, maximize it again, or remove it from the page. If you open a page, this mode is used by default.

If, for example, a user switches over into design mode via a corresponding link button, that user will be able to move a single Web Part within the zone and even across several zones.

Edit mode offers this possibility as well and additionally allows you to blend in a separate Editor Zone through which you may work on several properties of the individual Web Parts. Depending on the number of possibilities you want to give to your users to customize the page, you'll probably go for this mode or for design mode.

The fourth and last mode is catalog mode, which enables you to add new or previously removed Web Parts and show them on the page. In combination with the other modes, users can create a complete and individualized version of the page that will be stored permanently in combination with their user profile.

Introducing the New Personalization Controls

In the current Alpha version of ASP.NET 2.0, the Web Parts system consists of 11 new controls. And in the final version, there'll be even more. The controls are placed on one page, but their use depends on the chosen display mode. All controls are stored in the namespace System.Web.UI.WebControls. At present, however, a separate Web Parts namespace is being considered. All the controls can be found in the Personalization area of the Toolbox.

Controls Used in Normal View Mode

The administration of the whole Web Parts system is handled by the WebPartManager control, which has no visualization at all, yet is mandatory for the use of Web Parts. It handles the various zones and the content therein, view mode, and a lot more. You may place only one control of this type on a page.

The previously described zones are defined using one or several WebPartZone controls. Quite often zones are placed within table cells. They'll later take over the content to be shown and have a ZoneTemplate assigned that you can edit within VS .NET as usual. After all this, I'm sure you can easily imagine using Web Parts in combination with Master Pages.

You can add one or any number of server controls, including user controls, as content in a zone. Each control is automatically wrapped in a GenericWebPart control. Thus it can be treated as a Web Part that will allow the user to switch it on or off at a later time. If you want to add several elements instead of one control, the ContentWebPart control is recommended. This one contains a ContentTemplate, which you can edit visually in the development environment.

Used in combination, the three controls will enable you to build a portal in which users can individually move or hide content.

Controls Used in Catalog Mode

With catalog mode, users may add Web Parts that are new or have previously been removed from the page. To enable the users to do this, you must define a new zone of the type `CatalogZone` first. With `ZoneTemplate` you can configure this zone visually in the development environment.

If you place a PageCatalogPart control on the template of the zone, users will have the choice of adding Web Parts that they have previously removed from the page.

If you want to allow users to add Web Parts that aren't yet defined, you must implement one or several TemplateCatalogPart controls first. Each instance of this control type represents a kind of content group. You can add the desired Web Parts within the control by using a template. Apart from ContentWebPart, any other control will do as well.

Controls Used in Edit Mode

To edit form and content of displayed Web Parts visually, another zone type, `EditorZone`, is at your service. This zone is shown as soon as the WebPartManager appears in edit mode and one of the available Web Parts of the page has been chosen for editing. As usual, the zone contains a `ZoneTemplate` to store the content. At present, four integrated controls do the job:

- With the help of the AppearanceEditorPart control, users can influence the appearance of a Web Part at a later time. For example, they can define the size and the title and decide which type of frame should be shown.

- The LayoutEditorPart control can be used to define the desired display status of a Web Part (normal or minimized) as well as its membership to a zone together with its position.

- The BehaviorEditorPart control can be helpful for users to update the behavior of a Web Part—for example, whether it can be closed or exported.

- The PropertyGridEditorPart control offers very high flexibility and can handle custom properties of a Web Part control. This will work under the condition that the developer has marked them as changeable through the Web by using a special attribute.

Creating a Simple Web Parts Page

Okay, I've started out this chapter with a lot of theory! Web Parts, in fact, are quite easy to understand and use. A little example will give you an idea.

The example, based on those in previous chapters, will show you how to build a small portal page. It's essential to have an authenticated user session when working with Web Parts. Therefore, I've modified the web.config configuration file in a way that the login of the user is already required to access the starting page. This, however, isn't always mandatory, because the personalization feature, as described in the last chapter, works in combination with anonymous users as well. Additionally, I've activated the personalization of pages, which is deactivated globally by default.

```xml
<?xml version="1.0"?>
<configuration>
    <system.web>
        <compilation debug="true" />

        <authentication mode="Forms" />

        <authorization>
            <deny users="?" />
        </authorization>

        <roleManager enabled="true">
            <providers />
        </roleManager>

        <pages enablePersonalization="true" />

    </system.web>
</configuration>
```

Adding the WebPartManager Control

The complete administration of Web Parts is managed by the WebPartManager control. This control doesn't offer any visualization. Therefore, it's quite irrelevant where you place it on the page.

I'd like to recommend, however, placing the control in the head area of the page within the <head> tags. This way it's still available and won't disturb your layout at all. The same is possible in combination with Master Pages. In that case, you need to place the control just once, and it can then be used on all the pages of your web site.

```
<html>
<head runat="server">
    <title>Untitled Page</title>
    <asp:WebPartManager runat="server" id="WebPartManager"/>
</head>
<body>
...
```

NOTE *Please be aware that you can place only one WebPartManager control on each page. Furthermore, the control must get a unique ID as shown in the previous example.*

To activate personalization, you'll need direct access to the WebPartManager control within your source code. You can achieve this via a public property of the Master Page. A much easier way works like this:

```
WebPartManager manager = (this.Items[typeof(WebPartManager)] as WebPartManager);
```

Internally, the control adds its own instance to the new Items collection of the Page class during handling of the Page_Init event (by overriding OnInit()). Its own type instance is used as a key for the dictionary. This way the current instance can be accessed at any time within the page's life cycle as shown previously.

Adding Zones

Next, you can define the zones of your first content page. I've decided to enhance the starting page in this example, which now consists of a table with two columns and three lines. The first line goes right across both columns and consists only of one zone that I've dragged from the Toolbox as a regular WebPartZone control directly to the page. The second line has two equal zones: one appearing in the left cell and the other appearing in the right cell.

The source code of the updated content page is still quite simple, as Listing 8-1 demonstrates. Figure 8-3 shows the visual definition of the zones in VS .NET.

Listing 8-1. Zones Serving As a Kind of Container for Your Web Parts

```
<asp:content id="Content1"
    contentplaceholderid="ContentPlaceHolder1"
    runat="server">

    <table cellspacing="1" cellpadding="1"
        width="100%" border="1">
        <tr>
            <td colspan="2">
                <asp:webpartzone id="WPZ_TopZone"
                    runat="server"
                    width="100%"
                    draghighlightcolor="244, 198, 96">
                </asp:webpartzone>
            </td>
        </tr>
        <tr>
            <td>
                <asp:webpartzone id="WPZ_LeftZone"
                    runat="server" width="100%"
                    draghighlightcolor="244, 198, 96">
                </asp:webpartzone>
            </td>
            <td>
                <asp:webpartzone id="WPZ_RightZone"
                    runat="server" width="100%"
                    draghighlightcolor="244, 198, 96">
                </asp:webpartzone>
            </td>
        </tr>
        <tr>
            <td>
            </td>
            <td>
            </td>
        </tr>
    </table>
</asp:content>
```

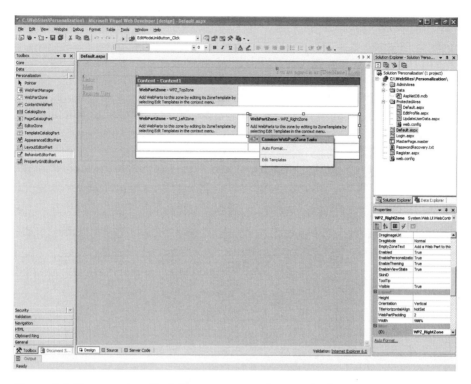

Figure 8-3. You can visually define your zones for any single page.

At first sight, you may think that the zone—same as the WebPartManager control—has no visualization of its own because these controls are shown as gray boxes only. This, however, isn't the whole truth. In edit mode the controls offer among other things a drag-and-drop functionality. Furthermore, they are responsible for the visualization of each single part and provide these parts with a header bar, for example.

Therefore, each zone control offers a considerable range of properties to modify its visualization. The easiest way to set these properties is to use the Auto Format dialog box from the Task List, which you already know from manipulating a bunch of other controls. In this dialog box, you can choose from two standard formats: SharePoint and IBuySpy. For the purposes of this example, I've decided to go with the first one. It's quite possible that this list will contain more items in the Beta version.

Adding Web Parts

Now that the WebPartManager control is in position and the zones are placed, I can show you what you've been waiting for: how to fill the zones with content.

As described previously, each zone has its own `ZoneTemplate` that carries the individual Web Parts, which you may edit as usual. Instead of placing text (literals) within the template, you may only use controls in this case. For example, I've placed a ContentWebPart control in the top zone to show some welcome text in the example. The ContentWebPart control also offers a template that accepts individual content. Figure 8-4 shows the embedded processing of both templates.

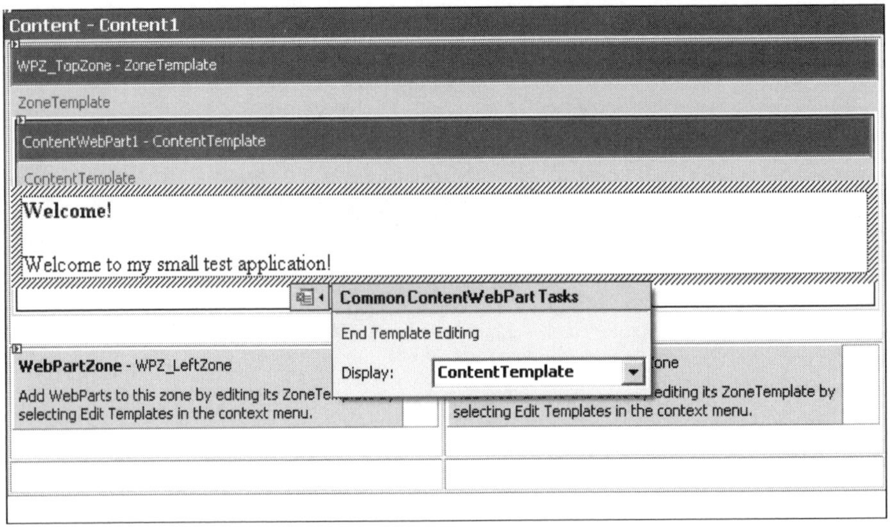

Figure 8-4. Edit the templates.

Beneath the Web Part controls that have been especially equipped to be part of a zone, you may as well place any other server control within a zone, as mentioned previously. By using traces, it's quite easy to recognize that a GenericWebPart control is wrapped automatically around each of these objects, so that such areas can be treated in the same way as other Web Parts.

I've equipped the two remaining Web Parts with a Calendar control (on the left) and a user control (on the right), which I took from the intranet project template of VS .NET. The user control shows a list with links by using a DataList control that has been data-bound to an XML file via a DataSetDataSource control. Of course, you may place more than one control in a zone.

After the page has been opened in the browser, it'll look somewhat similar to what is shown in Figure 8-5. Through the code in Listing 8-2, a frame is drawn around each single Web Part. In addition, the Web Parts each have a title bar in which the name is displayed and two links are offered to minimize and close them (which results in taking it off the page). With a click of the Minimize link, I deactivated the calendar before the screen shot was made. A click of the Restore link button would display it again.

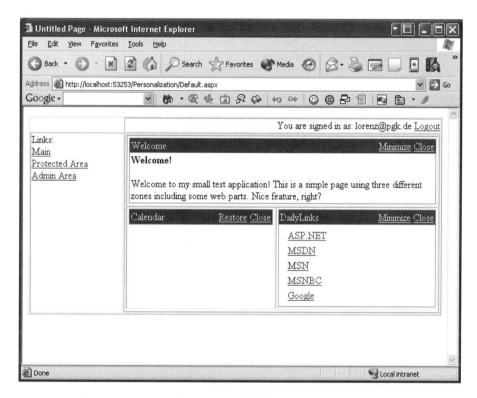

Figure 8-5. Congratulations! Your first ASP.NET version 2 portal page is ready.

Listing 8-2. A Comfortable Portal Page Without a Line of Code

```
<%@ page language="C#" master="~/MasterPage.master" %>
<%@ register tagprefix="uc1" tagname="DailyLinksWebPart"
    src="~/DailyLinksWebPart.ascx" %>

<asp:content id="Content1"
    contentplaceholderid="ContentPlaceHolder1"
    runat="server">

    <table cellspacing="1" cellpadding="1" width="100%" border="1">
```

```
<tr>
    <td colspan="2">
        <asp:webpartzone id="WPZ_TopZone" runat="server" width="100%"
            draghighlightcolor="244, 198, 96" >
            <zonetemplate>
                <asp:contentwebpart id="ContentWebPart1"
                    runat="server" width="100%" caption="Welcome">
                    <contenttemplate>
                        <strong>Welcome!</strong><br />
                        <br />
                        Welcome to my small test application!
                        This is a simple page using three different
                        zones including some web parts. Nice feature,
                        right?
                    </contenttemplate>
                </asp:contentwebpart>
            </zonetemplate>
        </asp:webpartzone>
    </td>
</tr>
<tr>
    <td valign="top">
        <asp:webpartzone id="WPZ_LeftZone" runat="server" width="100%"
            draghighlightcolor="244, 198, 96">
            <zonetemplate>
                <asp:calendar id="Calendar1" runat="server">
                </asp:calendar>
            </zonetemplate>
        </asp:webpartzone>
    </td>
    <td valign="top">
        <asp:webpartzone id="WPZ_RightZone" runat="server" width="100%"
            draghighlightcolor="244, 198, 96">
            <zonetemplate>
                <uc1:dailylinkswebpart id="DailyLinksWebPart1"
                    runat="server"></uc1:dailylinkswebpart>
            </zonetemplate>
        </asp:webpartzone>
    </td>
</tr>
<tr>
    <td>
        <asp:linkbutton id="LB_Personalize"
```

```
            runat="server"
            onclick="LB_Personalize_Click">
                Personalize this page!
        </asp:linkbutton>
      </td>
      <td>
      </td>
    </tr>
  </table>
</asp:content>
```

Customizing the Portal Page

The page now has some portal characteristics and can be modified a little bit by
the individual user. The result, however, isn't too exciting—is it? Wouldn't you like
to allow your users to modify the position of the content? It's probably easier than
you may think!

To follow along with this example, add a LinkButton control with the assigned
text "Personalize this page!" in an appropriate place of the page and take over the
event handling shown in the following code:

```
void LB_Personalize_Click(object sender, System.EventArgs e)
{
    WebPartManager manager = (this.Items[typeof(WebPartManager)]
                                        as WebPartManager);
    if (manager.DisplayMode == WebPartDisplayMode.Normal)
    {
        manager.SetDisplayMode(WebPartDisplayMode.Design);
        this.LB_Personalize.Text = "End Personalization";
    }
    else
    {
        manager.SetDisplayMode(WebPartDisplayMode.Normal);
        this.LB_Personalize.Text = "Personalize this page!";
    }
}
```

With a click of the button, the page will switch to design mode. This is
achieved by using the SetDisplayMode() method of the WebPartManager control.
The object has been queried from the new Page.Items dictionary as mentioned
earlier. Afterward, the user can visually define the position of each single Web
Part by dragging and dropping it to the desired position. The alpha blending

effect, which results in translucence as shown in Figure 8-6, helps you get the right look and feel for this maneuver. Another click of the button and you're finished with design mode.

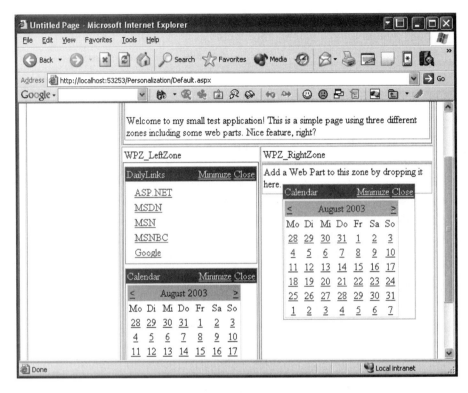

Figure 8-6. Just drag and drop to personalize your page.

Advanced Zone and Web Part Properties

Various properties allow you to individually set up defined zones as well as the Web Parts included therein. These can only be modified if you work directly with Web Parts and haven't placed a server or user control directly in the zone.

Customizing Your Web Part Zones

Although zones can be adapted to a fine level of detail, many changes don't affect the zone itself but have an overall influence on the integrated Web Parts. With the help of eight style properties, you can define the appearance of different areas in a sophisticated way. The arrangement of the Web Parts in a zone plays an important role with regard to the visuals. You set the Orientation property to either Vertical (default) or Horizontal. Even the drag and drop function can be adapted. The developer can choose among using the normal view of the content (including alpha blending), moving of the title bar, or displaying of a custom image.

The commands (or *verbs* in Microsoft terminology) shown in the title bar of each Web Part can be modified in a variety of ways. You can define the title, the description (shown as a tool tip), and a URL of an icon file for each and every verb.

The list of verbs can be enlarged, by the way, although I have to say that it takes some time to do that. Anyway, the WebPartZoneBase class offers the CreateVerbs event for this very purpose. You get access to a WebPartVerbCollection through the event arguments that are write-protected, however. To create a new verb, you must insert a new instance from the collection based on the existing one. Then you pass it back to the zone via the event arguments. Each verb contains a server-side event and, if needed, a client-side event-handling routine as well that starts upon a click of the verb.

The following code shows how to create a new verb displaying the text "Hello world". With a click of the automatically generated LinkButton control, the title of the corresponding Web Part will be changed programmatically, as shown in Figure 8-7.

```
void WPZ_TopZone_CreateVerbs(object sender,
    System.Web.UI.WebControls.WebPartVerbsEventArgs e)
{
    WebPartVerb verb = new WebPartVerb(
        new WebPartEventHandler(this.CustomWebPartVerb_ServerClick));
    verb.Text = "Hello world";
    e.Verbs = new WebPartVerbCollection(e.Verbs, new WebPartVerb[] {verb});
}

private void CustomWebPartVerb_ServerClick(object sender, WebPartEventArgs e)
{
    e.WebPart.Caption = "You clicked the custom verb!";
}
```

Figure 8-7. The way to add a new verb is a little unusal, but still easy to do.

Customizing Your Web Parts

Web Parts can be modified individually, too. For example, you can opt to assign a small and a large icon to the content. The presentation, including title bar and/or frame and the initial display mode (normal or minimized), can be influenced as well. You can even specify through various means which actions are allowed—for example, whether a Web Part can be moved, closed, or minimized.

Integration with Role Management has been done in very nice way. Through the Roles property, you may pass a list of roles separated by commas. Members of those roles now have access to the Web Part control. If a user is not a member of one of these roles, the Web Part will simply be hidden—the ideal basis for personalization.

Adding Web Parts

Maybe you've tested the example as it's been presented thus far in this chapter on your PC. Did you check what happens when you click the Close link? Well, the Web Part is closed and disappears from the page. How can it be shown again? So far not at all! The example can be enhanced to allow you do so, however.

Adding Web Parts Formerly Removed from the Page

If you want to allow users to add Web Parts, you'll first need a new zone, CatalogZone. This zone will only be shown if the WebPartManager control is in catalog mode. I've integrated a corresponding zone into the empty table cell on the example page on the lower-right side.

This zone control has a ZoneTemplate as well that holds the elements to be shown. They must derive (at least indirectly) from the CatalogBasePart class. Regular controls or Web Parts aren't allowed. One example of a control that is allowed is PageCatalogPart, which I've placed in the example. With the help of this control, you can add all the Web Parts to your page that you have removed from it earlier.

For the sake of a correctly functioning example, you need—apart from a new zone including PageCatalogPart—a second button that switches the WebPartManager control into catalog mode. The following event handling is being allocated to the LinkButton control:

```
void LB_AddWebParts_Click(object sender, System.EventArgs e)
{
    WebPartManager manager = (this.Items[typeof(WebPartManager)]
        as WebPartManager);
    if (manager.DisplayMode != WebPartDisplayMode.Catalog)
    {
        manager.SetDisplayMode(WebPartDisplayMode.Catalog);
        this.LB_Personalize.Text = "End Adding";
    }
    else
    {
        manager.SetDisplayMode(WebPartDisplayMode.Normal);
        this.LB_Personalize.Text = "Add web parts";
    }
}
```

In Figure 8-8, you can see the example in action. First I removed the welcome text from the page, and then I switched to catalog mode. Now the mentioned zone is shown. In the Page Catalog section, you can see the removed Web Part; if you were to check the check box beside it, choose a zone, and click the Add button, the text would be shown again.

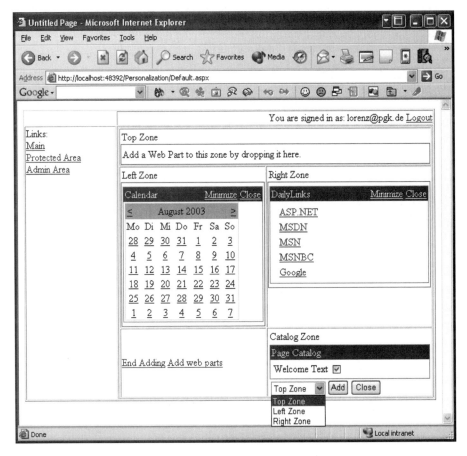

Figure 8-8. Add any removed web parts using the PageCatalogPart Control.

Adding New Web Parts

Apart from adding previously removed Web Parts, `CatalogZone` has a second role to fulfill: the insertion of new Web Parts. In the first step, you have to add a TemplateCatalogPart control to the existing `CatalogZone`. This control works similarly to the previously described `WebPartZone` and can take on Web Parts as well as any other controls. You can insert several TemplateCatalogPart controls within the `CatalogZone` and define content groups. The user can access a specific group through the LinkButton control and obtain a list of available entries afterward in the form of a CheckBoxList control.

On first view, the nesting of the control is sort of confusing. I hope that the following overview will make it more comprehensible for you:

```
CatalogZone
    TemplateCatalogPart
        Web Part 1
            Content
        Web Part 2
        Web Part 3
```

I've enhanced the example accordingly and added a TemplateCatalogPart titled "Money" as well as three ContentWebPart controls (see Listing 8-3). These have been titled according to three indexes—Dow Jones Industrial Average, S&P 500, and NASDAQ Composite—and could show the actual price. As you can see in this example and in Figure 8-9, however, functionality has not been integrated.

Listing 8-3. Adding Previously Removed Web Parts Using PageCatalogPart

```
<asp:catalogzone id="CatalogZone1"
    title="Catalog Zone" runat="server" width="100%">
    <zonetemplate>
        <asp:pagecatalogpart id="PageCatalogPart1" runat="server">
        </asp:pagecatalogpart>

        <asp:templatecatalogpart id="TemplateCatalogPart1"
            title="Money" runat="server" width="100%">
            <webpartstemplate>

                <asp:contentwebpart id="ContentWebPart2"
                    title="DOW" runat="server" width="100%"
                    caption="DOW">
                    <contenttemplate>
```

```
                    DOW
            </contenttemplate>
        </asp:contentwebpart>

        <asp:contentwebpart id="ContentWebPart3"
            title="S&P" runat="server" width="100%"
            caption="S&P">
            <contenttemplate>
                S&P
            </contenttemplate>
        </asp:contentwebpart>

        <asp:contentwebpart id="ContentWebPart1"
            title="NASDAQ" runat="server" width="100%"
            caption="NASDAQ">
            <contenttemplate>
                NASDAQ
            </contenttemplate>
        </asp:contentwebpart>


    </webpartstemplate>
  </asp:templatecatalogpart>
 </zonetemplate>
</asp:catalogzone>
```

> **CAUTION** *Please be aware that Web Parts defined within a TemplateCatalogPart control sometimes won't be correctly added to the page or even shown without content in the current version. This unattractive behavior will, of course, be solved in the Beta version.*

> **TIP** *You can spread the whole catalog, including the content to be shown within a user control. This way you can allow your users to add the same content to each personalized page without additional work.*

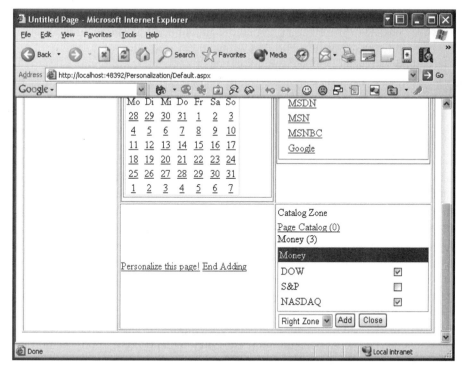

Figure 8-9. Just add all the Web Parts your users can select.

Editing Web Parts

Web Parts offer more than the opportunity to add or to delete content. You can give your users the option to edit several properties of the used Web Part. As already described briefly at the beginning of this chapter, you'll get good support from a third zone type, the `EditorZone`, and four editor controls to do this job. Like the `CatalogZone`, the `EditorZone` will only be shown if the corresponding mode is activated. In this case, `DisplayMode` must be set to `Edit`, which could be considered the big brother of `Design`.

> **TIP** *Due to the fact that the* `Edit` *setting of* `DisplayMode` *offers the same possibilities as* `Design` *and more, you should normally decide to use either one or the other mode depending on how many rights you want to give to your users for personalization. On the other hand, you can make the mode dependent on the roles the current user belongs to.*

I've enhanced the example again. Now it has a third table column, which contains the new EditorZone. I've stored all four existing editors therein: AppearanceEditorPart, BehaviorEditorPart, LayoutEditorPart, and PropertyGridEditorPart. Additionally, I've changed the event handling of the Personalize link buttons so that the page switches to editing mode with a button click.

```
void LB_Personalize_Click(object sender, System.EventArgs e)
{
    WebPartManager manager = (this.Items[typeof(WebPartManager)]
                                       as WebPartManager);
    if (manager.DisplayMode == WebPartDisplayMode.Normal)
    {
        manager.SetDisplayMode(WebPartDisplayMode.Edit);
        this.LB_Personalize.Text = "End Personalization";
    }
...
```

If you open the page and activate personalization with the already existing link, the page will appear to be unchanged at first. But there is a small difference, however: an additional link (verb) named "Edit" is shown in the title bar of each Web Part. With a click, you'll see the newly inserted zone with the different editors as shown in Figure 8-10. You can change the existing properties as you like and save them by clicking OK or Apply. Here again, I'm talking about verbs, which you obviously can adapt and localize if necessary. The insertion of new verbs, however, isn't implemented.

Figure 8-10 shows the possibilities of three editor parts that fulfill different purposes according to their names. What you *can't* see is the PropertyGridEditorPart control. I'll talk about this later in the chapter in the "Custom Web Parts" section.

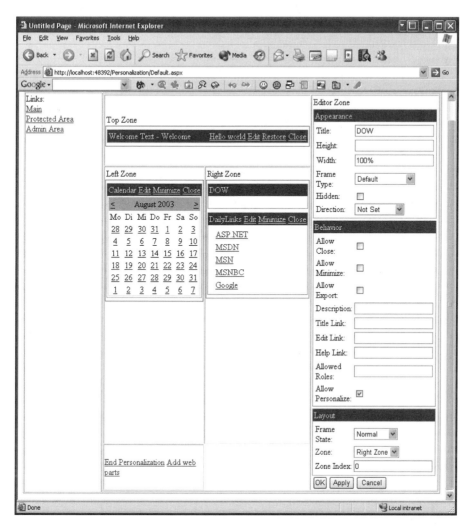

Figure 8-10. Several editor parts allow you to customize your page layout.

Integrating Editors with Role Management

It's imaginable that certain editing possibilities should only be allowed for exclusive user groups such as administrators. This could be the case with the BehaviorEditorPart control. It would be ideal to have role support equivalent to the Web Parts themselves. The latter has not been implemented yet, so you're facing some work ahead:

```
void EditorZone1_PreRender(object sender, System.EventArgs e)
{
    EditorPart editor = (EditorPart)
    ((Control)sender).FindControl("BehaviorEditorPart1");
    if (editor != null)
    {
        editor.Visible = this.User.IsInRole("Admins");
    }
}
```

Creating Custom Editor Parts

Two different approaches allow you to implement individual options for editing. First, you can use the PropertyGridEditorPart control to let users edit specially marked properties and store them within their personal page profiles. I'll show you how it works when I talk about the development of custom Web Parts in the next section of this chapter.

The second option to allow individual handling is creating a new EditorPart control that you integrate into the template of the EditorZone. The implementation is quite simple. Just derive the control from the abstract base class EditorPart, integrate the input elements, and implement the ApplyChanges and SyncChanges methods to store or to synchronize changes. You'll gain access to the selected Web Part through the property WebPartToEdit.

This approach will only be necessary if you need a large degree of control over what the EditorPart does. Many editing possibilities can be handled with the PropertyGridEditorPart control as well.

Custom Web Parts

At present, two Web Part classes are shipped with ASP.NET: ContentWebPart for visually editing content, and GenericWebPart, which will implicitly be used if you place other regular (user) controls into a WebPartZone. Additionally, you may create your own Web Parts by deriving a custom control class from the abstract base class WebPart. This is a regular web control deriving from the Panel control you already know.

You may ask yourself what the advantages of Web Parts are in comparison to a custom or user control. Well, with a Web Part control you have a direct access to the Web Part infrastructure. For example, you can implement properties that can be personalized as the following example shows.

Creating a Custom Web Part

Once more I've borrowed a small example from the intranet project template of VS .NET to demonstrate custom Web Parts. This particular Web Part can be used to show the actual weather conditions—a typical scenario for personalization because all users want their local weather conditions to be shown instead of generic ones. What could be more convenient than asking users for their zip code?

I've actually modified the original sample slightly so that it's structured quite simply. The overridden RenderContents() method holds a small JavaScript source snippet as a constant value that takes care of the weather data being taken over from another web site on the client side. The JavaScript method receives the content of the ZipCode property.

The property is marked with three attributes. Personalizable makes sure that the property is in fact personalizable and is stored individually for each user. Another attribute is named WebBrowsable, and it ensures that the value can be edited through the Web using the already mentioned PropertyGridEditorPart control. The third attribute, DisplayName, is assigned with the text that is shown as a title within the editor. Without an explicit definition, the name of the property would be displayed instead.

Listing 8-4 shows the source code—excluding the JavaScript—of the control. This can be registered with the page as usual and afterward placed in the ZoneTemplate of the WebPartZone control. After a click of the Edit button, the PropertyGridEditorPart control appears, and you can then use it to enter your own zip code (see Figure 8-11).

Listing 8-4. Creating Custom Web Parts with Only a Few Lines of Code

```
using System;
using System.ComponentModel;
using System.Web.Personalization;
using System.Web.UI;
using System.Web.UI.WebControls;

namespace PGK.Web.UI.WebControls.WebParts
{
    public sealed class WeatherWebPart : WebPart
    {
        private const string HtmlFormat = @"
            <div id=""weatherView""></div>
            <script id=""weatherScript"" language=""javascript""></script>
            <script language=""javascript"">

            ...

            CreateWeather('{0}');
            </script>
            ";

        private string _zipCode = String.Empty;

        [Personalizable]
        [WebBrowsable]
        [System.ComponentModel.DisplayName("Your ZIP Code")]
        public string ZipCode
        {
            get { return _zipCode; }
            set { _zipCode = value; }
        }

        protected override void RenderContents(HtmlTextWriter writer)
        {
            string text;

            if ((_zipCode == null) ||
                (_zipCode.Length == 0))
            {
                writer.Write(
                    "Please enter a zip code by personalizing this WebPart!");
```

```
            }
            else
            {
                writer.Write(String.Format(HtmlFormat, _zipCode));
            }
        }
    }
}
```

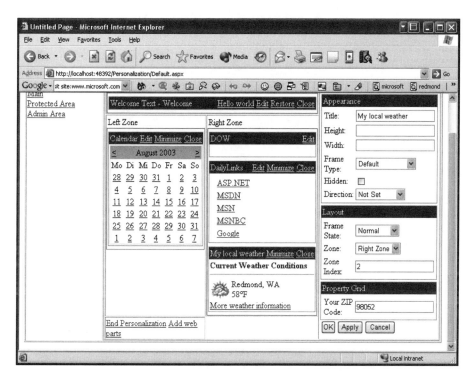

Figure 8-11. Maybe they'll get better weather tomorrow.

Sharing Data with Connection Points

Connection points are intended for the single-sided exchange of data between two
Web Parts that don't even have to know about each other. Each connection has a
provider that delivers the data and a consumer that uses it. The communication
is based on an interface, which has to be defined first and is controlled by the
WebPartManager.

> **TIP** *At present, the essential implementation for connection points is quite time-consuming, as the example shows. Presumably the system will be modified again in the Beta version to simplify the exchange of data for developers in the future. Probably the new way won't be completely compatible with the approach shown here.*

I've chosen the WeatherWebPart control presented earlier as the starting point for the example. This Web Part is a typical example in that it requires user-specific information, a zip code, to output weather data. To serve as a provider, I like to have another Web Part control that allows users to enter their zip code.

As mentioned previously, the basis for the communication relies on an interface that has to be known by the provider as well as by the consumer. IZipProvider implements the Zip property and the ZipHasChanged event that the provider can use to inform the consumer about a change.

```
using System;

public interface IZipProvider
{
    event EventHandler ZipHasChanged;

    string Zip
    {get; }
}
```

The provider shown here implements the IZipProvider interface to inform users about changes and give them the desired data. I'm talking about a composite control that is implemented as a Web Part with a TextBox control and a button. A click of the button activates the event that is defined in the interface. Overriding the ConnectionPoints property is important. In Listing 8-5, you can see that the Web Part control registers itself as provider for the mentioned interface. This is the only way to ensure a typed communication between the two Web Parts.

Listing 8-5. Allowing Users to Enter Their Zip Codes Through a Custom Provider

```
using System;
using System.ComponentModel;
using System.Web.Personalization;
using System.Web.UI;
using System.Web.UI.WebControls;
```

```
namespace PGK.Web.UI.WebControls.WebParts
{
    public class ZipProviderWebPart: WebPart, IZipProvider, INamingContainer
    {
        private string zip = string.Empty;
        private ConnectionPointCollection connectionPoints;
        private EventHandler zipHasChanged;
        private Button button;
        private TextBox textBox;

        public ZipProviderWebPart() { }

        string IZipProvider.Zip
        {
            get { return this.zip; }
        }

        event EventHandler IZipProvider.ZipHasChanged
        {
            add { this.zipHasChanged += value; }
            remove { this.zipHasChanged -= value; }
        }

        protected override void CreateChildControls()
        {
            this.textBox = new TextBox();
            this.textBox.AutoPostBack = true;
            this.textBox.Text = "90211";
            this.textBox.TextChanged += new EventHandler(this.OnZipChanged);
            this.Controls.Add(this.textBox);
            this.button = new Button();
            this.button.Text = "Submit";
            this.Controls.Add(this.button);
        }

        protected void OnZipChanged(object sender, EventArgs e)
        {
            this.zip = this.textBox.Text;
            if (this.zipHasChanged != null)
            {
                this.zipHasChanged(this, e);
            }
        }
```

```
        public override ConnectionPointCollection ConnectionPoints
        {
            get
            {
                if (this.connectionPoints == null)
                {
                    this.connectionPoints = new ConnectionPointCollection(this,
                        base.ConnectionPoints);

                    ConnectionProviderCallback provCallBack =
                        new ConnectionProviderCallback(GetIZipProvider);

                    ConnectionPoint connPoint =
                        new ConnectionPoint(typeof(IZipProvider), provCallBack);
                    connPoint.Name = "ZipProviderPoint";
                    this.connectionPoints.Add(connPoint);
                }
                return this.connectionPoints;
            }
        }

        private object GetIZipProvider()
        {
            return (IZipProvider)this;
        }
    }
}
```

This works in a similar way on the consumer side. The property must be over-ridden here as well so that the Web Part control can register as a consumer for the interface. A callback is also set here that will be called if the connection can be established. The WeatherWebPart control gets access to the provider through the interface and can register for the ZipHasChanged event. You can see all of this demonstrated in Listing 8-6.

Listing 8-6. TheWeb Part Consuming the Provider and Acquiring the Entered Zip Code

```
using System;
using System.ComponentModel;
using System.Web.Personalization;
using System.Web.UI;
using System.Web.UI.WebControls;
```

```
namespace PGK.Web.UI.WebControls.WebParts
{
    public sealed class WeatherWebPart: WebPart
    {
        private ConnectionPointCollection connectionPoints;
        private IZipProvider zipProvider;

        public override ConnectionPointCollection ConnectionPoints
        {
            get
            {
                if (this.connectionPoints == null)
                {
                    this.connectionPoints =
                        new ConnectionPointCollection(this, base.ConnectionPoints);

                    ConnectionConsumerCallback consCallBack =
                        new ConnectionConsumerCallback(ConnectToProvider);
                    ConnectionPoint connPoint =
                        new ConnectionPoint(typeof(IZipProvider),
                        consCallBack);

                    connPoint.Name = "ZipConsumerPoint";
                    this.connectionPoints.Add(connPoint);
                }

                return this.connectionPoints;
            }
        }

        public void ConnectToProvider(object obj)
        {
            if (obj == null && this.zipProvider == null)
                throw new Exception("Null interface");

            this.zipProvider = (IZipProvider) obj;
            if (this.zipProvider != null)
            {
                this.ZipCode = this.zipProvider.Zip;
                this.zipProvider.ZipHasChanged +=
                    new EventHandler(OnProviderZipChanged);
            }
        }
```

```
        public void OnProviderZipChanged(object sender, EventArgs e)
        {
            this.ZipCode = this.zipProvider.Zip;
        }


        ...

    }
}
```

Now the two web controls are in the position to communicate with each other, in principle. You only have to put them on a page and establish the connection between the two through the WebPartManager, as in Listing 8-7.

Listing 8-7. Establishing the Connection That Brings Provider and Consumer Together

```
<asp:content id="Content1"
    contentplaceholderid="ContentPlaceHolder1" runat="server">

    <asp:webpartmanager runat="server" id="WebPartManager">
        <connections>
            <asp:connection consumerid="WeatherWebPart1"
                providerid="ZipProviderWebPart1"
  enabled="true"
                providername="ZipProviderPoint"
                consumername="ZipConsumerPoint">
            </asp:connection>
        </connections>
    </asp:webpartmanager>

    <table cellspacing="1" cellpadding="1" width="100%" border="1">
        <tr>
            <td valign="top">
                <asp:webpartzone id="WPZ_LeftZone" runat="server" width="100%"
                    draghighlightcolor="244, 198, 96" title="Left Zone">
                    <parttitlestyle forecolor="White" backcolor="#2254B1">
                    </parttitlestyle>
                    <partstyle borderwidth="1px"
                        borderstyle="Solid"
                        bordercolor="#81AAF2">
                    </partstyle>
                    <partverbstyle forecolor="White">
                    </partverbstyle>
                    <zonetemplate>
```

```
                    <webparts:ZipProviderWebPart
                        id="ZipProviderWebPart1"
    runat="server" />
                    <WebParts:weatherwebpart
    id="WeatherWebPart1" runat="server" />
                        <asp:calendar id="Calendar1" runat="server">
                        </asp:calendar>
                    </zonetemplate>
                </asp:webpartzone>
            </td>
        </tr>
    </table>
</asp:content>
```

After all of this source code, you'll probably agree with my initial assessment. The implementation of connection points is still a little bit complex at present, although it looks quite easy in Figure 8-12. I certainly wouldn't have succeeded in implementing this example without the functioning template from AndreS of the ASP.NET team. Thank you very much for your help!

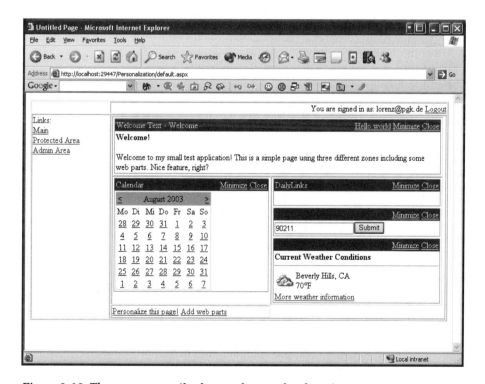

Figure 8-12. The user can easily change the weather location.

What to Expect Next?

The development of Web Parts is not completely finished yet. You can expect a couple of changes and new features with the Beta version. On one side, there'll be more personalization controls to complete the 11 existing ones. Furthermore, an Import/Export interface for Web Parts should be included. The connection points shown previously are subject to change as well. It may happen that the Beta version offers the possibility to reset a personalized page to its original state and to migrate the Page Personalization of an anonymous user.

Summary

Web parts allow users to customize a portal page in a very comfortable way. As the developer, you can easily create custom Web Parts and allow users to edit personalized data such as their zip code. You may already know this concept from the SharePoint Portal Server. Although the implementation of Web Parts in ASP.NET looks very similar to SharePoint, it is quite different under the hood.

CHAPTER 9

Applying Themes

THE NEW VERSION OF ASP.NET allows you to work with *Themes*, which enable you to globally define control designs. Control designs, called *Skins*, can be used to standardize the look and feel of a web site. Each Theme consists of one or several Skins for each of the desired server control types. The Skins in turn contain an empty control definition with individual property assignments. You can apply a Theme globally to a complete web site or just in some specific areas or for one of the site's pages. With each definition, you may decide whether it should be applied in general for all controls of a particular type or only for particular ones.

Themes always show their big advantages when an existing web site is about to be modified. In this case, you can make changes centrally, affecting all corresponding pages at once. The only requirement is the consequent use of Themes on all pages.

Understanding Themes

You can define many properties of a control with Themes and Skins respectively; among other things this includes color values for the background, foreground, and frame. Depending on the control, it's possible to assign pictures and other resources as for example the node icons of the new TreeView control. All assigned values are static in principle.

Properties that are primarily placed at run time, such as DataSource, and properties that directly influence the behavior of a control can't be defined by a Theme. The developer of a control must decide which properties can be defined in a Theme by marking the desired properties with a particular attribute.

One of the shipped Themes for the Label control looks like this:

```
<asp:Label runat="server"
    ForeColor="#000066"
    BackColor="transparent">
</asp:Label>
```

The code gets much more complex with the TreeView control, in which the displayed pictures are defined with a Theme. Both design templates have influence on all the controls of this type as long as nothing else has been specified (see Listing 9-1).

Listing 9-1. Defining a Bunch of Properties Through a Theme

```
<asp:TreeView runat="server" ForeColor="#000066" BackColor="transparent"
    BorderColor="#EEEEEE" ParentNodeImageUrl="images/basicblue_greysquare.gif"
    RootNodeImageUrl="images/basicblue_greysquare.gif" NodeIndent="10"
    LeafNodeImageUrl="images/basicblue_greysquare.gif">
    <NodeStyle horizontalpadding="5" ForeColor="#000066"
        verticalpadding="1" BackColor="#FFFFFF"></NodeStyle>
    <LeafNodeStyle ForeColor="#000066" BackColor="#FFFFFF"></LeafNodeStyle>
    <LevelStyles>
        <asp:TreeNodeStyle Font-Bold="True" BackColor="#FFFFFF"
            ForeColor="#000066" ChildNodesPadding="5"></asp:TreeNodeStyle>
    </LevelStyles>
    <RootNodeStyle Font-Bold="True" BackColor="#FFFFFF"></RootNodeStyle>
    <ParentNodeStyle ForeColor="#000066" BackColor="#FFFFFF"></ParentNodeStyle>
    <HoverNodeStyle Font-Underline="false" BorderColor="#EEEEEE"
        BackColor="#FFFFFF" ForeColor="#0000FF"></HoverNodeStyle>
    <SelectedNodeStyle BorderWidth="1px" ForeColor="#660066" BorderStyle="Solid"
        BackColor="#FFFFFF"></SelectedNodeStyle>
</asp:TreeView>
```

At first sight, Themes and Cascading Style Sheets (CSS) have a lot in common. Both allow the overall definition of primarily visual properties of an object. On closer inspection, however, you'll discover that the possibilities offered by Themes are quite different from those of classic CSS.

Unlike CSS, Themes can be directly integrated in ASP.NET and are optimized for its concepts. Therefore, Themes can define many properties that could not have been handled in this form with CSS. One example of this: the pictures of the TreeView control mentioned previously.

Unlike CSS, Themes aren't cascading. Properties that have been defined in one Theme will generally overwrite the corresponding values that had been assigned directly to the control.

Apart from this, Themes can contain CSS files. They are automatically referenced by individual pages if they've been saved in the Theme directory.

Using Global Themes

A couple of global, standard Themes are shipped with ASP.NET. You can integrate them directly into your web site. These Themes are stored in the following directory:

```
<windir>\Microsoft.NET\Framework\<version>\ASP.NETClientFiles\Themes\
```

Each of the available Themes has a separate subfile with the name of the Theme. The current Alpha version comes with two standard Themes: BasicBlue and SmokeAndGlass. It's expected that more Themes will come along with the Beta version.

Applying Themes to a Whole Web Site

You must choose a Theme in the web.config configuration file if you want to use it for the whole web site. The following entry in the <pages> tag will do the job:

```
<?xml version="1.0" encoding="UTF-8" ?>
<configuration>
    <system.web>
        <pages theme="BasicBlue" />
    </system.web>
</configuration>
```

Afterwards, all pages use the BlueBasic Theme unless something else has been defined. The effects are shown in Figure 9-1. The example consists of a TreeView, SiteMapPath, and GridView control to display the Northwind customers. If you take the same page and use the alternatively offered SmokeAndGlass Theme, the page will be shown with the brilliance and glamor you see in Figure 9-2.

Although the appearance of both figures is quite different, no modifications were made to the page itself. Only the configuration in the web.config file was modified to show a different Theme.

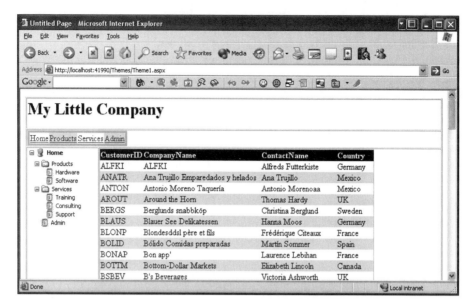

Figure 9-1. This Theme is called BlueBasic.

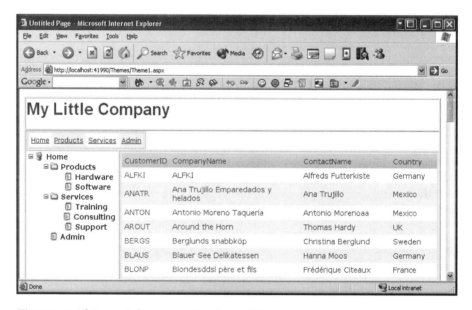

Figure 9-2. This one is known as SmokeAndGlass.

Applying Themes to a Web Site Area

Quite often you'll want to use different Themes for individual areas of a web site. In this case, you have two possibilities that the configuration system of .NET offers to you in the familiar way:

- You can store the subsections in separate directories and provide each of them with its own web.config configuration file that inherits the configuration of the root directory and overwrites the chosen Theme.

- Alternatively, you can use the <location> tag to define different Themes for a given path (either directory or page) within the root web.config file.

The following snippet shows the application of the <location> tag, which is used to assign an alternative Theme to the subdirectory named "subfolder".

```xml
<?xml version="1.0" encoding="UTF-8" ?>

<configuration>
    <system.web>
        <compilation debug="true" />
        <pages theme="BasicBlue" />
    </system.web>

    <location path="subfolder">
        <system.web>
            <pages theme="SmokeAndGlass" />
        </system.web>
    </location>

</configuration>
```

Applying Themes to a Single Page

As an alternative to the global assignment of a Theme, you can go for a differentiated design for each single page. To do so, you must assign the name of the desired Theme to the theme attribute of the @Page directive. When using Master Pages, this can naturally be done as well with the corresponding @Master directive.

```
<%@ page language="C#" theme="SmokeAndGlass" %>
```

> **CAUTION** *If you select a Theme through the configuration file as well as at page level, the @Page directive will overrule the global setting.*

Apart from the static assignment, the dynamic selection of a Theme is possible, too. Just pass the desired name to the Theme property of the Page class. Please be aware that the property must be set in the Page_PreInit event at the latest. Any changes at a later time in the page's life cycle, for example in the Page_Load event, will cause a run time exception.

```
void Page_PreInit(object sender, System.EventArgs e)
{
    this.Theme = "SmokeAndGlass";
}
```

In combination with personalization, the dynamic assignment of Themes is really getting interesting. As in the forums of www.asp.net, users may choose their desired view. Though this requirement indeed works, nevertheless the solution is quite tricky. You'll find an example later in this chapter in the "Using Themes with Personalization" section.

Themes Under the Hood

Despite what I discussed earlier regarding Themes and CSS, Themes frequently work with CSS behind the scenes! If you look at the source code of a generated ASP.NET page, you'll see the corresponding style definitions in the header. As long as your Theme uses some external CSS files, they'll automatically be referenced through the aspnet_client virtual directory.

```
<html>
<head id="Head1">
    <title>Untitled Page</title>
    <style>
        .aspnet_s0 { padding:1,5,1,5;color:#000066;...; }
        .aspnet_s1 { color:#000066;text-decoration:none; }
        ...
        .aspnet_s13 { color:Blue;text-decoration:none; }

    </style>
    <link rel="stylesheet"
        href="/aspnet_client/system_web/1_2_30703/Themes/BasicBlue/whatever.css"
```

```
        type="text/css" />
</head>
<body>
```

> **CAUTION** *If the example shown previously doesn't work properly with your own individually created pages, it may be that the server-side* <head> *tag is missing. This tag is absolutely necessary, because otherwise the styles can't be displayed.*
>
> ```
> <html>
>
> <head id="Head1" runat="server">
>     <title>Untitled Page</title>
> </head>
> <body>
> ```

Themes are administrated internally by two classes: PageTheme and ControlSkin. The latter offers a method, ApplySkin(), that applies a Skin to the control. In practice, however, you'll only rarely get in touch with these two classes.

Creating Themes

It would be quite boring if all web sites created with ASP.NET 2.0 used the same Themes. You have the choice, of course, to create your own Themes!

If you intend to use a newly created Theme globally for all the applications on your server, you can expand the list of global Themes. You just have to create a new subdirectory in the directory specified earlier. The name used later becomes the identifier of the Theme. Contrary to this approach, I recommend you create Themes exclusively for individual web sites and make copies available for other projects.

Creating a New Web Site Theme

You must create a new folder with the name "themes" in the root directory of your web site before you can apply a new Theme. Similar to the bin and code directories, this name is predefined. This fact can be visualized as well through a special icon in the VS .NET Solution Explorer. You must create another folder below the new directory if you want to create a new Theme. You can address the Theme across the chosen directory name later. For the purposes of this example, I've chosen HelloWorldTheme.

NOTE *If you choose the same name for a local and a global Theme, the local one has priority, and you can't address the global one anymore. Using the same name will* not *cause an inheritance to occur.*

Now you create a text file named theme.skin within the newly created directory that later on carries the design templates for the controls. The name of the file is irrelevant, however. Only the ending, skin, is important. Microsoft even recommends creating a separate file for each type of control. Concerning the global templates, the developers didn't apply their own recommendations. I agree with this convention and think that a single file will do in general.

You can define the desired design templates within the file. To do so, you must write down an empty control definition including the runat attribute for each desired control type (for example Label, GridView, TextBox, and so on) and assign the properties you want to it. Please be aware that an ID should *not* be noted.

The content of the file may look like the example in Listing 9-2. Two controls (TreeView and GridView) are being formatted in this case. As you can see in Figure 9-3, the Theme applied to the previously used page is showing its effects.

Listing 9-2. Creating a Custom Theme

```
<ASP:TreeView runat="server"
    Font-Size="12"
/>

<ASP:GridView runat="server"
    BorderColor="Red"
    BorderWidth="3"
    BorderStyle="Dashed"
    >

    <HeaderStyle
        BackColor="Red"
        ForeColor="Yellow"
        Font-Size="15"
    />

    <RowStyle
        ForeColor="Black"
    />

</ASP:GridView>
```

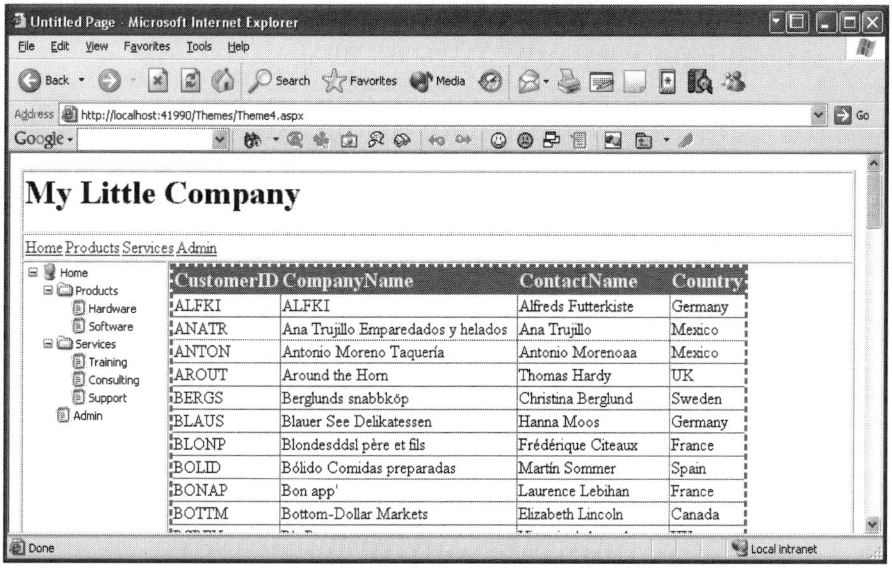

Figure 9-3. The same page shown earlier now uses a very special Theme.

> **TIP** *Instead of creating the controls manually within the Skin file and adding the desired properties afterwards, I recommend using the Design view of VS .NET. After you've edited the control according to your needs, you can copy it out of the HTML source code and insert it into the Theme, deleting unnecessary properties such as the ID afterwards.*

Using Cascading Style Sheets

With the help of Themes, it's quite easy to replace CSS files. You can use their defined styles within the Skin file(s) as well as within ASPX pages to specify, for example, the view of headlines and text. If you want to integrate a new CSS file in your page, you only have to copy it to the corresponding Theme directory. The ASP.NET engine takes care of the rest.

I've created a file named `styles.css` for demonstration purposes and filled it with the following data:

```
body, td
{
   font-family: Verdana;
   font-size: 11px;
}
```

```
h1
{
    font-size: 30px;
    color: blue;
}
```

The result is shown in Figure 9-4 as well as in the generated HTML source code of the page that automatically references the created file:

```
<html>
<head id="Head1">
    <title>Untitled Page</title>
    <style>
        ...
    </style>
    <link rel="stylesheet"
        href="Themes/HelloWorldTheme/styles.css"
        type="text/css" />
</head>
<body>
```

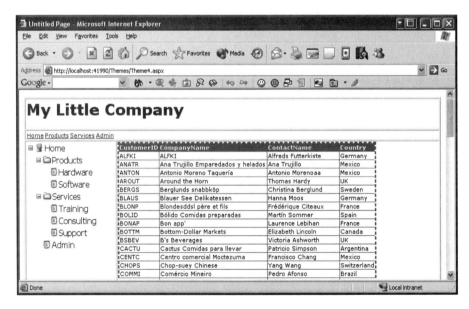

Figure 9-4. Using different stylesheet files with Themes is quite easy.

Creating Different Control Themes Called Skins

Up to now, I've shown only one Skin that has been defined for a control type in the examples. In reality, however, the controls of a type should often look a little different from each other. Therefore, you'll probably want to define additional Skins—apart from the so-called default Skins.

To differentiate between a default Skin and any number of additional Skins for a control type, you must assign them a unique identifier. For this purpose, you can use the SkinID property for the definition within the Skin file as well as later on when using the Skin within the page.

In Listing 9-3, I've enhanced the Theme of the preceding example as a test.

Listing 9-3. The Theme containing a Named Theme Called Skin

```
<ASP:GridView runat="server" SkinID="CommonGridView"
    BorderColor="Black"
    BorderWidth="1"
    BorderStyle="Solid"
    >

    <HeaderStyle
        BackColor="Blue"
        ForeColor="White"
    />

    <RowStyle
        ForeColor="Black"
    />

    <AlternatingRowStyle
        BackColor="#BBBBFF"
    />

</ASP:GridView>
```

I've implemented another GridView on the test page next to the existing one. It's identical and uses the same source code. Only the SkinID property has been directed to the additional Skin. Figure 9-5 shows the differences caused by this action.

```
<asp:gridview id="Gridview2" runat="server"
    autogeneratecolumns="False"
    datasourceid="SqlDataSource1"
    datakeynames="CustomerID"
    skinid="CommonGridView">
    ...
</asp:gridview>
```

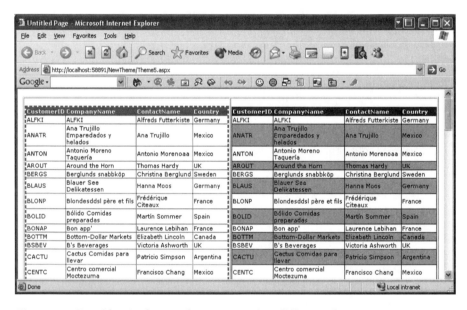

Figure 9-5. Two identical controls are now using different Skins.

Disabling Themes

As an alternative to the implementation of an additional Skin, you have the option to switch off the use of Themes for controls. As a result, all controls offer a property named EnableTheming that is activated by default and can be deactivated if desired.

```
<asp:gridview id="GridView1"
    runat="server"
    EnableTheming="false"
    ...
</asp:gridview>
```

If you want to deactivate Themes for a complete page, you should apply the homonymous attribute of the @Page directive as follows:

```
<%@ page language="C#" EnableTheming="false" %>
```

Using Themes with Personalization

The relationship of Themes and personalization is a very interesting topic. You may leave it up to users to decide the presentation of a portal. Maybe a little bit more of the blue color or rather some sort of dark green? The user will be able to decide which!

Listing 9-4 demonstrates such a choice, following the approach of Dave Sussmann, who cordially sent me his example. It contains a DropDownList control to choose a Theme. By setting up the AutoPostBack property, the selected value will be used immediately and stored in the profile, and the view will be updated accordingly.

Listing 9-4. Enabling the User to Select Which Theme to Use

```
<%@ page language="C#" %>

<script runat="server" language="c#">

void Page_PreInit(object sender, System.EventArgs e)
{
    this.Theme = Profile.Theme;
}

void Page_Load(object sender, System.EventArgs e)
{
    if (this.IsPostBack == false)
    {
        ListItem item = this.DDL_Theme.Items.FindByText(this.Profile.Theme);
        if (item != null)
        {
            item.Selected = true;
```

```
            }
        }
    }

    void DDL_Theme_SelectedIndexChanged(object sender, System.EventArgs e)
    {
        this.Profile.Theme = this.DDL_Theme.SelectedValue;
        this.Response.Redirect(this.Request.RawUrl, true);
    }

</script>

<html>
<head id="Head1" runat="server">
    <title>Untitled Page</title>
</head>
<body>
    <form id="Form1" runat="server">
        <asp:dropdownlist id="DDL_Theme" runat="server"
            onselectedindexchanged="DDL_Theme_SelectedIndexChanged"
            autopostback="True">
            <asp:listitem>BasicBlue</asp:listitem>
            <asp:listitem>SmokeAndGlass</asp:listitem>
        </asp:dropdownlist>

        ...

    </form>
</body>
</html>
```

As shown in the following snippet, I've attached a new property with a useful standard value to the profile in the web.config configuration file. This way I've ensured that the example works properly (see Figure 9-6).

```
<?xml version="1.0" encoding="UTF-8" ?>
<configuration>
    <system.web>
        <personalization>
            <profile>
                <property name="Theme" defaultValue="BasicBlue" />
            </profile>
        </personalization>
    </system.web>
</configuration>
```

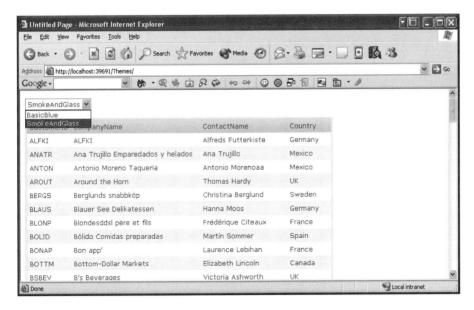

Figure 9-6. Your users can select which Theme to use.

Using Client Callback

The example just shown works, but there is a catch! A redirect must occur after the update of the profile, because the Theme can't be changed anymore at the time of the event handling. The assignment of the Page.Theme property would cause an InvalidOperationException. What can be done?

One of the new features of ASP.NET 2.0, called *Client Callback,* is applied in this situation. I'll go into the details of this feature in Chapter 11. In summary, this feature allows you to call a server-side method with JavaScript and without a post-back of the whole page. The approach is kind of similar to the IE Web Service behavior that you may already know. The system is based on XMLHTTP and can be used with the current versions of Internet Explorer and as well as Netscape.

Afterwards, you'll see the example, shown in Listing 9-5, that was modified on this basis. After selecting a new value in the DropDownList control, a client-side script will be initiated that activates the callback and, after successful completion, starts a postback to update the page.

Listing 9-5. Using Client Callback Is Another Way to Update the Profile Object

```
<%@ page language="C#" %>
<%@ implements interface="System.Web.UI.ICallbackEventHandler"%>

<script runat="server" language="c#">

void Page_PreInit(object sender, System.EventArgs e)
{
    this.Theme = Profile.Theme;
}

void Page_Load(object sender, System.EventArgs e)
{
    string callback = Page.GetCallbackEventReference(this, "arg",
        "MyCallBackHandler", null);
    string script = string.Format("function CallTheServerCallBack(arg)
        {{{0}; }}", callback);
    this.ClientScript.RegisterClientScriptBlock(this.GetType(),
        "CallTheServerCallBack", script, true);

    if (this.IsPostBack == false)
    {
        ListItem item = this.DDL_Theme.Items.FindByText(this.Profile.Theme);
        if (item != null)
        {
            item.Selected = true;
        }
    }
}

string ICallbackEventHandler.RaiseCallbackEvent(string eventArgument)
{
    this.Profile.Theme = eventArgument;
    return null;
}

</script>

<html>
<head id="Head1" runat="server">
    <title>Untitled Page</title>
```

```
<script language="javascript">
    function SetTheme(Theme)
    {
            CallTheServerCallBack(Theme);
    }
    function MyCallBackHandler(result, context)
    {
            __doPostBack('', '');
    }
</script>

</head>
<body>
    <form id="Form1" runat="server">
        <asp:dropdownlist id="DDL_Theme"
            runat="server" onchange="SetTheme(this.value);">
            <asp:listitem>BasicBlue</asp:listitem>
            <asp:listitem>SmokeAndGlass</asp:listitem>
        </asp:dropdownlist>


        ...


    </form>
</body>
</html>
```

You'll get further information about Client Callback in Chapter 11.

Using Themes for Custom Controls

The support of Themes within custom controls can be implemented extremely easily. First, you must decide whether each property should be available via a Skin or not. If the control derives from a base class like WebControl, then the decision has already been made with regard to a lot of existing properties. You just have to point the new Themeable attribute to all the other properties you want to allow to be assigned through a Skin. That's all you have to do!

```
[Themeable]
public string MyProperty
{
    get { return this.myProperty; }
    set { this.myProperty = value; }
}
```

Summary

The new Themes feature offers a load of possibilities that you can't handle with Cascading Style Sheets at all. Themes are fully integrated in the ASP.NET concept. In combination with personalization, you can even allow users to select their preferred Theme, which is then stored in their personal profile.

CHAPTER 10

Tracking Traffic with Site Counters

WHAT ARE *SITE COUNTERS*? In principle, they're a type of web site statistic. They aren't supposed to be in competition with web server log files. Rather, they provide additional and differentiated data, such as how often a button was clicked or whether an advertising banner has attracted visitors.

Site counters consist of three key elements: a couple of web controls that provide the essential statistical values, and a front-end for the evaluation of these statistics. Both are based on the Site Counter API.

The so-called page counters are a subfeature of site counters. The number of accesses on certain pages or on all pages is logged similarly to the log files of a web server.

The storage of all the gathered statistics is again taken care of by a place provider model. Providers for Access and SQL Server are included in the shipment, and Access is used by default. Because web sites with a high number of visitors will result in huge data volumes, the provider should be changed and SQL Server (or at least the MSDE version) should be used. Both providers offer data caching so that new values will be gathered and written to the database only every x seconds.

Using Site Counters

Using site counters is very easy. A couple of controls provide you with a set of properties for recording clicks. You can use different types of buttons for statistics with site counters—a DataList control doesn't offer an adequate measurement, of course.

The storage of recorded values works according to a predefined scheme with a total of eight values and the actual counter. The different values can be considered a kind of a hierarchy and in combination lead to the desired counter, the counter row. The hierarchy looks like this:

```
Application
    Counter Group
        Counter Name
            Page Url
                Counter Event
                    NavigateUrl
                        Start and End Time
```

The counter row is incremented with each new record. You can specify the number of counter rows that should be tracked each day to achieve more differentiated results. Figure 10-1 shows a cutout of the automatically generated database of the default provider for Access.

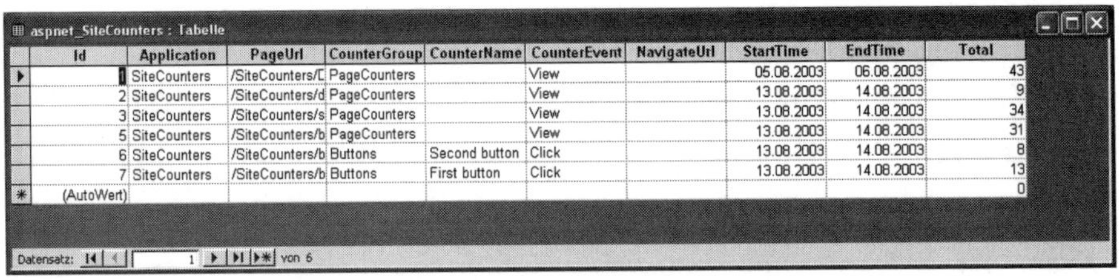

Figure 10-1. Site counters are tracked using counter rows.

Tracking Button Clicks

At present there are five button types to support the click recording via site counters: Button, LinkButton, and ImageButton, as well as the controls PhoneLink and ImageMap. The controls offer a uniform set of properties that are summarized in the Properties window in the category SiteCounters:

- CountClicks indicates whether or not site counters should be used for this control.

- CounterGroups defines the desired group.

- CounterName gives the name of the counter.

- RowsPerDay defines the number of counter rows per day. The default is −1, whereby the global setting from the machine.config file is used (one line per day).

- SiteCountersProvider allows you to specify an individual provider especially for the chosen control. Normally this property will *not* be assigned.

- TrackApplicationName indicates whether the name of the application should be saved.

- TrackPageUrl specifies whether the URL of the current page should be saved.

I've created a small example in Listing 10-1 with a Button and a LinkButton control to demonstrate the details. As you can see from the following listing, both controls log in to the same group, Buttons, but each uses a different counter name.

Listing 10-1. Automatically Logging Button Clicks to the Site Counter System

```
<%@ page language="C#" %>

<html>
<head runat="server">
    <title>Untitled Page</title>
</head>
<body>
    <form runat="server">
        <asp:button id="Button1" runat="server"
            text="Click me!"
            countergroup="Buttons"
            countclicks="True"
            countername="First button"
        />
        <br />
        <br />
        <asp:linkbutton id="LinkButton1" runat="server"
            countergroup="Buttons"
            countclicks="True"
            countername="Second button">
            Click me, too
        </asp:linkbutton>
    </form>
</body>
</html>
```

Each click on one of the buttons shown in Figure 10-2 will be logged automatically; nothing further is required from your side. This is also possible with the other counter-enabled controls mentioned previously.

Figure 10-2. Using site counters is quite easy.

Creating a Site Counter Report

A logging system without any kind of evaluation is useless. Unfortunately, there is no corresponding report tool being shipped with ASP.NET at present. However, the ASP.NET team plans to enhance the Web Application Administration Tool in this sense, probably in the Beta version. A corresponding register clip, "Reports," already exists, as you can see in Figure 10-3.

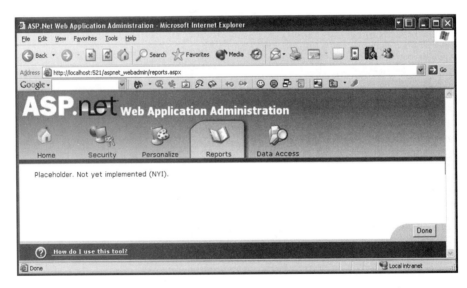

Figure 10-3. The Beta version will most likely ship with a reporting tool.

As long as there is no such reporting tool yet, you must make one yourself. I've created a very simple report page that lists all the saved counter rows of a group.

The page is based on the Site Counter API, which I cover later in this chapter. Figure 10-4 shows the page in action. Currently, the counter group Buttons from the last example is active.

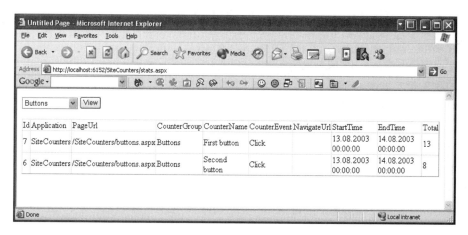

Figure 10-4. A simple reporting tool lists the button clicks.

Tracking Hyperlink Clicks

You may think that the site counter is limited to controls with server-side event treatment. This, however, is not the case, because the HyperLink control also allows you to measure clicks:

```
<asp:hyperlink id="HyperLink1" runat="server"
    countclicks="True"
    countergroup="HyperLinks"
    navigateurl="http://www.qualisite.de">
    Even HyperLinks are tracked
</asp:hyperlink>
```

The measurement is made possible with a particular URL that may in this example look like this:

```
http://localhost:6152/SiteCounters/counters.axd?d=046rKcoZNDzumM29BViU8ECjTGxIdA
    OKCJh5O5CXgYhXBGAwVujYRcKoU3FCE6vMr2iOF9uh4Bu2AiWQylV7fKrImlhidOUg-
    nwSIDAKZFtLIlGLsxK-*F*bxcADy8d2pdQrxrGfDBX7H8GsDYh351UJ-
    LOLZOUb2IY*7YSlVd*wOYbtab4NT7Wfzg7r7yfivhzag1so8oOGGaOmOOSHZ
    jPAhzi88dpjSHrxTPvBsBEiQQNZlwqlfq9qy1L4dGVxtXoWTQ*nvxw1
```

The URL is generated by the Site Counter API and refers to a special HttpHandler handler (System.Web.Handlers.SiteCountersHandler). The handler decrypts the data delivered as a query string, logs the click (including the source and destination address), and redirects to the actual destination.

Why such a long URL? Why isn't it sufficient to just pass an ID? Well, an ID would have to be stored in the application or in a database so that it still works, even after many months. In this URL, however, all information, such as source address, destination address, CounterGroup, and CounterName, is encrypted so that it can be used permanently without any additional dependency. Think of search engines and bookmarks in this context.

Tracking Ads

In combination with the AdRotator control that you may know from earlier versions, site counters make a lot of sense. The AdRotator control is different from the controls you've seen so far, as it can distinguish between the two counter events View and Click. You can activate tracking of these events independently by means of two properties.

The following cutout comes from the ASP.NET Internet Site template and is shipped with VS .NET. The logging of views and clicks was activated in the control. Additionally, a counter group was defined but not a counter name.

```
<asp:adrotator id="AdRotator2" runat="server"
    height="242px" width="122px" backcolor="#00C000"
    advertisementfile="advertisements\ads_tall.xml"
    countergroup="Ads"
    countclicks="True"
    countviews="True"
    trackapplicationname="true"
    tracknavigateurl="true"
    trackpageurl="true"
/>
```

You can define the counter name directly and differentiate it for each ad in the advertisement XML file. This way, you can clearly distinguish how often an advertisement has been shown and how many clicks it has received, as shown in the following code. Figure 10-5 shows the corresponding statistic.

```xml
<?xml version="1.0" encoding="utf-8" ?>
<Advertisements>
    <Ad>
        <ImageUrl>joesflowers.jpg</ImageUrl>
        <NavigateUrl>http://www.microsoft.com</NavigateUrl>
        <AlternateText>http://www.microsoft.net</AlternateText>
        <Keyword>Orange</Keyword>
        <Impressions>80</Impressions>
        <CounterName>Red Joe Flower</CounterName>
    </Ad>
    ...
</Advertisements>
```

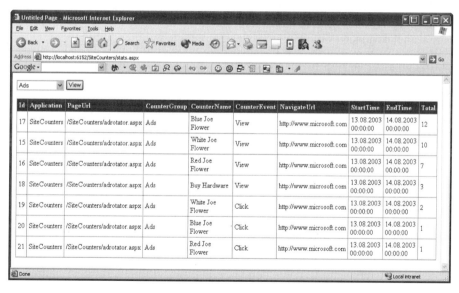

Figure 10-5. You can easily determine which ad is the most successful.

Using Page Counters

As I stated earlier, page counters are a subfeature of site counters. They allow you to log the request of pages within a web site. Because the expected data volume could be very high, page counters are deactivated by default and have to be activated first through the configuration file web.config:

```
<siteCounters
    enabled="true"
    ...
>
    <pageCounters
        enabled="true"
        rowsPerDay="1"
        trackApplicationName="true"
        trackPageUrl="true"
        counterGroup="PageCounters"
        counterName=""
    >
        <pagesToCount>
            <add path="*"/>
        </pagesToCount>
    </pageCounters>
</siteCounters>
```

Afterward, all the hits on a page are logged in the counter group PageCounters — namely one line per day and per page, as shown in Figure 10-6.

Alternatively, you can limit the logging to single pages or define certain areas with the help of wild cards:

```
    ...
    <pagesToCount>
        <clear />
        <add path="subdir/*.aspx"/>
    </pagesToCount>
</pageCounters>
</siteCounters>
```

Internally, by the way, page counters work with the System.Web.PageCountersModule module. This HTTP module logs the hits within an event handling of HttpApplication.EndRequest and passes them to the Site Counter API.

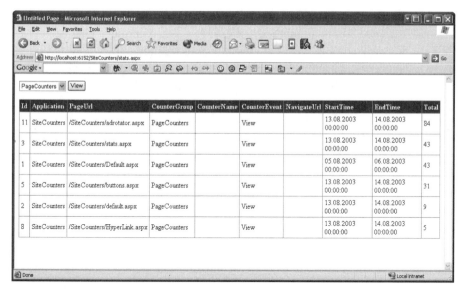

Figure 10-6. Page counters log every hit on every page of your web site.

> **NOTE** *Please be aware that only requests of files with the extension .aspx will be logged in the existing version. Web services or hits on files with an individual extension won't be part of the statistic.*

Introducing the Site Counter API

The Site Counter API consists of a single class, SiteCounters. You get the current instance across the homonymous property of the class HttpContext or from the local page, which is even easier. The class offers various methods that allow simplified access to three underlying methods:

- Flush signals the Site Counter Provider to take over the data from the cache and save it in the applied data store.

- GetRows allows read access on the saved data. The method redelivers a DataSet containing a single table.

- Write logs a new log entry and is used internally from various controls.

Nearly all the methods are overloaded several times and exist in different versions. With the GetGroupRows() method, for example, you can query all entries in a counter group with GetNameRows() for a specific counter name. Internally, however, GetRows() is used here as well. Just some of the parameters are passed over as null.

> **NOTE** *Please be aware that at this time the capability to query a listing of all counter groups or counter names isn't implemented. I hope this will be changed/enlarged in the Beta version.*

Creating a Reports Page

At the beginning of this chapter, I presented a simple page to query the statistical values to you. I have used it again and again in the various examples for the reporting. The page is based on the API and uses the FlushAll() method to acquire the statistical values that haven't been saved yet, and it uses the GetGroupRows() method to receive all the log values of the chosen group. As mentioned before, a listing of the latter can't be queried yet. Therefore, the groups are placed statically in the DropDownList control.

Listing 10-2. Accessing Reported Site Counter Data

```
<%@ page language="C#" %>

<script runat="server">

void BT_View_Click(object sender, System.EventArgs e)
{
    this.SiteCounters.FlushAll();
    this.GV_Rows.DataSource = this.SiteCounters.GetGroupRows(DateTime.MinValue,
        DateTime.MaxValue, this.DDL_Groups.SelectedValue);
    this.GV_Rows.DataBind();
}

</script>

<html>
<head runat="server">
    <title>Untitled Page</title>
</head>
<body>
    <form runat="server">
```

```
        <p>
            <asp:dropdownlist id="DDL_Groups" runat="server">
                <asp:listitem selected="True">Buttons</asp:listitem>
                <asp:listitem>HyperLinks</asp:listitem>
                <asp:listitem>Ads</asp:listitem>
                <asp:listitem>PageCounters</asp:listitem>
            </asp:dropdownlist>
            <asp:button id="BT_View" runat="server"
                text="View"
                onclick="BT_View_Click" />
        </p>
        <p>
            <asp:gridview id="GV_Rows" runat="server">
            </asp:gridview>
        </p>
    </form>
</body>
</html>
```

The two date parameters that are passed to the `GetGroupRows()` method are the start date and end date of the desired report. By indicating `MinValue` and `MaxValue`, you'll receive all the values. Otherwise, you may narrow down the delivered date block using the mentioned method.

Creating an Image Counter Control

The example in this section also demonstrates querying counter data. This time, however, it's in combination with page counters. You place the ImageCounter control shown in Listing 10-3 on each individual page to deliver a graphical hit counter for them.

Listing 10-3. Implementing a Graphical Page Counter

```
using System;
using System.Drawing;
using System.Drawing.Drawing2D;
using System.Web;
using System.Web.UI;
using System.Web.UI.WebControls;

[assembly:TagPrefix("PGK.Web.UI.WebControls.ImageCounter", "PGK")]

namespace PGK.Web.UI.WebControls.ImageCounter
{
    public class ImageCounter: CompositeControl
```

```
{
    protected DynamicImage dynamicImage;

    protected override void CreateChildControls()
    {
        this.dynamicImage = new DynamicImage();
        this.Controls.Add(this.dynamicImage);
    }

    protected override void OnPreRender(EventArgs e)
    {
        this.dynamicImage.Image = this.GenerateImage();
        base.OnPreRender(e);
    }

    protected virtual System.Drawing.Image GenerateImage()
    {
        int count = this.GetCounterValue();

        Bitmap bitmap = new Bitmap(100, 40);
        Graphics g = Graphics.FromImage(bitmap);
        g.Clear(Color.White);

        Font font = new Font("Tahoma", 20);
        g.DrawString(count.ToString(), font,
            new SolidBrush(Color.Black), new Point(0, 0));

        g.Flush();

        return bitmap;
    }

    protected virtual int GetCounterValue()
    {
        if (this.DesignMode == false)
        {
            SiteCounters counters = this.Page.SiteCounters;
            counters.FlushAll();
            return counters.GetTotalCount(DateTime.MinValue, DateTime.MaxValue,
                "PageCounters", null, null, null, null,
                this.Context.Request.Url.PathAndQuery);
        }
        else
        {
            return 123;
        }
    }
}
}
```

The ImageCounter control queries the overall counter value for the current URL with the GetTotalCount() method. This method of the SiteCounters class calls GetRows() internally and identifies the total number by simply adding the values delivered from the DataSet. The detected counter will be written with simple GDI+ routines into a bitmap and displayed by a DynamicImage control (the DynamicImage control is one of the novelties of ASP.NET 2.0 and is described in detail in the Chapter 11, which covers the enhanced Page Framework).

The implementation of the control is quite easy, as you'll see shortly. Figure 10-7 shows the result. The graphical details, however, aren't optimized yet.

```
<%@ page language="C#" %>
<%@ register namespace="PGK.Web.UI.WebControls.ImageCounter" tagprefix="PGK" %>

<html>
<head runat="server">
    <title>Untitled Page</title>
</head>
<body>
    <form runat="server"> Counter:<br />
        <pgk:ImageCounter runat="server" />
    </form>
</body>
</html>
```

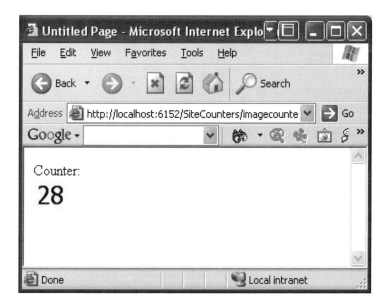

Figure 10-7. Here's my first ASP.NET 2.0 graphical counter (woo hoo!).

Using Site Counters with Custom Controls

If you've developed your own control and want to benefit from counters, I can recommend the implementation of a set of properties analogous to the standard buttons described in the beginning of this chapter. The real logging takes places with the SiteCounters.Write() method that was implemented with multiple overloads. In the easiest case, you deliver the counter group and counter name as well as the description of the event such as WClick or WView:

```
this.SiteCounters.Write(counterGroup, counterName, counterEvent);
```

Further overloads allow you, among other things, to deliver the address of destination and two Boolean parameters that define whether the current page and/or the name of the application should be recorded. By default, this information will be recorded.

Summary

I'm sure you've already implemented some kind of counting system in one or even several web projects. I actually did before. Site counters makes it easy now to add counting capabilities to a page, a button, or even a hyperlink. What I like most about the new feature is the way the developers in Redmond ensure a permanent use of tracked hyperlinks. All needed data is stored directly in the encrypted URL query string.

CHAPTER 11

The Enhanced Page Framework and Cool New Controls

IN THE EARLIER CHAPTERS you learned about some new features that will make your life as a developer much easier. Normally, however, you'll only discover many changes if you delve into the details. This chapter summarizes a couple of innovations that you probably haven't heard of yet or that I've just mentioned briefly in this book. A great deal of this chapter is devoted to new controls and the Page class.

Any New Controls Not Mentioned Yet?

Yep, there are some! As I mentioned in Chapter 1, there are more than 40 new controls in the new version of ASP.NET. I've already introduced most of them to you in the previous chapters—for example, the new Data Controls, the Security Controls, and the 11 controls used in the context of Web Parts. But there's more to discover. Let's go!

BulletedList

This control's name tells you what it's about—it renders a bulleted list. To do so, the common HTML tags (for example, <ul> and <li>) are used. In the easiest case, you assign the desired list items statically, as you already know from other data-bound controls such as DropDownList, ListBox, and so on:

```
<asp:bulletedlist id="BulletedList1" runat="server">
    <asp:listitem>First value</asp:listitem>
    <asp:listitem>Second value</asp:listitem>
    <asp:listitem>Third value</asp:listitem>
</asp:bulletedlist>
```

Many properties influence the design of the control. You can choose between different bullet characters or define your own image. It's also possible to create a numbered list and define its starting value:

```
<asp:bulletedlist id="BulletedList2" runat="server"
    bulletstyle="Numbered" firstbulletnumber="15">
    <asp:listitem>First value</asp:listitem>
    <asp:listitem>Second value</asp:listitem>
    <asp:listitem>Third value</asp:listitem>
</asp:bulletedlist>
```

The BulletedList control is a Data Control, so old and new concepts for data binding are fully supported. The following example shows the application of the control in combination with an XmlDataSource control that gets its content from the XML file `books.xml`:

```
<script runat="server">

void BulletedList3_Click(object sender,
    System.Web.UI.WebControls.BulletedListEventArgs e)
{
    ListItem item = this.BulletedList3.Items[e.Index];
    this.LB_SelectedBook.Text = string.Format("You selected '{0}'", item.Text);
}

</script>

...

<asp:bulletedlist id="BulletedList3" runat="server"
    datasourceid="XmlDataSource1"
    datatextfield="InnerText"
    bulletimageurl="arrow.gif"
    bulletstyle="CustomImage"
    displaymode="LinkButton"
    onclick="BulletedList3_Click"
/>
<asp:xmldatasource id="XmlDataSource1"
    runat="server" datafile="Books.xml"
    xpath="bookstore/genre/book/title">
</asp:xmldatasource>
<br />
<asp:label id="LB_SelectedBook" runat="server">
</asp:label>
```

In this example, the control displays the entries as LinkButton controls. If the user clicks one of the buttons, a central event is raised. In this case, the chosen book title is written to a Label control. Figure 11-1 shows the output of all three examples.

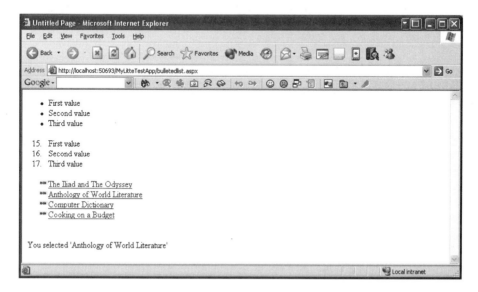

Figure 11-1. The new BulletedList control is very versatile.

DynamicImage

I've loved this new control since the day Scott Guthrie presented it at TechEd Europe. In the end it's not a big feature, but it's fun to dynamically create and deliver pictures this way. Naturally, this was already possible with earlier versions of ASP.NET. Up until now, however, you had to additionally create and register a separate handler. With version 2.0 this functionality comes right out of the box.

In the next sections, I discuss the practical uses of this control.

Scaling Existing Images

A simple and practical application is to use the DynamicImage control to adapt the size of a picture that already exists on your hard disk. To do so, you must pass the filename to the ImageFile property and assign the desired size of the output with Width and/or Height. The picture will be scaled dynamically and is sent to the browser in the desired format (the standard being JPEG).

```
<asp:dynamicimage id="DynamicImage1" runat="server"
    imagefile="paramount.gif"
    width="150px">
</asp:dynamicimage>
```

The picture shown in Figure 11-2 is delivered with a width of 150 pixels. The original one has a width of almost 300 pixels.

Figure 11-2. The DynamicImage control allows you to scale existing images.

In this context, the URL of the picture that was referenced in the browser is of interest. It refers to a special handler, CachedImageServiceHandler, of the System.Web.UI.Imaging namespace, to which an ID is passed. Internally, the picture is saved in the Cache of the HttpContext class in conjunction with the unique ID:

```
CachedImageService.axd?data=9a9a0768-a0ef-42d0-a895-3e87e41b5622
```

A nice example for an application is the generation of a thumbnail list. For this purpose, you can use the control with a data-bound DataList. The example in Listing 11-1 reads the names of all pictures out of the current directory and binds them to the DataList. Figure 11-3 shows the result.

Listing 11-1. A Thumbnail List

```
<%@ page language="C#" %>
<%@ import namespace="System.IO" %>

<script runat="server">

void Page_Load(object sender, System.EventArgs e)
{
    DirectoryInfo directory = new
        DirectoryInfo(Path.GetDirectoryName(this.Request.PhysicalPath));
    this.DL_Thumbnails.DataSource = directory.GetFiles("*.gif");
    this.DL_Thumbnails.DataBind();
}

</script>

<html>
<head runat="server">
    <title>Untitled Page</title>
</head>
<body>
    <form runat="server">
        <asp:datalist runat="server" id="DL_Thumbnails" repeatcolumns="2">
            <itemtemplate>
                <asp:dynamicimage runat="server"
                    imagefile='<%# Eval("Name") %>'
                    width="150px">
                </asp:dynamicimage>
            </itemtemplate>
        </asp:datalist>
    </form>
</body>
</html>
```

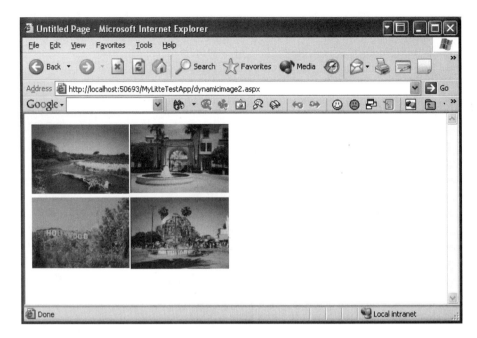

Figure 11-3. Creating a thumbnail list is fun now.

Passing Dynamically Created Images

You can use the DynamicImage control to display dynamically generated images. The example in Listing 11-2 shows the creation of a little smiley face with the help of the GDI+ classes from the System.Drawing namespace, and Figure 11-4 shows the result.

Listing 11-2. "Don't Worry, Be Happy!" (Thanks to the GDI+ Smiley Face)

```
<%@ page language="C#" %>
<%@ import namespace="System.Drawing" %>

<script runat="server">

void Page_Load(object sender, System.EventArgs e)
{
    this.DI_Image.Image = this.CreateImage();
}

private Bitmap CreateImage() {
    Bitmap b = new Bitmap(200, 200);
    Graphics g = Graphics.FromImage(b);
```

```
        g.Clear(Color.White);

        Pen pen = new Pen(Color.Red);
        pen.Width = 3;

        g.DrawEllipse(pen, 2, 2, 196, 196);

        Point[] points = {new Point(40, 140), new Point(100, 170),
            new Point(160, 140)};
        g.DrawCurve(pen, points);

        g.DrawLine(pen, 100, 70, 100, 130);

        Brush brush = new SolidBrush(Color.Black);
        g.FillEllipse(brush, 50, 60, 20, 20);
        g.FillEllipse(brush, 130, 60, 20, 20);

        g.Flush();
        return b;
}

</script>

<html>
<head runat="server">
    <title>Untitled Page</title>
</head>
<body>
    <form runat="server">
        This picture was created dynamically:<br /><br />
        <asp:dynamicimage id="DI_Image" runat="server" imagetype="Gif"/>
    </form>
</body>
</html>
```

In this example, the created picture is assigned to the `DynamicImage.Image` property. Alternatively, you might deliver a byte array to `ImageBytes`. This is particularly useful if you read the data out of a database, for example. Please be aware that you may only use *one* of the following properties: `ImageBytes`, `Image`, or `ImageFile`.

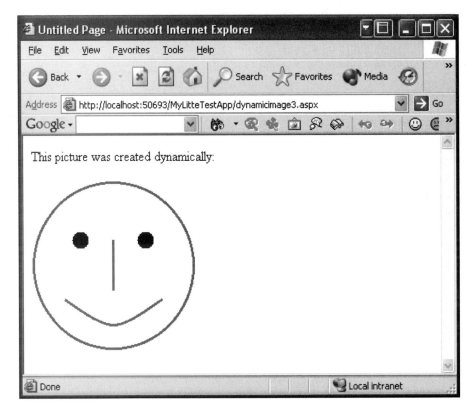

Figure 11-4. Say cheese!

> **TIP** *You'll find another example for a similar application of the DynamicImage control in Chapter 10. In that chapter, a DynamicImage control is used for the output of a page counter.*

Using an Image Generator Service

One more field of application of the control is the implementation of an Image Generator. This is a new file type with the extension `.asix`. The source code file contains a class that inherits from the abstract base `ImageGenerator` and acts as an `HttpHandler`. Within the abstract method `RenderImage()`, you can draw your image with the help of GDI+ into an instance of the `Graphics` class, which is passed as parameter.

Listing 11-3, which has the filename circlegenerator.asix, is based on source code from the official documentation. It draws a couple of randomized ellipses into the passed Graphics object.

Listing 11-3. The Image Generator Outputs a Couple Ellipses

```
<%@ Image class="CircleGenerator" Language="C#" %>

using System;
using System.Drawing;
using System.Drawing.Drawing2D;
using System.Drawing.Imaging;
using System.Web.UI.Imaging;

public class CircleGenerator : ImageGenerator
{
    protected override void RenderImage(Graphics g)
    {
        int width = (int)Style.Width.Value;
        int height = (int)Style.Height.Value;
        int w = Math.Max(DefaultWidth, width);
        int h = Math.Max(DefaultHeight, height);

        g.FillRectangle(Brushes.White, g.ClipBounds);

        int numberOfCircles = 1;

        if (Parameters["NumberOfCircles"] != null)
        {
            numberOfCircles = Int32.Parse(
                Parameters["NumberOfCircles"].ToString());
        }

        g.SmoothingMode = SmoothingMode.AntiAlias;
        Random random = new Random();

        for (int i = 0; i < numberOfCircles; i++)
        {
            int x = random.Next(w);
            int y = random.Next(h);
            int circleWidth = random.Next(w/2);
            int circleHeight = random.Next(h/2);
            int penWidth = random.Next(5);
```

```
        Color c = Color.FromArgb(random.Next(255), random.Next(255),
                            random.Next(255));
        g.DrawEllipse(new Pen(c,penWidth),x,y,circleWidth,circleHeight);
    }
  }
}
```

You reference the newly created Image Generator by using the
ImageGeneratorUrl property of the DynamicImage class, as shown in Listing 11-4.
The ability to pass values has been implemented in a very clever way.
ParameterCollection, which you already know from the DataSource controls,
serves as the basis. It can get its data from completely different sources, such as
cookies, sessions, query strings, and controls. The number of ellipses to be generated is managed by ControlParameter, which queries the value from a TextBox
control. Figure 11-5 shows the generated ellipses.

Listing 11-4. Using an Image Generator with the DynamicImage Control

```
<%@ page language="C#"%>

<html>
    <body>
        <form id="Form1" runat="server">
            <table>
                <tr>
                    <td valign="top">
                        Number of circles:<br />
                        <asp:textbox id="CircleCount" runat="server" text="15" />
                        <br />
                        <asp:button id="CreateImage" runat="server"
                            text="Create Image" />
                    </td>
                    <td>
                        <asp:dynamicimage id="Dynamicimage1" runat="server"
                            dynamicimagetype="ImageGenerator"
                            imagegeneratorurl="CircleGenerator.asix"
                            alternatetext="Generated image of circles."
                            height="400px" width="300px">
                            <parameters>
                                <asp:controlparameter
                                    name="NumberOfCircles"
                                    propertyname="Text"
                                    controlid="CircleCount">
```

```
                    </asp:controlparameter>
                </parameters>
            </asp:dynamicimage>
        </td>
    </tr>
</table>
</form>
</body>
</html>
```

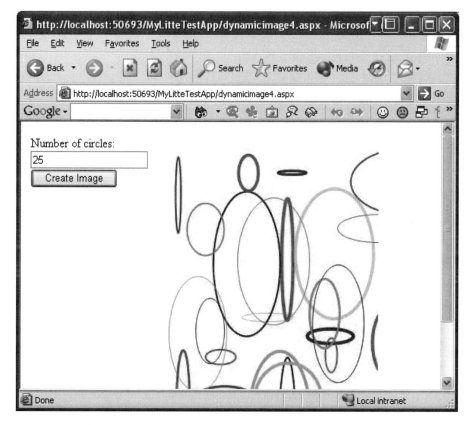

Figure 11-5. Custom Image Generators can use parameters.

ImageMap

A second new control from the field of graphics is called ImageMap. You can use this control to provide a picture with clickable hot spots that either act as regular links or initiate a postback. At present, you can define hot spots as circles, rectangles, or polygons. You can implement further types of hot spots if necessary by deriving from the synonymous abstract base class.

In Listing 11-5, the archway of the Paramount Studios is displayed in the browser. Various elements of the picture have been provided with hot spots. Clicking one of these hot spots will result in a postback and then display the description of the clicked zone through a Label control. Figure 11-6 shows the result.

Listing 11-5. Defining Hot Spots with the ImageMap Control

```
<%@ page language="C#" %>

<script runat="server">
void ImageMap1_Click(object sender,
    System.Web.UI.WebControls.ImageMapEventArgs e)
{
    this.LB_Message.Text = string.Format("You clicked the {0}.", e.Value);
}

</script>

<html>
<head runat="server">
    <title>Untitled Page</title>
</head>
<body>
    <form runat="server">
        <asp:imagemap id="ImageMap1" runat="server"
            imageurl="paramount.gif"
            onclick="ImageMap1_Click"
            hotspots-count="5"
            hotspotmode="PostBack">
            <asp:rectanglehotspot top="43" right="189"
                bottom="141" left="101" value="gate">
            </asp:rectanglehotspot>
            <asp:polygonhotspot coordinates="18,149,106,122,192,155,98,190"
                value="fountain">
            </asp:polygonhotspot>
            <asp:circlehotspot radius="30" x="273" y="92" value="tree">
```

```
                </asp:circlehotspot>
                <asp:rectanglehotspot right="295" bottom="145" left="190"
                    value="right building">
                </asp:rectanglehotspot>
                <asp:rectanglehotspot top="52" right="94" bottom="130"
                    value="left building">
                </asp:rectanglehotspot>
            </asp:imagemap>
            <br />
            <asp:label id="LB_Message" runat="server" font-size="20pt">
            </asp:label>
        </form>
    </body>
</html>
```

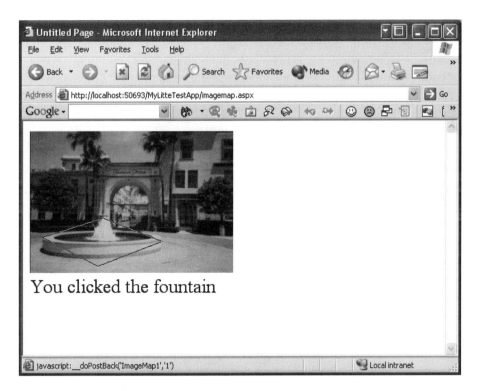

Figure 11-6. Welcome to Hollywood!

MultiView and View

In previous versions of ASP.NET, the Panel control was used quite often to switch different views of a single page—for example, for an entry form and the acknowledgement message if it has been handled successfully. Therefore, one panel was deactivated and the other one activated.

In cases like this, .NET version 2.0 offers two controls: MultiView and View. View can be compared with Panel, but it doesn't offer formatting. MultiView is the container for several View elements, and it takes care that only one of them is shown at a time. View controls are directly defined within the MultiView control and are placed visually there. The support in the development environment, however, isn't ideal yet. You can define the View control to be shown initially through the ActiveViewIndex property and you can change the View control programmatically with the ActiveViewIndex property's help or by means of the SetActiveView() method. Listing 11-6 demonstrates this with a simple input form including a confirmation message, and Figure 11-7 shows the result.

Listing 11-6. Switching Views of a Page with the MultiView and View Controls

```
<%@ page language="C#" %>

<script runat="server">
void Button1_Click(object sender, System.EventArgs e)
{
    this.LB_Name.Text = this.TB_Name.Text;
    this.MultiView1.ActiveViewIndex = 1;
}

</script>

<html>
<head runat="server">
    <title>Untitled Page</title>
</head>
<body>
    <form runat="server">
        <asp:multiview id="MultiView1" runat="server" activeviewindex="0">
            <asp:view id="View1" runat="server">
                Please enter your name:
                <br />
                <br />
                <asp:textbox id="TB_Name" runat="server">
```

```
            </asp:textbox>
            <asp:button id="Button1" runat="server" text="OK"
                onclick="Button1_Click" />
        </asp:view>
        <asp:view id="View2" runat="server">
            Your name is
            <asp:label id="LB_Name" runat="server">Label</asp:label>
        </asp:view>
    </asp:multiview> 

    </form>
</body>
</html>
```

Figure 11-7. You can use the MultiView and View controls to switch the interface.

If desired, you can leave it up to the control to choose the active view independently on basis of a query string variable. To do so, you must define the name of the variable through the QueryStringParam property and deliver the ID of the view to be shown in the query string.

> **NOTE** *The MultiView and View controls are ideal to use in combination with mobile devices. The two controls replace the MobileForm control, which was used in versions 1.0 and 1.1. Generally, usage of the Wizard control I describe in the next section is recommended for "regular" web sites.*

Wizard

In many scenarios for regular web sites, usage of the Wizard control may be preferred over the combination of MultiView and View controls. The Wizard control offers the possibility to automatically switch between views out of the box. Even the design support within the VS .NET environment is much better because the control fully integrates itself into the template concepts.

Listing 11-7 basically corresponds to Listing 11-6 for MultiView and View. In the first step of the Wizard control, the user's name has to be specified, and in the second step, the entered text will be displayed again.

Listing 11-7. Creating a Dialog Assistant Page with the Wizard Control

```
<%@ page language="C#" %>

<script runat="server">

void Wizard1_ActiveViewChanged(object sender, System.EventArgs e)
{
    this.LB_Name.Text = this.TB_Name.Text;
}

</script>

<html>
<head runat="server">
    <title>Untitled Page</title>
</head>
<body>
    <form runat="server">
        <asp:wizard id="Wizard1" runat="server"
            sidebarenabled="True"
            headertext="My Simple Wizard"
            activestepindex="0"
            width="100%"
            onactiveviewchanged="Wizard1_ActiveViewChanged">
            <headerstyle forecolor="White" backcolor="Blue"
                font-names="Verdana" font-size="15pt"
                font-bold="True">
            </headerstyle>
            <wizardsteps>
                <asp:wizardstep runat="server" title="Step 1">
                    Hello!<br />
```

```
            <br />
            Please enter your name:
            <asp:textbox runat="server" id="TB_Name">
            </asp:textbox>
            <br />
        </asp:wizardstep>
        <asp:wizardstep runat="server" title="Step 2">
            Thanks,<br />
            <br />
            your name is
            <asp:label runat="server" id="LB_Name">
            </asp:label>
        </asp:wizardstep>
    </wizardsteps>
  </asp:wizard>
 </form>
</body>
</html>
```

The possibilities of this control are far reaching. You can, for example, create the single steps through a Collection Editor and specify which task should be executed in each single step in a differentiated way—for example, Start, Step, or Finish. If you leave the value Auto unchanged, the control will define the sequence by itself.

As you can see in Figure 11-8, the control doesn't only show the current step but also takes cares of the headline and the buttons to move forward or backward. Furthermore, if you like you can display a SideBar, which allows the user to directly access each step through a link. All elements can either be taken over as default and adapted through styles or formatted individually with templates. In any case, events such as ActiveViewChanged, FinishButtonClicked, NextButtonClicked, PreviousButtonClicked, and SideBarButtonClicked enable you to interfere with the flow of the control.

Figure 11-8. The new Wizard control allows you to create easy-to-use wizard steps.

CAUTION *The only disadvantage with the Wizard control at present involves switching between single steps when you're working with VS .NET. At present, you have to temporarily change the* ActiveStepIndex *property if you want to work another view at a time. Hopefully this will change in the Beta version.*

Panel

The Panel control has been around for quite a while, and you surely have taken advantage of it now and then. In the future, it may become even more useful to you, because the new version of ASP.NET supports scrollbars (horizontally aligned, vertically aligned, or aligned in both directions).

Listing 11-8 shows the application of scrollbars. You must assign a size to the Panel control and activate scrolling. As you can see in Figure 11-9, the control takes care of the rest. Internally a HTML <div> tag with corresponding style sheets is used.

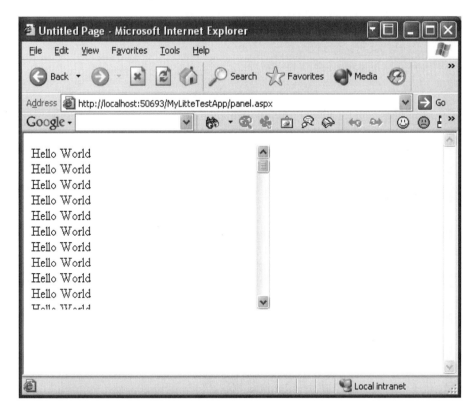

Figure 11-9. The Panel control now supports scrolling.

Listing 11-8. Scrolling with the Enhanced Panel Control

```
<%@ page language="C#" %>

<script runat="server">

void Page_Load(object sender, System.EventArgs e)
{
    StringBuilder sb = new StringBuilder();
    for (int i = 0; i < 100; i++)
    {
        sb.AppendLine("Hello World<br/>");
    }
    this.Panel1.Controls.Add(new LiteralControl(sb.ToString()));
}

</script>
```

```
<html>
<head runat="server">
    <title>Untitled Page</title>
</head>
<body>
    <form runat="server">
        <asp:panel id="Panel1" runat="server"
            width="300px" height="200px" scrollbars="Vertical">
        </asp:panel>

    </form>
</body>
</html>
```

Pager

Similar to the MultiView and View controls described previously, the Pager control is mainly used for mobile devices. I therefore describe it in detail in Chapter 12. You can use the Pager control to display (page by page) content placed in a control—for example, in the previously explained Panel control. Listing 11-9 shows the control's use.

Listing 11-9. Paging Content with the Pager Control

```
<%@ page language="C#" %>

<script runat="server">

void Page_Load(object sender, System.EventArgs e)
{
    for (int i = 0; i < 100; i++)
    {
        this.Panel1.Controls.Add(
            new LiteralControl(string.Format("Hello world ({0})<br/>", i + 1)));
    }
}

</script>

<html>
  <head>
  </head>
  <body>
    <form id="Form1" runat="server">

      <h3>Pager Class Example</h3>
```

```
        <asp:pager id="Pager1"
            controltopaginate="Panel1"
            runat="server" itemsperpage="10">
        </asp:pager>

        <asp:panel id="Panel1" runat="Server" />

    </form>
  </body>
</html>
```

In Listing 11-9, 100 instances of the class LiteralControl are added to a Panel control dynamically. The Pager control is used to display the subcontrols in blocks of ten elements each. This is possible because the Panel control supports the IPaginationInfo and IPaginationContainer interfaces. Beside the Panel control, the Pager control can also apply to Web Parts that inherit from the Panel control. Furthermore, the Page and HtmlForm classes support the interfaces.

The primary field of application of the Pager control, in my opinion, is in mobile devices. There you need to show a lot of content on a small display. The Pager's display can be adapted in detail to fulfill this purpose. But, of course, you could also use the control in "regular" web sites; for example, you could use it to list thumbnails on a page, as shown in Figure 11-10.

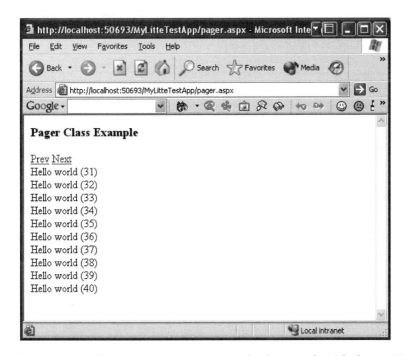

Figure 11-10. You can page content in multiple controls with the new Pager control.

FileUpload

With ASP.NET, uploading files has never been a problem. The corresponding control, however, was only available as a server-side HTML control. With the new version of ASP.NET, the ASP.NET team gives developers a "real" FileUpload web control, as shown in Listing 11-10 and Figure 11-11.

Listing 11-10. Uploading Files Is Now Supported by a "Real" Web Control

```
<%@ page language="C#" %>

<script runat="server">

void BT_Upload_Click(object sender, System.EventArgs e)
{
    if ((this.FU_Upload.PostedFile != null) &&
        (this.FU_Upload.PostedFile.ContentLength > 0))
    {
        this.LB_Message.Text = "Thanks!";
    }
    else
    {
        this.LB_Message.Text = "No file or empty file!";
    }
}

</script>

<html>
<head runat="server">
    <title>Untitled Page</title>
</head>
<body>
    <form runat="server">
        <asp:fileupload id="FU_Upload" runat="server" />
        <asp:button id="BT_Upload" runat="server"
                text="Upload" onclick="BT_Upload_Click" />
        <br />
        <br />
        <asp:label id="LB_Message" runat="server">
        </asp:label>

    </form>
</body>
</html>
```

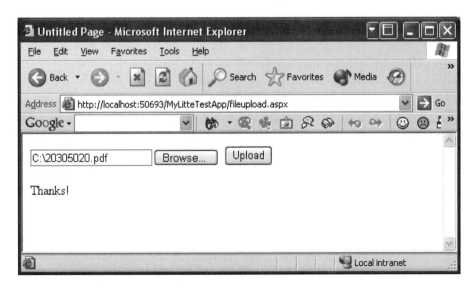

Figure 11-11. File upload is now controllable through the Web.

> **TIP** *The new FileUpload control has one important advantage: It automatically takes care of the correct setting of the* enctype *(encoding) attribute provided by the server-side* <form> *tag. This means no more annoying errors because of forgotten appendixes!*

HiddenField

The new HiddenField control does exactly what you would expect: It allows the use of a hidden field in the HTML source code of the page. This control is particularly helpful if you create it dynamically. Listing 11-11 shows the use of the HiddenField control.

Listing 11-11. The HiddenField Control

```
<asp:hiddenfield
    id="MyHiddenField"
    runat="server"
    value="Testvalue"
/>
```

Substitution

Internally, the new Substitution control is used in conjunction with output caching to allow dynamic content even with cached data. Perhaps the Beta version will include some practical "real world" example for its application too.

The only property assigned to this control is the name of a method. This method must correspond with a certain delegate (`HttpResponseSubstitutionCallback`) and it must be implemented statically within the local `Page` class. The method receives the current `Context` object as parameter and will be accessed within the `Render()` method of the control. This way, the returned string is printed out exactly at the position at which the control has been placed on the page. Listing 11-12 and Figure 11-12 show the use of this control.

Listing 11-12. Using the PlaceHolder to Output Text

```
<%@ page language="C#" %>

<script runat="server">

private static string MySubstitutionCallback(HttpContext context)
{
    return "Hello World";
}

</script>

<html>
<head id="Head1" runat="server">
    <title>Untitled Page</title>
</head>
<body>
    <form id="Form1" runat="server">
        Some text goes here.
        <br />
        <br />
        <asp:substitution id="Substitution1" runat="server"
            methodname="MySubstitutionCallback"
        />
        <br />
        <br />
        Some other text goes here.
    </form>
</body>
</html>
```

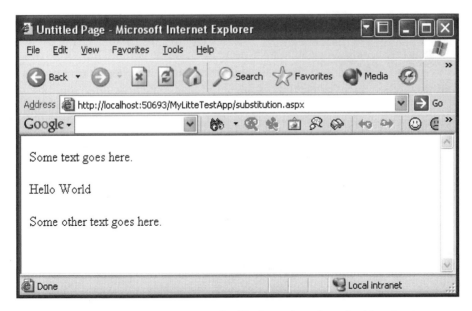

Figure 11-12. The Substitution control calls the assigned method just in time.

TextBox

The TextBox control is not new, of course. You know it already and you've surely used it many times. There is a small, but very nice, improvement for the input field. You can now use the AutoCompleteType property to define which VCard entry is used to automatically fill in the field. Internally, the vcard_name HTML attribute is used. If you don't want to use this feature, you can switch it off for the whole form. To do so, you must switch the AutoComplete property (see Listing 11-13) of the server-side form to "off."

Listing 11-13. The TextBox Control with Autocompletion Fields

```
<%@ page language="C#" %>

<html>
<head runat="server">
    <title>Untitled Page</title>
</head>
<body>
    <form runat="server" autocomplete="on">
        Email:
            <asp:textbox id="Textbox1" runat="server" autocompletetype="Email" />
    </form>
</body>
</html>
```

Control State

You already know about View State from previous versions of ASP.NET. What's new in this version is Control State. Here, I'm talking about data storage that's kept persistent in a hidden form field within the page:

```
<input type="hidden" name="__VIEWSTATE" value=" -- lots of data goes here -- " />
<input type="hidden" name="__CONTROLSTATE"
    value="/wEXAwUSRGVOYWlsc1ZpZXcxJF9jdGwwEGQC/////w9mBQlHcml
    kVmlldzEUKgAGZGRkZmRkBQ9HcmlkVmlldzEkX2NObDAQZAL/////D2Ysgb
    9McYV7cTOrIct23v91bs97qw==" />
```

The new Control State stores data of imminent importance for the control's use. If you deactivated the View State in version 1.0 or 1.*x*, you could use the former DataGrid control, for example, in a very limited way. This is no longer a problem with the new Control State, because very important information is stored in any case within Control State, while View State takes "only" less important information. What data is stored in what state system varies from control to control.

You can use Control State in your own controls, of course. For that purpose, you must register it first while you handle the OnInit event:

```
this.Page.RegisterRequiresControlState(this)
```

In addition, you must overwrite the LoadControlState and SaveControlState methods to store and retrieve the desired data.

Anything New for Validation Controls?

There is really no big news regarding validation controls, but there are two really useful small items of interest.

First, you can define several validation groups on one page to allow the validation of several independent forms, for example. To define a group, you have to set the ValidationGroup property of all participating controls (input fields, validation controls, and buttons) to an identical unique value—for example, "ContactForm." Everything else is done by the Framework, on the client side as well as on the server side. The second feature is a nice goodie that ensures that the first invalid input field automatically gets the focus.

Both features are included in Listing 11-14. Two identical forms are placed here on a single page. Both are validated independently according to which button is clicked. Figure 11-13 shows the output.

Listing 11-14. Using Validation Groups to Create Several "Virtual" Forms

```
<%@ page language="C#" %>

<script runat="server">

</script>

<html>
<head runat="server">
    <title>Untitled Page</title>
</head>
<body>
    <form runat="server">
        <h1>First form</h1>
        <p>
            <asp:textbox id="TextBox1" runat="server" validationgroup="firstform">
            </asp:textbox>
            <asp:requiredfieldvalidator id="RequiredFieldValidator1"
                runat="server" display="Dynamic"
                setfocusonerror="True"
                validationgroup="firstform"
                controltovalidate="TextBox1">***</asp:requiredfieldvalidator>
            <br />
            <br />
            <asp:button id="Button1" runat="server"
                validationgroup="firstform" text="Submit" />
        </p>


        <h1>Second form</h1>
        <p>
            <asp:textbox id="TextBox2" runat="server" validationgroup="secondform">
            </asp:textbox>
            <asp:requiredfieldvalidator id="RequiredFieldValidator2" runat="server"
                display="Dynamic"
                setfocusonerror="True"
                    validationgroup="secondform"
                    controltovalidate="TextBox2">***</asp:requiredfieldvalidator>
            <br />
            <br />
            <asp:button id="Button2" runat="server"
                validationgroup="secondform"
```

```
                    text="Submit" />
        </p>

    </form>
</body>
</html>
```

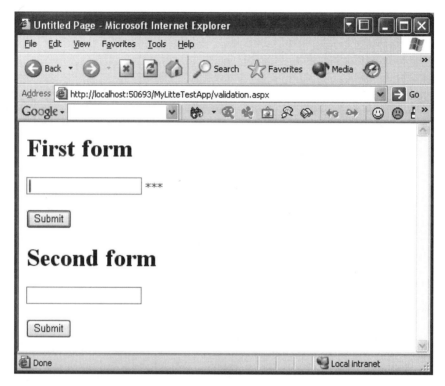

Figure 11-13. Validation groups are definitely a missing feature of version 1.0.

What's New to the Page Framework?

Again, only some small changes were made for the Page Framework. Nevertheless, it's worth a closer look at the Framework surrounding the class Page class.

New Page Events

The Page class offers some new events that allow you even more interaction with the page's life cycle:

- PreInit is raised before the initialization of the page. At this time, you may, for example, still define the desired Theme.

- InitComplete is raised after the initialization is finished.

- PreLoad is raised before the loading of the page.

- LoadComplete follows the loading of the page.

- PreRenderComplete is raised as soon as the PreRender event is completely handled. Here, for the last time you have the chance to make changes on the page before it's rendered.

Adding Headers

With the help of the new Header property of the Page class, you can make changes to the HTML head area in a very convenient way. The property holds an object that supports the IPageHeader interface. This way you can attach external style sheets, include style sheets, directly and define metadata. The latter happens as follows:

```
<script runat="server">

void Page_Load(object sender, System.EventArgs e)
{
    this.Header.Metadata.Add("author", "Patrick A. Lorenz");
}

</script>
```

In the HTML source code delivered to the browser, it will look as follows:

```
<html>
<head>
    <title>Untitled Page</title>
    <meta name="author" content="Patrick A. Lorenz" />
</head>
```

Setting Control Focus

The new possibility to set the cursor focus on an input control is very convenient. Validation controls make use of them as described previously. To do this, the abstract Control class implements a Focus method. Support for this method depends upon the control that is used. If you want to assign the focus to a text field, for example, you use the following command:

```
this.Textbox1.Focus();
```

Alternatively, you can set the focus through the Page class. Here as well, a post-back to the server will be done.

```
this.SetFocus(this.Textbox1);
```

You may additionally determine the initial focus by defining the defaultfocus attribute of the server-side HTML <form> tag:

```
<form runat="server" defaultfocus="TextBox2">
```

Defining a Default Button

The missing possibility to set a standard button is a real deficit in previous versions of ASP.NET. In version 2.0, you may now very easily define if a button will be activated and then specify which button will be activated when a user presses the Enter key in a form.

The selection of the default button works in a similar way as setting the default focus through the `defaultbutton` attribute of the server-side HTML `<form>` tag:

```
<%@ page language="C#" %>

<script runat="server">

void Button1_Click(object sender, System.EventArgs e)
{
    this.LB_Message.Text = "You clicked button1";
}

</script>

<html>
<head runat="server">
    <title>Untitled Page</title>
</head>
<body>
    <form runat="server" defaultbutton="Button1">
        <asp:textbox id="Textbox1" runat="server">
        </asp:textbox>
        <asp:button id="Button1" runat="server"
            text="Button" onclick="Button1_Click" />
        <asp:label id="LB_Message" runat="server"></asp:label>
    </form>
</body>
</html>
```

> **NOTE** *This implementation of the default button is made in a way that could be refitted easily on the former ASP.NET versions. Unfortunately, form groups aren't considered, for example, in a similar way as validation groups. This feature will probably be reworked in the Beta version.*

Accessing Validation Controls

While I'm covering validation groups, I should mention that the Page.Validators property returns a collection of all validation controls on page up to now. If you only need the controls assigned to a certain validation group, you should use the new method Page.GetValidators() instead and pass the name of the desired group.

The New Page.Items Dictionary

If you want to exchange data within a page, you can use the new dictionary offered by the Page.Items property. You can add any object to the dictionary during the life cycle of the page and access it anytime, for example, within user controls or custom controls.

One control that already uses this new possibility is WebPartManager, which I presented to you in Chapter 8. This control stores a reference for itself in the dictionary and is this way accessible for all the Web Parts on the page.

> **CAUTION** *Please be aware that the content of the dictionary* can't *be kept persistent between postbacks, but it has to be created anew on every request (comparable to* Context.Items*).*

Using Cross-Page Posting

You could have used the Server.Transfer method in previous versions of ASP.NET to switch from one page to another on the server side. The new version allows you to make a real cross-page posting so that you can post from one page to another within the current web site. This can be useful, for example, if you want to explicitly share a form or its processing on several pages.

If you want to post to another page, you must assign the desired URL to the PostTargetUrl property, which is presently being supported by the three controls: Button, LinkButton, and ImageButton. A small JavaScript function takes care that the target address of the form will be changed accordingly on the client. This functionality is used in Listing 11-15 by button1.

Listing 11-15. Posting the Form to a Different Page with the Button

```
<%@ page language="C#" %>

<script runat="server">

void Button2_Click(object sender, System.EventArgs e)
{
    Label1.Text = "Hi " + TextBox1.Text + " you selected: " +
        Calendar1.SelectedDate;
}

</script>

<html>
<body>
    <form id="Form1" runat="server">
        Enter Name:
        <asp:textbox id="TextBox1" runat="server"></asp:textbox>
        <asp:button id="Button1" runat="server"
            text="Postback to Another Page"
            posttargeturl="~/crosspost2.aspx" />
        <br /><br />
        Pick Date:
        <br /><br />
        <asp:calendar id="Calendar1" runat="server">
        </asp:calendar>
        <br /><br />
        <asp:button id="Button2" runat="server"
            text="Postback to Same Page"
            onclick="Button2_Click" />
        <br /><br />
        <asp:label id="Label1" runat="server" font-size="Large">
        </asp:label>
        <br /><br />
    </form>
</body>
</html>
```

The button refers to a second page with the filename crosspost2.aspx. Inside this second page, the previous page is accessible through the PreviousPage property. You can, for example, access the contained controls with the help of the FindControl() method and reuse their content in the second page. As shown in Figure 11-14 and Listing 11-16, this is used to display the entered name and the selected date of the first page.

Figure 11-14. You can now post to different target pages.

Listing 11-16. Accessing the Previous Page with the Cross-Post Destination Page

```csharp
<%@ page language="C#" %>

<script runat="server">

void Page_Load(object sender, System.EventArgs e)
{
    TextBox textBox1 = (TextBox) PreviousPage.FindControl("TextBox1");
    Calendar calendar1 = (Calendar) PreviousPage.FindControl("Calendar1");
    this.Label1.Text = string.Format("Hi {0} you selected {1}",
        textBox1.Text, calendar1.SelectedDate);
}

</script>

<html>
<body>
    <form id="Form1" runat="server">
        <asp:label id="Label1" runat="server" font-size="X-Large"></asp:label>
    </form>
</body>
</html>
```

As long as you already know the original page on the target page, you can reference it through the use of the new directive @PreviousPage. You can either enter the page's virtual path or its type name. This way, you get type-safe access to the previous page so that you can exchange data by using properties:

```csharp
<%@ page language="C#" %>

<script runat="server">

public string Text
{
    get { return this.TextBox1.Text; }
}

public DateTime SelectedDate
{
    get { return this.Calendar1.SelectedDate; }
}

</script>
```

You can access the properties on the target page directly through the PreviousPage property:

```
<%@ page language="C#" %>
<%@ previouspage virtualpath="crosspost3.aspx" %>

<script runat="server">

void Page_Load(object sender, System.EventArgs e)
{
    if (this.IsCrossPagePostBack)
    {
        this.Label1.Text = string.Format("Hi {0} you selected {1}",
            this.PreviousPage.Text, this.PreviousPage.SelectedDate);
    }
}

</script>
```

As you can see from the previous listing, you can use the IsCrossPagePostBack property to find out if the page has been accessed using a cross-page postback or not. Outside of the Page class, by the way, you get access to the current or previous pages through the Context.CurrentHandler and the Context.PreviousHandler properties.

> **CAUTION** *Please be aware that at present cross-page posting is only possible between two pages of the same web site. You can't define external addresses. This limitation will presumably be gone in the Beta version.*

Setting Properties in the @Page Directive

With the new version of ASP.NET, the @Page directive got a reasonable enhancement. You can not only assign its attributes, but also any properties of the Page class or of an inherited class.

You can use the new capability, for example, to assign an individual title to a page. I've already presented some possible solutions for this frequently asked feature in Chapters 4 and 5. The following example goes one step further and allows you to set the title through the @Page directive.

The example in Listing 11-17 consists of three files:

- The TitledPage base class, which derives from Page and implements a single property, Title.

- The masterpage5.aspx Master Page, which requests the chosen title through the TitledPage class and assigns it to a Literal control.

- The contentpage5.aspx Content Page, which allows the assignment of an individual title without any source code just by using the @Page directive.

Listing 11-17. @Page allows setting of any page properties.

```
// Code/ TitledPage.cs
using System;

public class TitledPage : System.Web.UI.Page
{
    private string title;

    public string Title
    {
        get { return this.title; }
        set { this.title = value; }
    }
}


// masterpage5.master
<%@ master language="C#" %>

<script runat="server">

void Page_PreRender(object sender, System.EventArgs e)
{
    this.LT_HtmlTitle.Text = ((TitledPage)this.Page).Title;
}

</script>

<html>
<head runat="server">
    <title><ASP:Literal id="LT_HtmlTitle" runat="server" /></title>
```

```
</head>
<body>
    <form runat="server">
        <asp:contentplaceholder id="ContentPlaceHolder1" runat="server">
        </asp:contentplaceholder>
    </form>
</body>
</html>

// contentpage5.aspx
<%@ page language="C#"
    master="~/MasterPage5.master"
    inherits="TitledPage"
    Title="Hello World!" %>

<script runat="server" language="c#">

</script>
<asp:content id="Content1"
    contentplaceholderid="ContentPlaceHolder1"
    runat="server">
    Just a simple content page
</asp:content>
```

The title was used properly, as you can see in Figure 11-15. If you want to use this approach for your own web site, you can assign the new page TitledPage base class for the whole site through the configuration file web.config. This way, you don't have to assign it on each single page.

Figure 11-15. The page's title is set using the @Page directive.

> **TIP** *Setting properties works not only with the* @Page *directive, but also with the* @Control *directive and even the new* @Master *directive in Master Pages.*

Adding Default Namespaces

As in the previous versions of ASP.NET, a couple of frequently used namespaces are imported on all pages by default. This way, you can use classes from, for example, System.Web, System.UI, System.Web.UI.WebControls, and so on directly. Importing additional namespaces is possible as before through the @Import directive.

Additionally, the new version gives you the chance to enlarge the listing of default namespaces. Just add the desired namespaces to the corresponding section in the configuration file, web.config, as follows. The import will be considered during the compilation, and it's well supported by IntelliSense in the VS .NET development environment.

```
<?xml version="1.0"?>
<configuration>
    <system.web>
        <pages>
            <namespaces>
                <add namespace="System.IO" />
            </namespaces>
        </pages>
    </system.web>
</configuration>
```

What About Client Scripting?

In Chapter 2, you saw that the new development environment offers great support for client-side programming. Even dynamic generation of client scripts has become easier, as you'll see in the next section. Furthermore, a new Client Callback function is ready to use.

Client Scripting

In the future you can leave the definition of client-side scripts to the `ClientScriptManager`, which you can access through the `Page.ClientScript` property. The object returned offers the scripting methods that you already know from the existing `Page` class and some new ones. Among others there are, for example, `RegisterArrayDeclaration()`, `RegisterClientScriptBlock()`, `RegisterClientScriptInclude()`, `RegisterClientScriptResource()`, `RegisterHiddenField()`, `RegisterOnSubmitStatement()`, and `RegisterStartupScript()`.

As of now, the scripts are handled through several dictionaries internally to avoid the double definition of common scripts. With the help of various `Is ... Registered` methods, you can check if a script already exists. In addition to the existing approach, you can now pass a type instance that's used as additional key value:

```
this.ClientScript.RegisterClientScriptBlock(this.GetType(), "myscript", myScript);
```

The annoying creation of script blocks that are needed again and again is a thing of the past. If desired, the `ClientScriptManager` will create the common JavaScript tags `<script> ... </script>` automatically for you. A new Boolean parameter does the job for several methods:

```
this.ClientScript.RegisterStartupScript(this.GetType(),
    "startupalert",
    "alert('Hello world!');",
    true);
```

Client Callback

Until now, a postback of the complete page is required for each server-side action, including all the corresponding difficulties such as the eventual loss of the current scroll position and the control focus. Also, the user can interact with the page without waiting for the entire reload. The new Client Callback feature was built to be used in those cases when only single data values have to be sent and reloaded rather than the entire page. Therefore, a request is sent to the server through JavaScript and XMLHTTP similarly to what has been done by the Internet Explorer WebService behavior in the past.

In comparison with the Internet Explorer WebService behavior, Client Callbacks are available in the current version of the Internet Explorer as well as for Netscape (using its own technique). You can use the Client Callback in custom controls as well as directly within your page. One control that already benefits from this feature today is the TreeView. It can dynamically load nodes as needed.

The implementation of a Client Callback is relatively easy and consists of only two steps. First, the control or the page must support the `ICallbackEventHandler` interface by implementing the `RaiseCallbackEvent` method. This method is accessed as soon as the Callback is initiated. It receives a character string as parameter. Also, the value returned by the method (that will later be available on the client side) is defined as a string. Additionally, you need two client-side script functions that initiate the Callback and process the (asynchronously delivered) return value.

Listing 11-18 shows the proceeding steps in a comprehensive way. In this case, the local page uses the Callback itself and implements the already mentioned interface to fulfill this purpose. The Callback is used to invert a string value (character by character) that was entered by the user in a TextBox control and display it afterward in the input box again.

Listing 11-18. Server-Side Page Callback Reverses Entered Text

```
<%@ page language="C#" %>
<%@ implements interface="System.Web.UI.ICallbackEventHandler"%>

<script runat="server">

void Page_Load(object sender, System.EventArgs e)
{
    string callback = Page.GetCallbackEventReference(this, "this.value",
        "ProcessReverse", null);
    this.Textbox1.Attributes.Add("onchange", callback);
}

string ICallbackEventHandler.RaiseCallbackEvent(string eventArgument)
{
    char[] chars = eventArgument.ToCharArray();
    Array.Reverse(chars);
    return new string(chars);
}

</script>

<script language="javascript">

function ProcessReverse(result, context)
{
```

```
        document.forms[0].Textbox1.value = result;
}

</script>

<html>
<head runat="server">
    <title>Untitled Page</title>
</head>
<body>
    <form runat="server">
        <asp:textbox id="Textbox1" runat="server">
        </asp:textbox>
    </form>
</body>
</html>
```

The Callback function is created through the Page.GetCallbackEventReference() method and assigned to the input box's onchange client event. Apart from the parameter, the method includes the name of the second client function that will receive the asynchronously delivered result of the callback. In this case, it's the ProcessReverse() function that puts the return value of the Callback into the TextBox on the client side. Sounds complicated, doesn't it? A glance at Figure 11-16 and Listing 11-18 will show you that it is quite easy indeed, however.

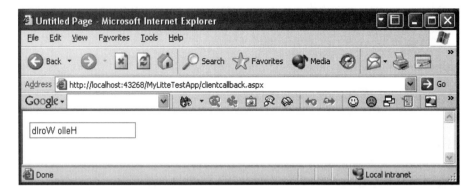

Figure 11-16. The text "Hello World" was reversed by a server-side callback method.

> **TIP** *You'll find another example for the use of Client Callbacks in Chapter 9, which covers Themes. There you will find a solution in which a Theme chosen by a user is stored in his Personalization Profile using the Callback.*

Caching and SQL Server Invalidation

The DataSource controls described in Chapter 3, which covers the new and enhanced data access, offer the capability for integrated caching (except for the SiteMapDataSource control). The approach of these controls corresponds in principle to the ones you already know from versions 1.0 and 1.1. The data is held in memory either absolutely or sliding, depending on a specific time value. This is a possible approach, but it doesn't correspond with the practical requirements.

The new SQL Server Cache Invalidation feature will close the gap. Now you can have the caching depend on changes in an entire database table or even a single line. The latter approach will work only in combination with Yukon notifications (Yukon is the code name for the successor of SQL Server 2000, currently in Beta as well). Table-based invalidation works as well with SQL Server 2000 and even 7.0. Here, the table is polled internally with a configurable time span (standard is 60000 and minimum is 500 milliseconds) and is tested for changes.

Configuring SQL Server Cache Invalidation

To use SQL Server Cache Invalidation you must configure the monitored database first. This is done by the program aspnet_regsqlcache, which you'll find in the following directory:

```
<windir>\Microsoft.NET\Framework\<version>\
```

The command-line program knows various parameters. To configure the Northwind database on the local SQL server, for example, you can use the following command:

```
aspnet_regsqlcache -d Northwind -ed –E
```

In a second call of the program, you must activate the desired table:

```
aspnet_regsqlcache -d Northwind -t Customers -et –E
```

To receive a listing of the currently activated tables, you can use the following command:

```
aspnet_regsqlcache -d Northwind -lt –E
```

> **CAUTION** *Please note that all parameters are currently case sensitive. If you have any difficulties activating the invalidation, please double-check your input.*

The program will create a new table with the (endless) name AspNet_SqlCacheTablesForChangeNotification within the specified database. For each table to be monitored, the table contains an entry with name of the table, a timestamp of the creation, and a version number. This number is incremented with each change through a trigger within the database to be monitored. By polling and comparing, the version changes can be identified and the cache gets invalidated.

```
CREATE TRIGGER dbo.[Customers_AspNet_SqlCacheNotification_Trigger]
    ON [Customers]
FOR INSERT, UPDATE, DELETE AS
BEGIN
    IF NOT EXISTS (SELECT tableName FROM
        dbo.AspNet_SqlCacheTablesForChangeNotification
        WHERE tableName = 'Customers')
        RETURN
    ELSE
    BEGIN
        UPDATE dbo.AspNet_SqlCacheTablesForChangeNotification
            SET changeId = changeId + 1
            WHERE tableName = 'Customers'
    END
END
```

Once the database, including the table, is configured, you must add both to the web.config configuration file. To allow you to do this, the new section <sqlCacheDependency> works together with the also new section <connectionStrings>. If you want to get monitoring on the Northwind database on the local SQL Server for example, your web.config file looks like this:

```
<configuration>
    <connectionStrings>
        <add name="Northwind" connectionString="server=.;
            database=Northwind;Integrated Security=SSPI;" />
    </connectionStrings>

    <system.web>
        <cache>
            <sqlCacheDependency enabled="true" pollTime="5000">
                <databases>
                    <add name="Northwind" connectionStringName="Northwind" />
                </databases>
            </sqlCacheDependency>
        </cache>
    </system.web>
</configuration>
```

Using SQL Server Cache Invalidation with Data Source Controls

Although it's quite time consuming to configure the new caching possibility, it's much easier to use afterward, as the example in the following listing clearly shows. In principle, you must only activate the caching of the used SqlDataSource control and assign the desired dependency to the SqlCacheDepedency property. The dependency consists of the database name configured in the web.config file as well as the table name. Both values are separated by colon—in this case, Northwind:Customers.

```
<%@ page language="C#" %>

<html>
<head runat="server">
    <title>Untitled Page</title>
</head>
<body>
    <form runat="server">
        <asp:gridview id="GridView1" runat="server" allowpaging="True"
            datasourceid="SqlDataSource1" allowsorting="True"
                autogeneratecolumns="False"
            selectedindex="0" datakeynames="CustomerID">
        </asp:gridview>
        <asp:sqldatasource id="SqlDataSource1" runat="server"
            selectcommand="SELECT CustomerID, CompanyName,
```

```
                ContactName FROM Customers "
            providername="System.Data.OleDb"
            connectionstring="..."
              sqlcachedependency="Northwind:Customers"
              enablecaching="True">
        </asp:sqldatasource>
    </form>
</body>
</html>
```

You can test this example very easily by setting the polling value in the configurations file to 5 or more seconds, and afterward you can change any value in the table.
If you refresh the page in the browser, the change will only become effective after a
few seconds. A look at the table AspNet_SqlCacheTablesForChangeNotification
shows that the version has been incremented.

Using SQL Server Cache Invalidation Programmatically

You can use the new SqlCacheDependency class directly in the source code to place
any elements in the cache. This is particularly useful for data that should be globally available.

Listing 11-19 shows the query and the caching of a DataSet within the cache
object. An instance of the new SqlCacheDependency class is passed as a parameter
when you add the object to the cache. Similar to the SqlDataSource control, the
class was prepared for the Northwind database. In case of changes, the object will
be invalidated in the cache, which results in a new creation of the DataSet through
CacheItemRemovedCallback.

Listing 11-19. Yukon Allows Line-Based Cache Invalidation

```
<%@ page language="C#" %>
<%@ import namespace="System.Data" %>
<%@ import namespace="System.Data.SqlClient" %>

<script runat="server">

void Page_Load(object sender, System.EventArgs e)
{
    if (this.Cache["ds"] == null)
    {
        this.CreateDataSet();
```

```
    }
    if (this.IsPostBack == false)
    {
        this.LB_Customers.DataSource = this.Cache["ds"];
        this.LB_Customers.DataBind();
        this.LT_LastUpdate.Text = ((DateTime)this.Cache["LastUpdate"]).ToString();
    }
}

void CreateDataSet()
{
    string connString = ConfigurationSettings.ConnectionStrings["Yukon"];
    string cmdText = "Select CompanyName FROM Customers";

    SqlConnection connect = new SqlConnection(connString);
    SqlDataAdapter adapter = new SqlDataAdapter(cmdText, connect);

    DataSet ds = new DataSet();
    adapter.Fill(ds);

    SqlCacheDependency dependency = new SqlCacheDependency("Yukon",
                                                "Customers");
    this.Cache.Add("ds", ds, dependency, DateTime.MaxValue, TimeSpan.Zero,
        CacheItemPriority.Default, new CacheItemRemovedCallback(
        this.DataSetRemoveFromCache));

    this.Cache.Insert("LastUpdate", DateTime.Now);
}

void DataSetRemoveFromCache(string key, object value,
                            CacheItemRemovedReason reason)
{
    this.CreateDataSet();
}

</script>

<html>
<head runat="server">
    <title>Untitled Page</title>
</head>
<body>
    <form runat="server">
```

```
        <p>
            <asp:listbox id="LB_Customers" runat="server"
                height="200px" width="300px" datatextfield="CompanyName">
            </asp:listbox>
        </p>
        <p>
            Last update:
            <asp:literal id="LT_LastUpdate" runat="server">
            </asp:literal>
        </p>
    </form>
</body>
</html>
```

If you're using Yukon, you can pass a `SqlCommand` (instead of the specified name of the database and the index) to the constructor of the `SqlCacheDependency` class, in a way similar to this example. This way, you can use single-line-oriented SQL Cache Invalidation.

> **TIP** *If you want to use the SQL Server Invalidation without caching, you can use the* `SqlDependency` *class from the* `System.Data.SqlClient` *namespace.*

Other Caching Enhancements

In previous version of ASP.NET, you already had the option to cache depending on a time span, a file, or a different cache entry using the `CacheDependency` class. Beyond this, the caching system couldn't be enhanced by developers, however, because the class was marked as `sealed`.

In the new version of the Framework, the class isn't sealed anymore and even offers some overridable methods. By inheriting from the class, you can now implement totally individual cache dependencies and integrate them seamlessly in the caching framework.

Two classes deriving from `CacheDependency` are already shipped with ASP.NET. You have already learned about the `SqlCacheDependency` class. The second class is called `AggregateCacheDependency`. This class allows the aggregation of several other dependencies. This way, you can, for example, make a cached object depend on two different tables. You aren't limited to a specific type; you can even mix the existing ones with custom dependencies.

Using Page and Control Caching

Do you remember the @OutputCache directive? Of course you do! This directive allows you to specify a SQL Server dependency for complete pages as well as for controls. You can place the desired dependency through the new sqldependency attribute in the familiar form *database:table*. Listing 11-20 shows you how it works, and Figure 11-17 shows you how it looks.

Listing 11-20. The @OutputCache Directive Now Supports SQL Server Cache Invalidation

```
<%@ page language="C#" %>
<%@ outputcache duration="600" varybyparam="none"
    sqldependency="Northwind:Customers" %>

<script runat="server">

void Page_Load(object sender, System.EventArgs e)
{
    this.LT_LastUpdate.Text = DateTime.Now.ToString();
}

</script>

<html>
<head runat="server">
    <title>Untitled Page</title>
</head>
<body>
    <form runat="server">
        <asp:gridview id="GridView1" runat="server" allowpaging="True"
            datasourceid="SqlDataSource1" allowsorting="True"
                autogeneratecolumns="False"
            selectedindex="0" datakeynames="CustomerID">
        </asp:gridview>
        <asp:sqldatasource id="SqlDataSource1" runat="server" selectcommand="SELECT
            CustomerID, CompanyName, ContactName FROM Customers"
            providername="System.Data.OleDb" connectionstring="...">
        </asp:sqldatasource>
        <p>
            Last update:
            <asp:literal id="LT_LastUpdate" runat="server"/>
        </p>
    </form>
</body>
</html>
```

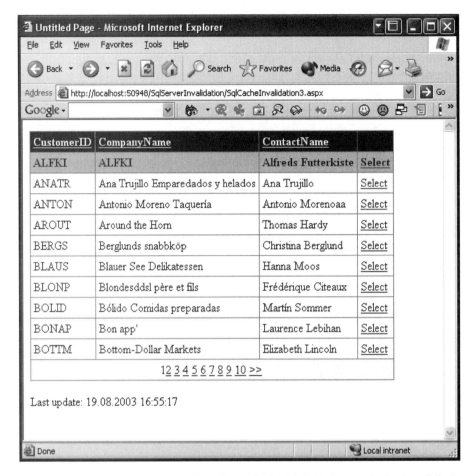

Figure 11-17. Any page or control can be cached with SQL Server Cache Invalidation.

Summary

This chapter described a bunch of new, very useful features, concepts, and enhancements. There are many new controls that makes it more convenient to develop state-of-the-art web sites. Programming on both sides—client and server—is much easier now. Also, the new SQL Server Cache Invalidation helps you optimize your web sites.

CHAPTER 12

Going Mobile

THE CHANGES THAT COME WITH ASP.NET 2.0 will affect mobile controls as well. But that's what we developers are used to. No support for mobile devices existed in the first version. Then the Microsoft Mobile Internet Toolkit (MMIT) was introduced. With version 1.1, the MMIT was directly integrated in the framework under the name ASP.NET Mobile Controls.

In version 2.0, the mobile controls with the corresponding System.Web.Mobile namespace are still available, but only for compatibility reasons. It shouldn't be used any more for new web sites.

Mobile Development ASP.NET 2.0 Style

The new ASP.NET version offers a completely new concept for the development of mobile web sites. Instead of using special mobile controls as you've had to do up to now, you'll work with already known controls such as Label, TextBox, Button, and so on—the same as if you were developing a web site for regular desktop browsers. Depending on the device used, the controls are delivered in the required format, regardless of whether you're using (X)HTML, WML, or CHTML (short for Compact HTML, which is used with i-mode in Japan). Just forget about the separate <mobile:...> controls!

Instead of rendering their content individually, the controls utilize a set of adapter classes that have been assigned to them during configuration. This new concept is called *adaptive rendering*. Many adapters are already included with ASP.NET for all the standard controls.

Due to the separation of control and adapter, support for new or individual target devices can be added without any problems. You can even modify the output of a control to serve different purposes without changing the control itself.

Adaptive Rendering in Action

Just access any page in different devices or emulators to see adaptive rendering in action. I've created the page in Listing 12-1 as a test. It consists of a simple input form, Button control, and Label control.

Listing 12-1. Creating Mobile Pages Using the Regular Web Controls

```
<%@ page language="C#" %>

<script runat="server">

void BT_Submit_Click(object sender, System.EventArgs e)
{
    this.LT_Name.Text = string.Format("Your name is: {0}", this.TB_Name.Text);
}

</script>

<html>
<head runat="server">
    <title>Untitled Page</title>
</head>
<body>
    <form runat="server">
        <p>Please enter your name:
            <br /><br />
            <asp:textbox id="TB_Name" runat="server"/>
            <asp:button id="BT_Submit" runat="server"
                text="OK"
                onclick="BT_Submit_Click" />
        </p>
        <p><asp:literal id="LT_Name" runat="server"/></p>
    </form>
</body>
</html>
```

The result isn't really exciting, though. Much more exciting is the fact that you can access the page through completely different browsers without any changes. Figures 12-1 through 12-3 show the example page in the regular desktop Internet Explorer, the Internet Explorer for Pocket PCs, and the Openwave WAP Emulator.

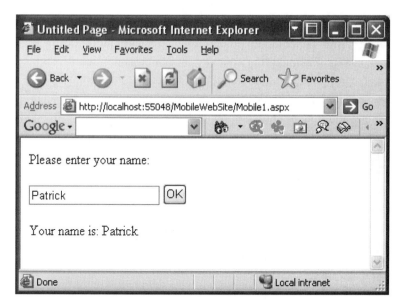

Figure 12-1. The same page in Internet Explorer ...

Figure 12-2. ... in Internet Explorer for Pocket PC ...

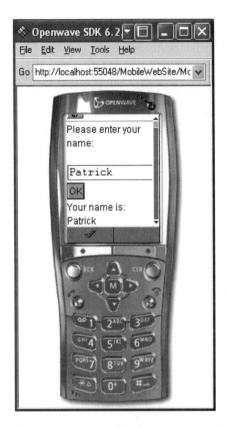

Figure 12-3. . . . and in Openwave WAP Emulator.
(Image courtesy Openwave Systems Inc.)

TIP *Check out the Mobile area on the* www.asp.net *web site if you want to get a good overview of emulators. The Pocket PC Emulator is included with the Microsoft Pocket PC 2003 SDK. This SDK requires Microsoft eMbedded Visual C++ 4.0, including Service Pack 2. All of the three setups are shipped as a part of MSDN Subscription or can be downloaded (at a total of more than 400MB) from the Microsoft web site.*

One UI for Different Devices?

When faced these new possibilities, one urgent question comes to mind: Will it be sufficient in the future to develop only one UI for all devices? The answer is absolutely clear: No! In 90% or more of all cases you'll still need a UI for regular desktop browsers and one for mobile devices. A unique surface doesn't make sense because the differences are just too big.

However, you can now use the same controls and the identical programming model without any problems. Maybe you can even port some parts of the UI more easily.

Device Filter

Another option that the new controls offer is the so-called Device Filter. You can use it to assign properties in a declarative way for different target devices. For this purpose, you just have to assign the unique ID of the device in front of the parameter name. The ID is defined by the configuration. This may look as follows:

```
<asp:image imageurl="foo.jpg" netscape:imageurl="foomozzila.jpg" />
```

This approach works for any properties as well as for attributes and templates. The filter can even be used on many attributes offered by the @Page and @Control directives.

Browser Configuration

By including the new adaptive rendering feature, the configuration possibilities have become remarkably more numerous. Also, administrators have access to any of these settings so that they can quickly make changes and enhancements. Until recently, configuration was integrated in the machine.config file. From now on it will be placed in a separate directory:

```
<windir>\Microsoft.NET\Framework\<version>\CONFIG\Browsers
```

In this directory, you'll find a separate file for each browser type with the extension .browser that contains the necessary settings.

The configuration for the emulator of Openwave used earlier is stored in the openwave.browser file and partially looks as shown in Listing 12-2. The assigned unique ID is marked in bold.

Listing 12-2. The Browser Configuration File Used to Assign the Adaptive Rendering Class

```
<browsers>
    <!-- sample UA "UP.Browser/3.1.03-DS13 UP.Link/5.0.2.7" -->
    <browser id="up" parentID="default">
        <identification>
```

```
        <userAgent match="(UP\.Browser)|(UP/)" />
        <userAgent nonMatch="Go\.Web" />
    </identification>

    <capture>
        <userAgent match="..." />
    </capture>

    <capabilities>
        <capability name="browser" value="Phone.com" />
        <capability name="canInitiateVoiceCall" value="true" />
        ...
    </capabilities>

    <controlAdapters markupTextWriterType="System.Web.UI.WmlTextWriter">
        <adapter controlType="System.Web.UI.Page"
                adapterType="System.Web.UI.Adapters.WmlPageAdapter" />

        <adapter controlType="System.Web.UI.DataBoundLiteralControl"
                adapterType="System.Web.UI.Adapters.
                WmlDataBoundLiteralControlAdapter"/>

        ...
    </browser>
</browsers>
```

Creating Mobile Web Sites

Unlike what you get with Visual Studio 2003, no special project template for
mobile web applications is being shipped with VS .NET anymore—at least none
exists in the current Alpha version. This makes sense; due to merging the controls,
a separate treatment has become dispensable. If you want to make a project suitable for mobile devices, you just create a new web site as usual and add the
desired pages.

Thanks to adaptive rendering, you can use all known web controls in mobile
web sites. Additionally, more controls are included that focus especially on the
needs of mobile devices.

Working with MultiView/View

In the scenarios up to this point, you've seen several forms within a mobile web page created. In the new version, however, you'll only work with one server-side form, the same way you would with regular pages. Nevertheless, you may want to switch between different views as you would with the cards used in WML, for example. For this purpose, the MultiView and View controls can be used in combination. I already talked about these controls in Chapter 11. The real target for their use, however, is mobile devices.

The example in Listing 12-3 is based on the one in Listing 12-1 with the difference being that now a MultiView and two View controls are used to switch between editing and displaying the user's name. Further on, I've added a button to jump back to the previous view. Figure 12-4 shows the output of the example.

Listing 12-3. The MultiView and View Controls Optimized for Mobile Scenarios

```
<%@ page language="C#" %>

<script runat="server">

void BT_Submit_Click(object sender, System.EventArgs e)
{
    this.LT_Name.Text = string.Format("Your name is: {0}", this.TB_Name.Text);
    this.MV_Main.ActiveViewIndex = 1;
}

void LB_Back_Click(object sender, System.EventArgs e)
{
    this.MV_Main.ActiveViewIndex = 0;
}

</script>

<html>
<head runat="server">
    <title>Untitled Page</title>
</head>
<body>
    <form runat="server">
        <asp:multiview id="MV_Main" runat="server" activeviewindex="0">
            <asp:view id="View1" runat="server">
                <p>
```

```
                        Please enter your name:
                        <br /><br />
                        <asp:textbox id="TB_Name" runat="server"/>
                        <asp:button id="BT_Submit" runat="server"
                            text="OK" onclick="BT_Submit_Click" softkeylabel="OK" />
                    </p>
                </asp:view>
                <asp:view id="View2" runat="server">
                    <p>
                    <asp:literal id="LT_Name" runat="server"/>
                    <br /><br />
                        <asp:linkbutton id="LB_Back" runat="server" softkeylabel="Back"
                            onclick="LB_Back_Click">Back</asp:linkbutton>
                    </p>
                </asp:view>
            </asp:multiview>
        </form>
    </body>
</html>
```

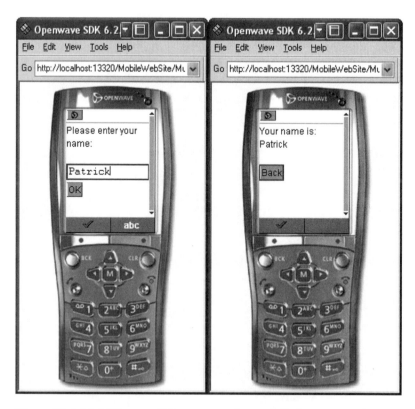

Figure 12-4. MultiView and View are used to switch the current view.
(Image courtesy Openwave Systems Inc.)

Switching between various views results from the use of the MultiView control's ActiveViewIndex property. In the development environment, however, all the views are displayed in parallel and can be visually edited, as shown in Figure 12-5.

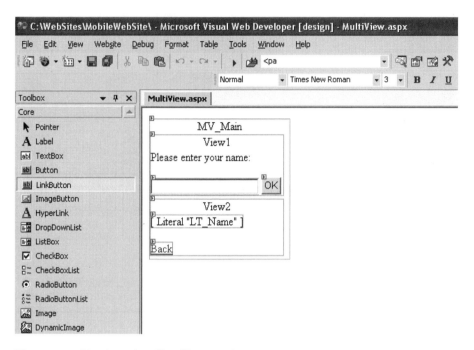

Figure 12-5. You can visually edit your views.

TIP *Many mobile devices support soft keys, which are nothing but physical buttons that enable you to perform desired actions. The different Button controls have a property called SoftwarekeyLabel that will enable you to define labeling if the (mobile) browser supports it.*

Using the Pager Control

I briefly presented the Pager control to you in Chapter 11. The application of this control is particularly useful for mobile web applications with a limited bandwidth and a small viewing display because you can paginate the content.

Listing 12-4 shows the usage of the Pager control in combination with a DataList control, which doesn't support paging itself. The Customers table of the Northwind database is shown with company name and telephone number.

Listing 12-4. Serving Large Amounts of Data to Small Clients Through the Pager Control

```
<%@ page language="C#" %>

<html>
<head runat="server">
    <title>Untitled Page</title>
</head>
<body>
    <form runat="server">
        <asp:sqldatasource id="SqlDataSource1" runat="server"
            providername="System.Data.OleDb"
            selectcommand="..."
            connectionstring="...">
        </asp:sqldatasource>
        <asp:panel id="PNL_Customers" runat="server">
            <asp:datalist id="DL_Customers" runat="server"
                datasourceid="SqlDataSource1">
                <itemtemplate>
                    <asp:label text='<%# Eval("CompanyName") %>' runat="server" />
                    <br />
                    Phone:
                    <asp:label text='<%# Eval("Phone") %>' runat="server"/>
                </itemtemplate>
            </asp:datalist>
        </asp:panel>
        <asp:pager id="Pager1" runat="server"
            controltopaginate="PNL_Customers" itemsperpage="5" mode="NextPrev">
        </asp:pager>
    </form>
</body>
</html>
```

This source code will work without any problems in the both the desktop and Pocket PC versions of Internet Explorer. Unfortunately, the Openwave simulator still shows the very long customer list, regardless of the paging (see Figure 12-6). Due to this example being heavily based on the examples in the documentation, I presume this involves a bug in the current version that will be eliminated in the Beta version.

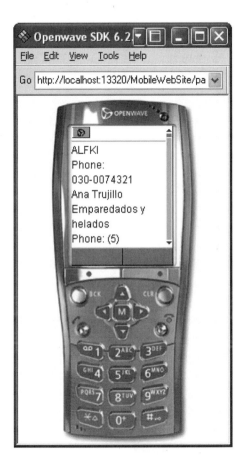

Figure 12-6. In the Openwave WAP Emulator, the list won't be paged. (Image courtesy Openwave Systems Inc.)

Making a Phone Call

It is reasonable to enlarge the list shown previously with the capability to call the individual companies directly. The example doesn't work as easily as I thought. Therefore, I've made an easier example to demonstrate a new control (see Listing 12-5). This one, called PhoneLink, enables you to initiate a telephone call as long as the current device will support it.

Listing 12-5. Enabling Phone Calls Through the PhoneLink Control

```
<%@ page language="C#" %>

<html>
<head runat="server">
    <title>Untitled Page</title>
</head>
<body>
    <form runat="server">
        <asp:phonelink id="PL_Contact" runat="server"
            phonenumber="004976339239990"
            navigateurl="contact.aspx">
            Call me!
        </asp:phonelink>
    </form>
</body>
</html>
```

As you can see in the listing, you can specify a URL as well as a telephone number. Depending on the device and its capabilities, either a call is initiated or the given address will be opened in the browser, as shown in Figure 12-7.

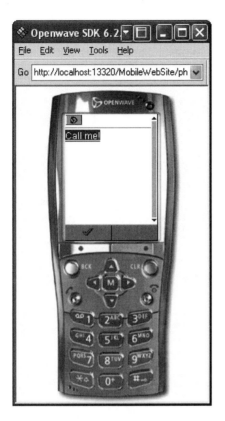

Figure 12-7. Hello, this is me. Who are you?
(Image courtesy Openwave Systems Inc.)

Summary

This chapter has introduced you to the most important news for the development of mobile web sites. A significant change is the merging of regular and mobile controls by the introduction of adaptive rendering. This system allows you to address any device without worrying about additional concepts or controls—which means your productivity will go up!

All web controls being shipped can be used for mobile scenarios without any grave problems. By developing your own adapter classes, you may modify the output of existing controls or make your own controls usable for mobile devices.

CHAPTER 13

Configuration for Developers and Administrators

YOU'LL HAVE TO ADJUST quite a lot of things with ASP.NET version 2.0. You've heard about new options and features in the various chapters of this book, all of which are waiting for you to configure them to your liking. Due to space restrictions, however, this book can't completely cover this topic. Therefore, I'd like to recommend taking a look at the `machine.config` configuration file. There really is a lot to discover in this file.

This chapter isn't dedicated to configuration settings, but demonstrates the various new possibilities they provide and how to edit them. Naturally, you can still edit the `web.config` configuration file directly within the development environment or even by means of a simple text editor. But maybe there is a little more convenience ahead for you?

Web Application Administration

You've already heard about the new Web Site Administration tool in Chapter 6. As I also discussed in that chapter, the Security Setup Wizard can be used to configure the security settings of a web site. Actually, the possibilities of the tools are limited to these settings. Some further developments are being planned for the Beta version.

You can reach the tool, shown in Figure 13-1, through the following URL:

```
http://localhost/<application>/webadmin.axd
```

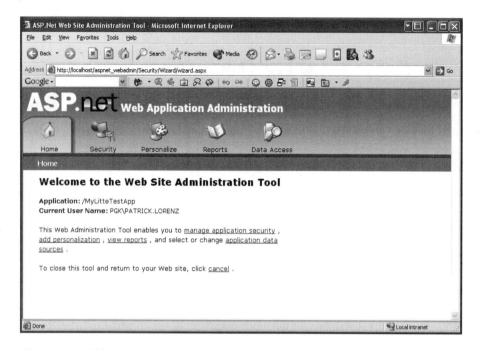

Figure 13-1. This new tool is intended to be used by administrators.

Of course, this tool has been created completely in ASP.NET and is available in the following directory in the source code:

```
<windir>\Microsoft.NET\Framework\<version>\ASP.NETWebAdminFiles
```

The source code will help you to get a better understanding of ASP.NET with regard to configuration on the one hand. On the other hand, it forms the basis for individual changes and above all for enhancements. Instead of developing your own admin tool for your web site, you can expand the existing tool with the required functions from now on. ISPs as well can offer an enhanced tool to their customers this way.

Actually, you can only set up and enhance the tool globally with the `machine.config` configuration file. Within the `<webSiteAdministrationTool>` section, you can not only define whether the tool is active, but also who will get the right to access it. According to the default setting, all users have the right to access the tool from the local machine. Any access from outside the machine will be declined. Integration with the user management system makes particularly sense for productive systems.

MMC Administration Tool

Apart from the tool for administration exists another one for configuration. This one is integrated into the IIS snap-in for the Microsoft Management Console (MMC). Consequentially, this tool is only available in combination with IIS, but not for projects that have been stored in the local file system.

A new tab, ASP.NET, has been integrated in the Properties dialog box of each application and of each (virtual) directory. The tab shows the current version that is being used for the selected web site: ASP.NET version 1.0, 1.1, or 1.2 (which means 2.0). Later on it will be possible to change the version directly in the dialog box.

TIP *This tool is, by the way, not just at your disposal on the local machine, so you can even directly configure remote systems this way, as you can see in Figure 13-2.*

Figure 13-2. You can configure your web site even via remote access.

The Edit configuration button brings up a voluminous dialog box with many register tabs. You can use them to edit or overwrite almost every allowed setting of the web.config configuration file for the application respective to the current sub-directory (see Figure 13-3). The choices go from connection strings to application settings, authentication and authorization, up to tracing and the loaded HTTP modules.

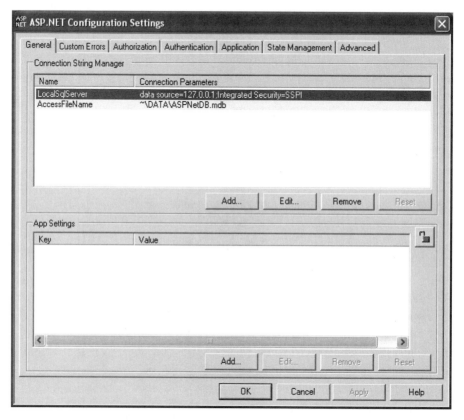

Figure 13-3. The Configuration Settings Editor allows modifying of virtually every setting in your web.config file.

CAUTION *Please bear in mind that the configuration tool is still at a very early stage and therefore not all of the features have been implemented yet. Some dialog boxes, for example, are still without functionality at present. This will certainly change with the Beta version.*

Configuration API

The new .NET Framework offers a big API to allow typed access to the configuration settings. More than in the earlier version of the .NET Framework, you can not only read, but also update and write the settings. This way, you can change the configuration for your web site very conveniently without needing to work manually with the `web.config` file. Even changes of the configuration in subdirectories are possible this way. Both of the tools that I've presented to you in this chapter are already intensively using this new API.

Accessing Configuration

The starting point for reading settings is the `Configuration` class taken from the `System.Configuration` namespace. You can obtain an instance of the class for the desired configuration area by using one of its several static methods.

For example, to detect the root configuration for the current application, you can use the `GetConfigurationForUrl()` method and pass the virtual path of the application:

```
string appPath = this.Request.ApplicationPath;
Configuration config = Configuration.GetConfigurationForUrl(appPath);
```

By means of a couple of properties from the returned class instance you can get some information on the configuration file. With the `HasFile` property, for example, you can detect whether the file already exists (if this isn't the case, the inherited settings will be used) and identify its physical filename with the help of `FilePath`.

Naturally, the current possibilities for accessing the settings will be supported further, but with the API a new way is offered to you. Depending on the application area, you must make up your mind which way to go.

Accessing Application Settings and Connection Strings

You know application settings from the first version of ASP.NET. They are nothing but a simple NameValueCollection by which you can deposit individual configuration settings in the web.config file and provide it with a unique key. This looks like the following:

```
<?xml version="1.0"?>
<configuration>
    <appSettings>
        <add key="test1" value="This is my first v2 app settings value"/>
        <add key="test2" value="And this is my second one"/>
    </appSettings>
</configuration>
```

Access to the settings through the API is shown in the following example. AppSettingsSection class used in the following code snippet comes from the System.Web.Management namespace, which is used for the configuration of web sites in addition to the System.Web.Configuration.

```
string appPath = this.Request.ApplicationPath;
Configuration config = Configuration.GetConfigurationForUrl(appPath);
AppSettingsSection appSettings = config.AppSettings;

foreach (string key in appSettings.Settings)
{
    this.Response.Write(string.Format("<p><b>{0}</b> = {1}</p>",
        key, appSettings.Settings[key]));
}
```

You can also use the existing query options through the ConfigurationSettings class without directly using the API, as you can see in Figure 13-4. In this case, however, you won't have the option to change data as described in the "Updating Configuration" section.

```
foreach (string key in ConfigurationSettings.AppSettings)
{
    this.Response.Write(string.Format("<p><b>{0}</b> = {1}</p>",
        key, ConfigurationSettings.AppSettings[key]));
}
```

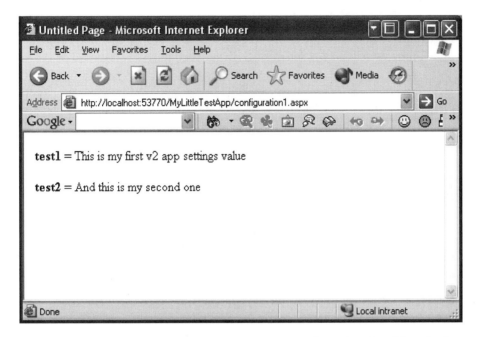

Figure 13-4. You can access the application settings either using the old method or with the new Configuration API.

In the past, application settings have frequently been used to store connection strings. This way, they are saved at a central position outside of the source code and can be switched easily between the development and the live platform. The new version, however, has a separate area that is exclusively designated for the storage of connection strings.

This new area is used by different providers employed for site counters, Membership Management, and Role Management, as well as for personalization. For example, if you want to replace the SQL Server that is being used by the providers, you just have to modify one single connection string in the machine.config file or overwrite it in the local web.config file.

And here's how the new section with its two default values in the machine.config looks like:

```
<?xml version="1.0" encoding="UTF-8" ?>
<configuration>
    <connectionStrings>
        <add name="LocalSqlServer"
            connectionString="data source=127.0.0.1;Integrated Security=SSPI" />
        <add name="AccessFileName" connectionString="~\DATA\ASPNetDB.mdb" />
    </connectionStrings>
</configuration>
```

The usage of connection strings with the new API looks similar to the usage of application settings. The `Configuration` class doesn't offer typed access, though. Therefore, they have to be queried through the collection that is returned by the `Sections` property.

```
string appPath = this.Request.ApplicationPath;
Configuration config = Configuration.GetConfigurationForUrl(appPath);
ConnectionStringsSection connStrings =
    (ConnectionStringsSection) config.Sections["connectionStrings"];

foreach(ConnectionStringSettings connString in connStrings.ConnectionStrings)
{
    this.Response.Write(string.Format("<p><b>{0}</b> = {1}</p>",
        connString.Name, connString.ConnectionString));
}
```

In case of a read-only access, you can use the following abbreviation:

```
foreach(string key in ConfigurationSettings.ConnectionStrings)
{
    this.Response.Write(string.Format("<p><b>{0}</b> = {1}</p>",
        key, ConfigurationSettings.ConnectionStrings[key]));
}
```

You must use the following line if you want to query a named and specific connection string within your web site or even from a custom provider (see Figure 13-5):

```
ConfigurationSettings.ConnectionStrings["key"]
```

NOTE *At present, the* SqlDataSource *and* AccessDataSource *classes don't incorporate the connection strings that have been deposited in the configuration. It is foreseen that such support will be given with the Beta version so that you can centrally exchange the applied connection strings.*

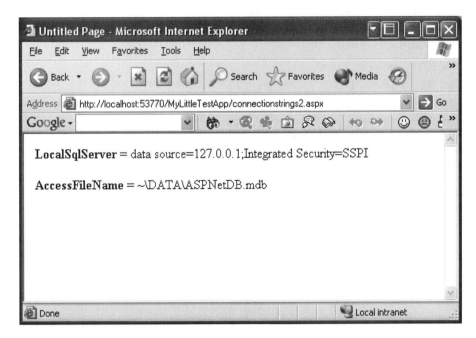

Figure 13-5. Accessing the new connection string section is very easy, too.

Accessing Other (Well-Known) Web Configurations

It's really worth it to take a good look at the Web property of the Configuration class. It returns a big object model that covers the complete standard configuration of an ASP.NET web site. The property returns a class of the type WebConfigurationSectionGroup whose properties reflect the already-known configuration sections: AnonymousIdentification, Authentication, Authorization, Compilation, and many, many more. Each property again delivers an object that allows typed access on each and every attribute and subelement of the section the object represents.

The page implemented in Listing 13-1 and shown in Figure 13-6 uses the new API with the intention of displaying all the active authorization rules. It becomes quite clear how detailed the object that has been implemented is because there is a class for the section, one for the rules, and a collection to hold the rules. The rule type is defined through an enumeration.

Listing 13-1. Acquiring and Displaying All Authorization Rules in the Browser Window

```
<%@ page language="C#" %>
<%@ import namespace="System.Web.Management" %>

<script runat="server">

void Page_Load(object sender, System.EventArgs e)
{
    string appPath = this.Request.ApplicationPath;
    Configuration config = Configuration.GetConfigurationForUrl(appPath);
    AuthorizationSection authorization = config.Web.Authorization;

    this.DL_Rules.DataSource = authorization.Rules;
    this.DL_Rules.DataBind();
}

</script>

<html>
<head runat="server">
    <title>Untitled Page</title>
</head>
<body>
    <form runat="server">
        <asp:datalist id="DL_Rules" runat="server">
            <itemtemplate>
                Action: <asp:literal id="Literal1" runat="server"
                    text='<%# ((AuthorizationRule) Container.DataItem).Action %>'/>
                <br />
                Users:
                <asp:repeater runat="server"
                    DataSource='<%# ((AuthorizationRule)
                        Container.DataItem).Users %>'>
                    <itemtemplate><%# Container.DataItem %></itemtemplate>
                    <separatortemplate>-</separatortemplate>
                </asp:repeater>
                <br />
                Roles:
                <asp:repeater runat="server"
                    datasource='<%# ((AuthorizationRule)
                        Container.DataItem).Roles %>'>
```

```
            <itemtemplate><%# Container.DataItem %></itemtemplate>
            <separatortemplate>-</separatortemplate>
          </asp:repeater>
        </itemtemplate>
      </asp:datalist>
    </form>
  </body>
</html>
```

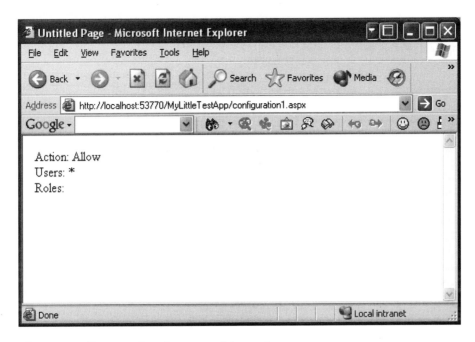

Figure 13-6. Everyone is welcome to visit my site.

Access to many other configuration values is done in a similar way. No wonder the System.Management namespace consists of more than 100 different classes and enumerations.

Accessing Other (Not Well-Known) Web Configurations

You can access not only the known standard elements through the new API, but also any others as well. Access takes place through the two Sections and SectionsGroups properties of the Configuration class, as demonstrated in Listing 13-2. A SectionGroup object again contains Sections as well as additional subgroups. The objects will be used in this example to list all the groups including their first-level subsections in a ListBox control (see Figure 13-7).

Listing 13-2. Giving Access to Any Configuration Section Through the Configuration Class

```
<%@ page language="C#" %>

<script runat="server">

void Page_Load(object sender, System.EventArgs e)
{
    string appPath = this.Request.ApplicationPath;
    Configuration config = Configuration.GetConfigurationForUrl(appPath);

    for (int i = 0; i < config.SectionGroups.Count; i++)
    {
        ConfigurationSectionGroup group = config.SectionGroups[i];
        this.LB_Sections.Items.Add(group.Name);

        for (int j = 0; j < group.Sections.Count; j++)
        {
            ConfigurationSection section = group.Sections[j];
            this.LB_Sections.Items.Add(string.Format("...{0}", section.Name));
        }
    }
}

</script>

<html>
<head id="Head1" runat="server">
    <title>Untitled Page</title>
</head>
<body>
    <form id="Form1" runat="server">
        <asp:listbox id="LB_Sections" runat="server" width="300px" height="300px">
        </asp:listbox>
    </form>
</body>
</html>
```

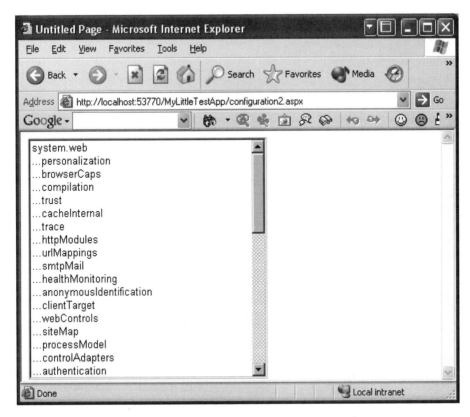

Figure 13-7. The nested collections allow you to dive deep into the configuration.

All sections are represented by classes derived from the abstract base ConfigurationSection, as shown in Listing 13-3. You can access the contained data by the offered properties in each case, or alternatively query the underlying configuration directly as XML (see Figure 13-8).

Listing 13-3. Accessing the Configuration Data As Raw XML Data

```csharp
<%@ page language="C#" %>

<script runat="server">

void Page_Load(object sender, System.EventArgs e)
{
    string appPath = this.Request.ApplicationPath;
    Configuration config = Configuration.GetConfigurationForUrl(appPath);
```

```
        ConfigurationSection section = config.Sections["appSettings"];
        this.TB_XML.Text = section.GetRawXml().OuterXml;
    }

    </script>

    <html>
    <head runat="server">
        <title>Untitled Page</title>
    </head>
    <body>
        <form runat="server">
            <asp:textbox id="TB_XML" runat="server"
                textmode="MultiLine" width="300px" height="100px">
            </asp:textbox>
        </form>
    </body>
    </html>
```

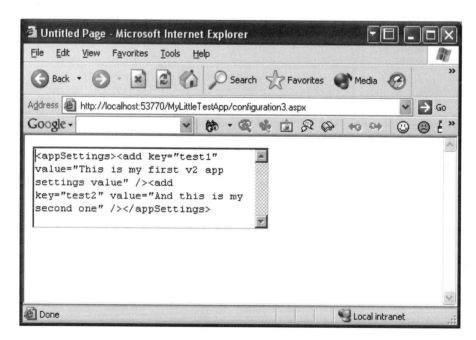

Figure 13-8. This is really a raw configuration XML.

Updating Configuration

The real innovation of the API is the possibility to update entries and write the configurations back to the corresponding web.config file. The properties of the various section objects are therefore implemented as get *and* set. The various collections as well allow you quite often to delete or to add entries. After you have made the desired changes directly in the object model, you can write them back in one step using the Configuration.Update() method.

> **CAUTION** *Please be aware that changes take effect directly with the next request of the page. In case of an incorrect application, it might happen that the web site won't work any more. For example, I deactivated the anonymous authentication in a test project, although the anonymous user was activated for some properties of the profile. The result was that the page couldn't be requested any more and I had to undo the change manually.*

Updating Application Settings and Connection Strings

Application settings is one of the collections you can modify and enhance very easily. The following example shows the addition of a new entry to the web.config configuration file:

```
string appPath = this.Request.ApplicationPath;
Configuration config = Configuration.GetConfigurationForUrl(appPath);
AppSettingsSection appSettings = config.AppSettings;

appSettings.Settings.Add("test3", "This one was created using the new API");
config.Update();

foreach (string key in appSettings.Settings)
{
    this.Response.Write(string.Format("<p><b>{0}</b> = {1}</p>",
        key, appSettings.Settings[key]));
}
```

The changes will be saved at once and are available with the next request of the page—without a complete and annoying restart of the application, of course! After running the example, the configurations file looks as follows:

```
<?xml version="1.0"?>
<configuration>

    <appSettings>
        <add key="test1" value="This is my first v2 app settings value" />
        <add key="test2" value="And this is my second one" />
        <add key="test3" value="This one was created using the new API" />
    </appSettings>

    <system.web>
        ...
    </system.web>

</configuration>
```

The procedure is quite the same with connection strings. Here you can update the delivered collection as well. Additionally, the inherited entries can be removed as you can see in the second example in this code snippet:

```
string appPath = this.Request.ApplicationPath;
Configuration config = Configuration.GetConfigurationForUrl(appPath);
ConnectionStringsSection connStrings =
    (ConnectionStringsSection) config.Sections["connectionStrings"];

connStrings.ConnectionStrings.Remove("LocalSqlServer");

ConnectionStringSettings connString = new ConnectionStringSettings();
connString.Name = "test";
connString.ConnectionString = "data source=127.0.0.1;Integrated Security=SSPI";
connStrings.ConnectionStrings.Add(connString);

config.Update();
```

The current configuration file now contains a <remove> tag:

```xml
<?xml version="1.0"?>
<configuration>

    <connectionStrings>
        <remove name="LocalSqlServer" />
        <add name="test"
            connectionString="data source=127.0.0.1;Integrated Security=SSPI" />
    </connectionStrings>

    <system.web>
        ...
    </system.web>

</configuration>
```

Updating Other Web Configurations

Analogous to the preceding examples, you can make changes in the configuration settings for web sites through the shown object model. The following listing shows, for example, the creation of a new authorization rule.

```csharp
string appPath = this.Request.ApplicationPath;
Configuration config = Configuration.GetConfigurationForUrl(appPath);
AuthorizationSection authorization = config.Web.Authorization;

AuthorizationRule rule = new AuthorizationRule();
rule.Action = AuthorizationRuleAction.Allow;
rule.Users.Add("TestUser");
rule.Roles.Add("TestRole");
authorization.Rules.Add(rule);

config.Update();
```

Or do you want to switch the debug mode of the example on or off? No problem at all! Simply change the settings and call Update()!

```
string appPath = this.Request.ApplicationPath;
Configuration config = Configuration.GetConfigurationForUrl(appPath);

CompilationSection compilation = config.Web.Compilation;
compilation.Debug = (!compilation.Debug);

config.Update();
```

Summary

The new .NET version offers a rich feature set for configuring your applications. You can not only access the settings, but also update and write them back to the configuration file—without restarting the whole application. The new API is already used by two new configuration tools, which offers developers and administrators a convenient way to manage their web sites.

CHAPTER 14

Fun Pet Tricks

THIS CHAPTER OFFERS a series of so-called Fun Pet Tricks that were originally published in the protected Alpha forums for Whidbey by Scott Guthrie and myself. These tricks will give you interesting insights to various features of the new version of ASP.NET and can in most cases be adopted within minutes. Some of my own Fun Pet Tricks have been created during the work on this book, and I've directly embedded them in chapters with related topics rather than list them in this chapter.

Many thanks to Scott, who allowed the publication of his samples. You can definitely find more of my tricks in the forums of www.asp.net in the near future. I hope you enjoy them!

Fun Pet Trick #1: HTML Source Preservation

By Scott Guthrie

One of the biggest new features of Visual Studio Whidbey is the fact that the designer no longer reformats or rearranges your HTML source code.

To see a fun example of this in action, try these steps:

1. Create a new ASP.NET page.

2. Paste the following code into Source view (notice that the button is custom formatted in a nondefault way to have one attribute per line):

```
<%@ page language="VB" %>
<html>
<body>
    <form runat="server">
        <asp:button id="Button1"
                    runat="server"
                    text="Button"
                    backcolor="Red"
                    font-italic="True" />
    </form>
</body>
</html>
```

3. Switch to design mode.

4. Type some text before the button, press Enter, put the cursor after the button, press Enter, type some more text.

5. Flip back to source mode. The code now looks as follows (notice the button wasn't reformatted):

```
<%@ page language="VB" %>
<html>
<body>
    <form runat="server">
        Some random text<br />
        <br />
        <asp:button id="Button1"
                    runat="server"
                    text="Button"
                    backcolor="Red"
                    font-italic="True" />
        <br />
        <br />
        some more random text
    </form>
</body>
</html>
```

6. Flip back to design mode, select the button, and then change the text property in the Properties grid.

7. Flip back to source mode and notice that even when the button text was updated, the designer *did not* reformat the indentation of the attributes:

```
<%@ page language="VB" %>
<html>
<body>
    <form runat="server">
        Some random text<br />
        <br />
        <asp:button id="Button1"
                    runat="server"
                    text="Push Me"
                    backcolor="Red"
                    font-italic="True" />
        <br />
```

```
        <br />
        some more random text
    </form>
  </body>
</html>
```

Cool stuff. You can now use the design surface with confidence.

Fun Pet Trick #2: Selection Preservation on View Switch

By Scott Guthrie

One of the nice new features in Visual Studio is that the cursor position is now maintained when switching views between design and source mode.

Specifically, if you have a control selected in design mode, and then switch to source mode, the cursor in source mode will automatically be positioned to the first character of the server control tag.

If you move the cursor onto another server control or HTML element, and then switch to design mode, that control will be selected by default.

If you highlight any text in source mode, and then switch to design mode, that text range will show up selected in design mode. Likewise, if you select a different block of text in design mode and then switch to source mode, that text will be highlighted in the editor.

The end result of this feature is that you can rapidly switch back and forth between design and source mode—without having to spend time scrolling or figuring out where you are in the document.

To try this out, save and load the following file inside the IDE. Move the cursor around in source mode onto the calendar, and then flip into design mode. Notice the calendar is automatically selected. Select the button, and switch into source mode. Notice the cursor position on the button. Highlight "est" from the simple test string at the top, and then switch into design mode and notice the text selection.

```
<%@ page language="VB" %>

<html>
<body>
    <form runat="server">
        This is a simple test of control selection<br />
        <br />
        <asp:button id="Button1" runat="server" text="Button" />
```

```
        <br />
        <br />
        <asp:calendar id="Calendar1" runat="server">
        </asp:calendar>
    </form>
</body>
</html>
```

A small feature, but it adds a nice touch to the editing experience.

Fun Pet Trick #3: Client-Side Script IntelliSense by Browser Type

By Scott Guthrie

VS .NET provides full client-side IntelliSense on pages. To see this in action, just follow these steps:

1. Create a new page.

2. Flip to source view.

3. Click the drop-down list on the top left (default selection is Server Objects & Events).

4. Select the window object from the drop-down list (it is indented under Client Objects & Events).

5. From the second drop-down list (to the right of the first one), select the onload event. This will automatically generate a client-side `window_load` event handler.

6. Within the `window_onload()` event handler type **document**. You should then get full IntelliSense against the `document` client-side object property.

7. Now change the validation target of the document by clicking the validation link on the bottom-right side of the window. By default, it is set to IE 6.0. Try clicking it, and then changing it to Netscape Navigator 4.0.

8. Now go back to the event handler and reenter the "." after the document object—notice that the client-side object model has shrunk. This is because the IntelliSense engine is filtering to only show those methods, events, and properties of the client-side elements that are available with the currently selected validation target. Because Navigator 4.0 has less client JavaScript support than IE 6.0, the IntelliSense list is smaller.

A small touch—but one that makes doing client-side scripting a lot easier, and ensures that the JavaScript you write works with the browsers you target.

Fun Pet Trick #4: The Code Directory (and Its Cross-Language Usage)

By Scott Guthrie

One of the fun improvements made in ASP.NET 2.0 is the introduction of the code directory. This directory lives immediately underneath the application root of an ASP.NET application, and enables you to easily add non-UI code, resources, and web services to your application without requiring developers to manually compile a DLL to do so.

Note that you can use this feature within any development tool (Notepad, Emacs, Dreamweaver, FrontPage 11, and so on). It really shines, though, with VS .NET—which has native IntelliSense support for it.

Here are some steps to see this in action:

1. Launch Visual Studio and create or open a blank web page.

2. Within the Solution Explorer, create a new code directory.

3. Within the code directory, right-click and add a new class. Select C# as the language.

4. Add an Add() method to the class in the file you just created:

```
using System;
public class Class1
{
    public int Add (int x, int y)
    {
        return x + y;
    }
}
```

5. Click the Save button.

6. Now create a new C# page within the application (example: `page1.aspx`).

7. Add a button to the design surface, and then double-click it to generate the event handler.

8. Within the event handler, you can now instantiate and call the class you just created. Notice that you get full IntelliSense support for it.

9. Call the method and update the button's text:

```
void Button1_Click(object sender, System.EventArgs e)
{
    Class1 test = new Class1();
    Button1.Text = "Add Method: " + test.Add (6, 5);
}
```

10. Press Ctrl+F5 and notice that the code works—no compilation is required.

11. Keeping the browser open, try changing the values passed to the `Add()` method to 7 and 5. Click Save in the ASPX file, then click the button again in the browser. Notice that the change is immediately updated—no explicit recompile is required.

12. Now create a new page within your web site—this time create the page using VB .NET.

13. Drag and drop a button onto the design surface, and then double-click the button to add an event handler.

14. Now try using the C# class you previously created. Notice that you get full IntelliSense support, despite the fact that you are using two different languages within the same project (something VS has never done before).

15. Call the `Add()` method and update the Button control:

```
Sub Button1_Click(ByVal sender As Object, ByVal e As System.EventArgs)
    Dim test As New Class1
    Button1.Text = "Add Method: " & test.Add(5, 6)
End Sub
```

16. Run the page (press Ctrl+F5) and notice that everything works.

17. Now set a breakpoint on the `Dim` statement just shown (press F9 on the line), and then debug the page (press F5). Note that you might need to click Yes to add a `web.config` file with debugging enabled if you don't have that already set up.

18. Once the page comes up, click the button. The debugger will now break on the first line of the event handler. Press F10 to step over it to the second line.

19. Then press F11 to step into the `Add` call. Notice that you can seamlessly debug from C# to VB within the same project.

20. Hover the cursor over the `x` and `y` variables to see their values show up in the debugger (without having to look at the watch/local window). Press F5 when you are done to complete the page request.

The two big benefits of the code directory are that it enables much quicker development (no long compiles required—just click Save to update things), and you can now move to cross-language development within your web sites (which can be awfully nice). In a shared project scenario (using source control), you also now no longer need to check out and check in the project file when adding a component (which leads to contention or collisions when multiple people do it)—just add it to the code directory and away you go.

Fun Pet Trick #5: WSDL Files and the Code Directory

By Scott Guthrie

One of the nice new features of the code directory is that it now supports the ability to automatically generate a web service proxy class for you from a WSDL file. This enables you to quickly drag and drop a web service description file (with the extension `.wsdl`) into your web site—and immediately start to take advantage of it without having to run a proxy generation tool, or jump through any hoops to use it.

Suppose I wanted to use the Google search engine from within my ASP.NET application; I could simply download the Google WSDL file and save it as `GoogleService.wsdl` within my code directory, and then call the `googleSearch.doGoogleSearch()` method from within any of my pages or classes in order to invoke it. Visual Studio will of course provide full IntelliSense for me when going against this dynamically generated proxy class.

Following are the steps to see this in your own projects:

1. Create a code directory underneath your web application.

2. Copy the WSDL file called `GoogleSearchService.wsdl` underneath the code directory.

3. Click the refresh button within the Solution Explorer if you've created this file outside the IDE to make sure the project system sees the file.

4. Create a new VB page called `Google.aspx`, and paste in the code that follows to use it:

```vb
<%@ page language="VB" %>

<script runat="server">

    Sub Button1_Click(ByVal sender As Object,
    ByVal e As System.EventArgs)
        Dim GoogleKey As String = "/2NPhvVQFHLVehciRntdHOcJIVYJlrJS"
        Dim googleService As New GoogleSearchService
        Dim results As GoogleSearchResult =
            googleService.doGoogleSearch( _
                GoogleKey,
    TextBox1.Text, 0, 10, True, "", True, "", "", "")
        DataList1.DataSource = results.resultElements
        DataList1.DataBind()
    End Sub

</script>

<html>
<body>
    <form id="Form1" runat="server">

        Search Term:
        <asp:textbox id="TextBox1" runat="server"></asp:textbox>
         
        <asp:button id="Button1" runat="server" text="Button"
            onclick="Button1_Click" />
        <br />
        <br />
        <asp:datalist id="DataList1" runat="server">
```

```
        <ItemTemplate>
            <asp:label id="Label1" font-size="15pt" font-bold="true"
                text="<%# Container.DataItem.title %>"
                runat="server" />
            <br />
            <asp:label id="Label2"
                text="<%# Container.DataItem.snippet %>"
                runat="server" />
            <br />
            [<asp:hyperlink id="Hyperlink1"
                navigateurl="<%# Container.DataItem.URL %>"
                text="<%# Container.DataItem.URL %>"
                runat="server"/>]
            <br /><br />
        </ItemTemplate>
    </asp:datalist>
</form>
</body>
</html>
```

5. Click Run within Visual Studio.

6. Enter a search term on the page, and then click the button to retrieve the
    results of that search term from Google. The results will then be displayed
    on the page by data binding them to an ASP.NET DataList control.

Note that the preceding code sample has a `googlekey` value. Visit this
URL to register your own free account with Google and receive your own key
(the one shown in the example is Scott's): `https://www.google.com/accounts/`
`NewAccount?continue=http://api.google.com/createkey&followup=http://`
`api.google.com/createkey`.

A pretty easy way to add search to your site . . . and a nice little demo of a cool
new ASP.NET version 2.0 feature.

Fun Pet Trick #6: Precompilation of ASP.NET Applications

By Scott Guthrie

ASP.NET has always supported a dynamic compilation model, in which pages and
resources are dynamically compiled the first time they are accessed. This was true
in ASP.NET version 1.0 (even in code-behind scenarios where the ASPX page was
always compiled the first time the page was hit), and even more true in ASP.NET

version 2.0 (where dynamic compilation is now supported for even more types of files and resources).

Dynamic compilation has two downsides:

1. A small first-time hit occurs when accessing a page or resource (since a compiler is spinning up). The compiled output is persisted (so the hit only occurs once), but the overall time to compile can add up significantly on large sites of thousands of pages.

2. When you dynamically compile, you need to have the source code deployed on the production server. This makes it harder to resell applications—because your customers then effectively get your source code (resulting in your having less control over it).

ASP.NET solves both of these issues by supporting a precompilation option. This precompilation option supports precompiling *all* resources within an ASP.NET application—ASPX pages; code-behind; inline code; code, themes, and resources directories; ASCX, ASMX, ASAX, files; and so on.

This ensures that no runtime hit whatsoever happens when a page is first requested off of a server; everything is compiled and ready to go when the files are copied up on the system.

The precompilation utility also automatically strips out all source code from the application; this includes both new code-behind as well as code within the ASPX page, and even the markup within the files. This provides total protection of all of your intellectual property (IP).

The following steps walk you through how to precompile an application using the Alpha version. Note that VS .NET will automatically have a Build Menu option within Beta (so that you can easily kick-start the build within the IDE). For now, though, you need to use a command-line option to enable this (note that this will continue to ship in the Beta and final release to enable batch compile options, as well as automated, script-based compile scenarios).

1. Build an ASP.NET application in a directory called c:\PetTrick. Note that if you don't have an existing application lying around, try copying and using the one available at this URL:
   `http://www.asp.net/Forums/ShowPost.aspx?tabindex=1&PostID=300870`.

2. Open a command-line window.

3. Use the `aspnet_compiler.exe` utility within the Framework's redistribution directory to compile the application to a new target directory (note that this isn't on the default system path, so you'll need to fully qualify the compiler name).

Multiple options are enabled when using `aspnet_compiler.exe`—try just adding a `-?` to the end of the arguments list to see all of them.

```
c:\WINDOWS\Microsoft.NET\Framework\v1.2.30703\aspnet_compiler.exe
-v /PetTrick -p c:\PetTrick c:\PetTrickCompiledTarget
```

The preceding statement compiles an existing application that lives in the PetTrick directory into the PetTrickCompiledTarget directory.

To run the built application, go into `InetMgr` and set up an IIS virtual root application called PetTrick to point at the PetTrickCompiledTarget directory (note that the `-v` option on the tool asks for the final virtual root name in order to make sure you get the virtual hierarchy right when burning in references).

When you browse to the PetTrick root directory, the application will work as normal. When you open the PetTrickCompiledTarget directory, though, you'll notice that no ASPX source code is left. Instead, you'll just find marker files. All code within the pages, code, and resources directories have been precompiled down into assemblies in the bin directory.

You can now deploy this on a remote machine and get fast startup performance (no compile-time hit), and all your source code IP is safe.

Fun Pet Trick #7: Creating a Thumbnail List in About 1 Minute

By Patrick A. Lorenz

This Fun Pet Trick shows how to create a thumbnail list of all images placed in a given directory. All you need is the DynamicImage control, a DataList, and the `System.IO` namespace. Here you go:

```
<%@ page language="C#" %>
<%@ import namespace="System.IO" %>

<script runat="server">

void Page_Load(object sender, System.EventArgs e)
{
    DirectoryInfo directory = new
        DirectoryInfo(Path.GetDirectoryName(this.Request.PhysicalPath));
    this.DL_Thumbnails.DataSource = directory.GetFiles("*.gif");
    this.DL_Thumbnails.DataBind();
}
```

```
</script>

<html>
<head runat="server">
    <title>Untitled Page</title>
</head>
<body>
    <form runat="server">
        <asp:datalist runat="server" id="DL_Thumbnails" repeatcolumns="2">
            <itemtemplate>
                <asp:dynamicimage runat="server"
                    imagefile='<%# Eval("Name") %>'
                    width="150px">
                </asp:dynamicimage>
            </itemtemplate>
        </asp:datalist>
    </form>
</body>
</html>
```

What the sample actually does is scale all GIFs in the pages directory to 150 pixels width and displays them in the browser.

Have I already mentioned that I love the new DynamicImage control? Well, I do! ;-)

Fun Pet Trick #8: Implementing a Login System in Only 3 Minutes

By Scott Guthrie

ASP.NET version 2.0 includes built-in Membership Management and Role Management systems that provide automatic credential storage and role mapping support against multiple data store providers.

To access Membership Management and Role Management, you can use the Membership and RoleManager classes that are in the System.Web.Security namespace (which is imported by default for pages).

For example, you can use these classes to add new users to the application simply by calling Membership.CreateUser(username, password).

On top of these APIs, the ASP.NET team has added a suite of cool Login controls that live on the Security tab of the VS .NET toolbox. These internally call the Membership Management and Role Management APIs—and eliminate the need to write any code for common security tasks.

In the Alpha version, the following controls appear on the Toolbox:

- *Login:* Login form

- *LoginView:* Templated control to vary output based on logged-in state

- *PasswordRecovery:* Control that enables passwords to be retrieved when forgotten

- *LoginStatus:* Control that toggles a login/logout message with a link to the login page

- *LoginName:* Control that outputs the login name of the current user

The ASP.NET team will add two more controls in the Beta—one for creating new users on the system, and one for changing passwords (for the Alpha version you'll need to use the Membership API and write a little bit of code to enable these scenarios).

Following is a simple example of how to use all of the preceding features to implement a security system with the Alpha version that uses Forms Authentication and stores usernames and passwords in a membership store. (By default it will use the AccessProvider—you can update the configuration file to point it at SQL without having to change any code.)

Step 1

Update web.config to enable Forms Authentication and the role provider.

```
<?xml version="1.0" encoding="UTF-8" ?>
<configuration>
    <system.web>
        <authentication mode="Forms" />
        <roleManager enabled="true" />
    </system.web>
</configuration>
```

Step 2

Build a `Default.aspx` page that has both a LoginStatus control and a templated
message for anonymous and logged-in users.

```
<%@ page language="VB" %>

<html>
<body>
    <form runat="server">
        <table id="Table1" cellspacing="1" cellpadding="1" border="1">
            <tr>
                <td width="500">
                    <h1>Put Site Logo/Banner Stuff Here</h1>
                </td>
                <td width="100" align="center">
                    <asp:loginstatus id="LoginStatus1" runat="server" />
                </td>
            </tr>
        </table>

        <br />

        <asp:loginview id="LoginView1" runat="server">
            <anonymoustemplate>
                <h2>Welcome to My Site</h2>
            </anonymoustemplate>

            <loggedintemplate>
                <h2>
                    Welcome <asp:loginname id="LoginName1" runat="server" />
                </h2>
            </loggedintemplate>
        </asp:loginview>
    </form>
</body>
</html>
```

Step 3

Build a `Login.aspx` page that uses the Login control.

```vb
<%@ page language="VB" %>

<html>
<body>
    <form runat="server">
        <asp:login id="Login1" runat="server"
            font-names="Verdana" font-size="10pt" borderwidth="1px"
            bordercolor="#CCCC99" borderstyle="Solid" backcolor="#F7F7DE"
            createusertext="Register New Account" createuserurl="CreateUser.aspx">
            <titletextstyle font-bold="True" forecolor="White" backcolor="#6B696B">
            </titletextstyle>
        </asp:login>
    </form>
</body>
</html>
```

Step 4

Build a `CreateUser.aspx` page that uses the Membership APIs to add new users into the application. Note that this will be made easier in the Beta version with a new CreateUser control.

```vb
<%@ page language="VB" %>

<script runat="server">

    Sub Button1_Click(ByVal sender As Object, ByVal e As System.EventArgs)
        Try
            Membership.CreateUser(UserName.Text, Password.Text)
            FormsAuthentication.RedirectFromLoginPage(UserName.Text, False)
        Catch ex As Exception
            Label1.Text = "Unable to create user - user may already exist"
        End Try
    End Sub

</script>

<html>
```

```
<body>
    <form runat="server">
        UserName:
        <asp:textbox id="UserName" runat="server">
        </asp:textbox>
        <br />
        <br />
        Password:
        <asp:textbox id="Password" textmode="Password" runat="server">
        </asp:textbox>
        <br />
        <br />
        <asp:button id="Button1" runat="server"
            text="Create User"
            onclick="Button1_Click" />
        <br />
        <br />
        <asp:label id="Label1" runat="server" font-size="Large"
forecolor="#FF0033">
        </asp:label>
    </form>
</body>
</html>
```

All in all, very little code is required (none will be needed with the Beta version). The resulting implementation is very secure (passwords are automatically hashed with salts to avoid retrieval in the event of a database hack) and very fast.

Should make building secure sites with Whidbey a breeze . . .

Fun Pet Trick #9: Profile Object

By Scott Guthrie

The Profile Management feature within ASP.NET 2.0 is pretty cool. Basically it enables you to save and retrieve properties about incoming users to your application.

Unlike session state, this profile information is saved within a personalization store database and not deleted unless the administrator explicitly gets rid of it. As such, you can use it to store information about users for days, weeks, or years at a time. You can also do back-end data mining on the information to help optimize your application's experience even further.

To enable this feature, create a web.config file within your web application virtual root that looks like this:

```
<configuration>
    <system.web>
        <personalization>
            <profile>
                    <property name="NickName" type="string"/>
            </profile>
        </personalization>

        <authentication mode="Windows"/>

        <authorization>
            <deny users="?"/>
        </authorization>

    </system.web>
</configuration>
```

This will define a personalization store with a single property called NickName that can be accessed or stored for any user hitting the system.

To update the NickName property for a calling user, just write code within your page as follows (note that VS .NET provides full IntelliSense support on the Profile object):

```
Profile.NickName = TextBox1.Text
```

You can then print the nickname like so:

```
Label1.Text = "Hello " & Profile.NickName
```

Under the covers, ASP.NET then handles saving and restoring the profile settings to and from a database. This makes it incredibly easy to add or update personalization settings for users and provide a much richer browsing experience within applications as a result.

Fun Pet Trick #10: Data Binding the New BulletedList Control to an XML File

By Scott Guthrie

One of the new server controls in Whidbey is the BulletedList control, which enables you (not surprisingly) to display a list of bulleted items.

One of the nice features of the control is a `displaymode` property that enables you to toggle the control in a few interesting ways. The default value is `text`, which causes plain text to be rendered. You can also toggle it into `HyperLink` mode, which will generate hyperlinks.

A simple trick is to use the BulletedList control (in `HyperLink` mode) to generate a list of links to other sites within your page, by dynamically binding it to an XML file on disk (where the links are encapsulated).

The following example shows how to easily do this using the new DataSetDataSource control:

```
<%@ page language="VB" %>

<html>
<body>
    <form runat="server">
        <asp:bulletedlist id="BulletedList1" runat="server"
            datatextfield="Name" datasourceid="DataSetDataSource1"
            datavaluefield="Url" displaymode="HyperLink">
        </asp:bulletedlist>
        <br />
        <br />
        <asp:datasetdatasource id="DataSetDataSource1"
            runat="server" datafile="MyLinks.xml">
        </asp:datasetdatasource>
    </form>
</body>
</html>
```

where the `MyLinks.xml` file is defined as follows:

```
<?xml version="1.0" encoding="utf-8" ?>
<Links>
    <Link>
        <Name>ASP.NET Site</Name>
        <Url>http://www.asp.net</Url>
    </Link>
```

```
<Link>
    <Name>MSDN</Name>
    <Url>http://msdn.microsoft.com</Url>
</Link>
<Link>
    <Name>ASPAdvice</Name>
    <Url>http://www.aspadvice.com</Url>
</Link>
</Links>
```

Updating the XML file on disk will then automatically update the list of links on your site.

A very simple trick—but kind of useful on content sites.

Fun Pet Trick #11: Data Binding to Generics

By Scott Guthrie

One of the great new features in Whidbey is Generics, which basically provide a mechanism that enables developers to build classes whose signature and internal data types can be templatized.

For example, rather than use an ArrayList (which is a collection of type Object), or force developers to create their own strongly typed list collection class (such as the OrderCollection class), developers using Whidbey can employ the new List class implemented within the System.Collections.Generic namespace, and specify the type of the collection when using or referencing it.

For example:

```
// Use the built-in "List" collection within
// the System.Collections.Generic namespace
// to create a collection of type "Order"
List<Order> orders = new List<Order>();

// Add Order objects into the list
orders.Add(new Order(123, "Dell"));
orders.Add(new Order(345, "Toshiba"));
orders.Add(new Order(567, "Compaq"));

// Lookup the "OrderId" of the first item in the list -
// note that there is no cast below,
// because the collection items are each an "Order" object
// (as opposed to "Object"
// which they would be with an ArrayList
int orderId = orders[0].OrderId;
```

```
// The following statement will generate a compile error, but would have
// compiled (but generated a runtime exception) if the collection was
// an ArrayList
orders.Add("This will not work because it isn't an order object");
```

The following code is a richer example of how to use Generics with the new ASP.NET ObjectDataSource control, and then bind the list to a GridView control.

First is the OrderSystem.cs file, which should be saved within the code directory immediately underneath the application root:

```
// OrderSystem.cs: Save within "code" directory
using System;
using System.Collections.Generic;

public class Order
{
    private int _orderId;
    private string _productName;

    public Order(int orderId, string productName)
    {
        _orderId = orderId;
        _productName = productName;
    }

    public string ProductName
    {
        get
        {
            return _productName;
        }
    }

    public int OrderId
    {
        get
        {
            return _orderId;
        }
    }
}

public class OrderSystem
```

```
{
    public List<Order> GetOrders()
    {
        List<Order> orders = new List<Order>();
        orders.Add(new Order(123, "Dell"));
        orders.Add(new Order(345, "Toshiba"));
        orders.Add(new Order(567, "Compaq"));

        return orders;
    }
}
```

I can then write a simple ASPX page that uses the ObjectDataSource control to bind against the GetOrders() method to retrieve a list of Order objects. I can then point the GridView at the ObjectDataSource control:

```
<%@ page language="C#" %>

<html>
<body>
    <form runat="server">
        <asp:gridview id="GridView1" runat="server"
            datasourceid="ObjectDataSource1" bordercolor="#CC9966"
            borderstyle="None" borderwidth="1px" backcolor="White" cellpadding="4">
            <headerstyle forecolor="#FFFFCC" backcolor="#990000"
                font-italic="False" font-bold="True">
            </headerstyle>
        </asp:gridview>

        <asp:objectdatasource id="ObjectDataSource1" runat="server"
            typename="OrderSystem"
            selectmethod="GetOrders">
        </asp:objectdatasource>
    </form>
</body>
</html>
```

Enjoy . . .

Index

Symbols

' (comment character), 26
@ (at) symbol, for comments, 26

A

absolute caching, 79
Access (Microsoft)
  for personalization profiles, 180
  for user management data, 142
AccessDataSource control, 62
active user count, determining, 170–171
ActiveViewIndex property, 278
  of MultiView control, 323
adaptive rendering, 10, 315–318
Add New Item command, in Solution
    Explorer, 52
administrative user, Security Setup
    Wizard for setup, 140
AdRotator control, 256
ads tracking, site counters for, 256–257
AfterLogin event, for Login control, 150
AggregateCacheDependency class, 312
allowAnonymous attribute, 195
AllowPaging property, of GridView
    control, 67
AllowSorting property, of GridView
    control, 67
anonymous methods, as new C# feature,
    22–24
anonymous users, 159–160
  conditional page display for, 154–155
  personalization with, 194–197
    activating profile properties,
      194–195
    migrating profiles to authenticated
      users, 196–197
AnonymousID property, of HttpRequest
    class, 160
Answer template, 153
AnswerLookupError event, for
    PasswordRecovery control, 153
AppearanceEditorPart control, 203, 219
applications
  deployment, 12–13
  migrating existing 2002/2003, 38–39
  precompilation, 355–357
  settings in web.config file, 334
  updating configuration, 343–345
ApplySkin() method, of ControlSkin
    class, 239

AppSettingsSection class, 334
app.sitemap XML file, 127–128, 158
As keyword, 27
.asix namespace, 270
ASP.NET 2.0
  architecture stack, 2
  new features, 1–13
    configuration, 11–12
    controls, 2–4
    deployment, 12–13
    master pages, 4
    mobile devices, 10
    personalization, 7–8
    site counters, 11
    site navigation, 5
    themes/skins, 8–10
    user management, 6
ASP.NET Configuration Settings dialog
    box, General tab, 332
aspnet.mdb file, 174
aspnet_regsql.exe tool, 174
at (@) symbol, for comments, 26
Attributes collection, of SiteMapNode
    class, 135
Authenticate event, for Login control, 150
authentication of users
  conditional page display after,
    154–155
  Login control for, 145–150
  as Web Parts requirement, 204
authorization rules
  acquiring and displaying in browser,
    338–339
  creating, 345
<authorization> tag, 143
Auto Format dialog box, for zone control,
    207
AutoCompleteType property, of TextBox
    control, 289
AutoFormat command, 97
AutoGenerateColumns property, 66
AutoGenerateDeleteButton property, of
    GridView control, 72
AutoGenerateRows property, of
    DetailsView control, 83
automatic code generation, splitting files
    and, 25
AutoPostBack property, of DropDownList
    control, 245

369

forums.apress.com